PRAISE *for*

Many Hands Make Light Work:
A Memoir

"Written in the tradition of *Cheaper by the Dozen* and in the spirit of Erma Bombeck, *Many Hands Make Light Work* is a valentine, pure and simple, to the large, boisterous, old-fashioned family from which the author happily hails."

—Madeleine Blais, Pulitzer Prize-winning journalist and author of *To the New Owners*

"Part childhood memoir, part parenting manual, and part home-improvement guide, this nostalgic and charming Midwest coming-of-age story makes one yearn for a bygone era. This large and boisterous family, led by a most endearing patriarch, is utterly delightful."

—Mary Carlomagno, author of *Best Friend for Hire*

"Try not to be too jealous of a childhood spent with eight siblings, great parents, a Midwestern town that gave kids free-range, and an era that trusted all children to rise to the occasion (even occasions involving real, live lions). Anyone who remembers—and longs for—a free-range childhood will love sinking into *Many Hands*. A gem of a book."

—Lenore Skenazy,
president of Let Grow and founder of Free-Range Kids

"The 1970s might have been the Me Decade for the rest of the world, but the nine Stritzel kids discover their best and truest selves not as wayward individualists but as a unified team. In the college town of Ames, Iowa, led by their frugal father and hardworking mother, these kids welcome the world with open arms, high spirits, and hard work. *Many Hands Make Light Work* is the most cheerful childhood memoir you will ever read."

—Laura Kalpakian, National Endowment for the Arts Fellowship recipient and award-winning author of *The Great Pretenders*

"*Many Hands Make Light Work* is the laugh-out-loud tale of a regimented yet happy-go-lucky, large Catholic Midwestern family. Masterfully written, this charming, nostalgic story is a blueprint for the modern family, showing how family bonds can steer each of us to our true north."

—Colleen Haggerty, finalist for the Indie Excellence Book Award, and author of *A Leg to Stand On: An Amputee's Walk Into Motherhood*

many

hands

make

light

work

many
hands
make
light
work

a memoir

Cheryl Stritzel McCarthy

SHE WRITES PRESS

Published 2019
Printed in the United States of America
ISBN: 978-1-63152-628-2 pbk
ISBN: 978-1-63152-629-9 ebk
Library of Congress Control Number: 2019937595

For information, address:
She Writes Press
1569 Solano Ave #546
Berkeley, CA 94707

She Writes Press is a division of SparkPoint Studio, LLC.

Book design by Stacey Aaronson

for Dad, to whom nothing was impossible
and
for Mom, who made everything possible

NOTE

This is a true story, more or less. Very few details have been altered, and a handful of names have been changed. Dialogue had to be imagined but remains true to the spirit of what actually happened.

In chapter 23, "King of the Jungle," know this: everything (aside from names) including details is true.

CONTENTS

prologue

E arly on a June morning in 2012, Welch Avenue lay peaceful and serene in slanting sunlight, before the grinding motor of a massive machine roared to life. The backhoe raised its monstrous yellow arm and lofted its great iron claw. The arm poised like a bird of prey over the third-story attic of house number 412. For a second, positioned over the roof corner, the arm paused. For that second, the house stood as it had for a century. Then the backhoe opened the blocky metal teeth of its claw and bit.

Shingles, clapboard, plaster, lumber: it all crumpled, splintered, and heaved inward. The arm reached higher and the claw extended, clutching and crunching into the center of the roof. The claw lifted, then smashed down like a fist. Dust billowed up, rolling outward in a gritty cloud.

The attic of our old house saw daylight. Massive framing joists, their heft as toothpicks against the arm, tumbled down into the house. Wood-framed windows, glass panes wavy from age, exploded as the house buckled, the tinkling fall of their shards muted by the backhoe's roar.

The yellow backhoe didn't care about noise or destruction. It maneuvered around the house, doing the job we'd hired it to do. It trundled down the long, broad concrete driveway alongside of what had once been our childhood home, pausing to strike before repositioning to a new spot for a fresh mouthful. The machine's broad feet, encased in rolling belts of ridged metal, thumped off the driveway onto the backyard, pressing deep tracks through grass into black soil. The yellow arm reached up and pushed at exterior walls. They folded inward like origami.

the victorian lady and
the baseball team

*E*arly on a June morning in 1969, Welch Avenue lay peaceful and serene in slanting sunlight. Old frame houses lining
both sides of the street seemed to be snoozing. Down the street, a
man in a bathrobe shuffled out a screen door to retrieve the morning newspaper from the worn floorboards of a broad front porch.
Lofty shade trees, fully leafed out in the abundant growth of early
summer, formed a Gothic green arch as they met their mates across
the street. The lush canopy hid cicadas clinging to the ridged bark
of the maples, elms, basswoods, and oaks, but this early in the day,
the cicadas' song was only a soft trill. Even the fraternity house
across the street was quiet, its residents moved out for the summer.

Just after seven on that weekday morning, any noise on Welch
Avenue emanated from house number 412, a rambling, gold-painted
clapboard house with one full-width addition already tacked onto
the back and another on the drawing board. The old house kept
expanding, just like the family it sheltered. This morning, as every
morning, a rushing pack of children and teenagers quickly pattered
down number 412's front and back stairwells, thundered through

the little living room, and converged in the sunny kitchen at the rear of the house. We nine siblings, all on time for breakfast—but just barely—slid into our places by our parents around our home-made nine-by-four kitchen table like a whole team of baseball play-ers sliding into home. Breakfast could start.

"Bless us, O Lord, and these Thy gifts," Dad intoned in one breath as soon as the last of his offspring slid into place.

Dad was lean and quick, his face and hard-muscled forearms already tan from outdoor work. Today, he wore a dress shirt and tie for a long day teaching summer classes at Iowa State University. He kept his early receding, salt-and-pepper hair close-cropped to avoid upkeep. At five foot ten and one hundred fifty pounds, he was spare, wiry, and strong. His physical being radiated drive, efficiency, and action: Dad would have had no time or patience for anything as superfluous as an ounce of extra flesh. He seemed to create an invisible force field of forward motion around his body. You couldn't be near him without getting drawn into that momentum yourself and sud-denly finding your own operating speed ramped up several notches.

Now he swiftly continued the prayer, "which we are about to receive." Dad never wasted a second, and so we didn't either.

We tented our hands and joined in the prayer, finishing in unison "throughChristourLordAmen"—before our voices splintered into a cacophony of chatter. Mom, neat and trim in Bermuda shorts and a sleeveless, white buttoned blouse, her black hair in natural short curls, had been up well before us prepping the eggs and bacon that lay steaming on the table. Mom radiated calm as powerfully as Dad radiated action. Mom was just as productive as Dad, but without any of his urgency. It was Mom who had crafted the myriad house-hold-chore schedules taped inside kitchen cabinet doors. This morning, as per written schedule, one of us had gotten up early to clear the dishwasher and set the table while Mom made breakfast.

The prayer complete, Dad delivered our work instructions in the staccato manner of a machine gun. Dad was a full-time, year-round professor of agronomy. That was his career. His second job, of much more importance to the nine of us, was running our family business of acquiring, remodeling, and managing old houses, mostly in our Campustown neighborhood, for rental to Iowa State students.

"Denise, I want you to ramrod the show over at 2304," he began, quickly swallowing the last of a tiny glass of orange juice and nodding at seventeen-year-old Denise, our second-oldest sibling. By "ramrod the show," Dad meant that Denise would be in charge of us on our construction work site today. Maryanne, age eighteen and the oldest, would stay home today to help Mom with housework.

"2304," in our family's parlance, was the tenth and most recent addition to our family's growing collection of rental houses. We referred to all our houses by street numbers only, which gave rise to a colloquial patois among us; our speech was peppered with references to 410, 420, 535, 508, for example, and now 2304. The last, a once-stately Victorian manse on the corner of Knapp and Lynn streets in our neighborhood, was an ancient, genteel lady that had fallen on hard times. The house was a great bargain. That was why we'd bought it.

A month ago when Mom and Dad had finalized the purchase of 2304, they'd given us kids a tour of the work we'd be doing on it over the summer. That day, Dad had stood on the sagging porch, patted the rotting gingerbread trim on its carved posts, and told us, "This old house just needs love." From long experience, we suspected this particular Victorian lady needed a good deal more than that.

The number of rental houses our family owned (or, more accurately, were paying on) changed over time as Mom and Dad sold one or bought another. The number of children in the family changed over time too, though they never sold any of us.

Mom and Dad hadn't planned on running a home-based busi-ness of buying old houses, renovating them, and renting them to students. It just started to make sense. College attendance across the country was rising. In 1950, 17 percent of the US population was enrolled in college. By 1960, that number was 22 percent, and by 1970, 33 percent. Burgeoning numbers of students bound for Iowa State University clamored for housing close to campus—where we lived. At the same time, families on Welch began to move out to the edges of Ames, where new houses sprang up in former cornfields. Venerable houses along streets in Campustown sprouted For Sale signs. These old houses, which like 412 dated from the early 1900s, began to look like aging wives. They couldn't compete with the sweet young things beckoning from the outskirts of town. Neighbors stampeded out to air conditioning, avocado appliances, and concrete patios. The Grand Old Girls of Campustown were left empty, their porches forlorn, their paint flaking down into flower beds where weeds muscled in on peony and iris.

Mom and Dad had no intention of following the crowd—or letting our neighborhood devolve into disrepair. Instead, starting in the early sixties, they began to buy the old houses, both to keep up our area and to provide much-needed housing for students. In the early years, our family had little extra money, so Mom and Dad would get a bank loan or buy on contract with the seller. As thrift and labor fattened their hard-won savings, they could buy houses in our neighborhood with cash. But that was years in the future.

"Take Marla, Greg, Clare, and Cheryl as your crew," Dad in-structed Denise, listing us in descending birth order. We four in the middle, ages sixteen, thirteen, twelve, and ten, constituted the core of what Mom and Dad called their Baseball Team: nine kids born within a span of eleven years.

Dad scraped the last vestiges of scrambled eggs out of the skillet on the table. "Many hands make light work!" he proclaimed as he deposited the eggs on Greg's plate. Of Dad's many and varied pithy sayings, this was his favorite.

Mom and Dad hadn't planned on forging us nine into our own informal wrecking crew and construction company, either. It simply became necessary. For our business to succeed, we had to do everything ourselves—remodeling, maintenance, painting, lawn mowing, shrub trimming, and snow shoveling. Even so, with mortgages, insurance, and taxes, profit margins could be knife-thin. Dad worked on the houses anytime he wasn't working at the university. Mom worked on them whenever the demands of running our own gigantic household allowed. We kids worked on them every summer day that wasn't Sunday. By the time each of us was in fourth grade, we knew how to hammer a nail, spackle a wall, prune a shrub.

We were certainly many hands, and that made the work, if not exactly light, at least manageable. From early on, each of us had a paintbrush in our hands and a song in our hearts. We missed the memo on family dysfunction, and actually sang on the job. Somehow, instead of rebelling, we sang as we dipped paint rollers into trays and rolled smooth latex onto old plaster walls. We sang as we wielded flat metal scrapers high on a scaffold, scraping peeling paint off exterior clapboard. We sang as we mopped up after students moved out, as we wiped out moldy refrigerators, as we scrubbed greasy gunk off stoves. We harmonized our way through the sixties and seventies, immersed in our little world of spackle and paint, as the larger world around us careened through those tumultuous decades.

Dad passed a pitcher of milk to Mom while still rapid-firing instructions to us. "Load up the station wagon with crowbars and hammers. All those tools are in 410 garage."

Most of our rental houses included separate one-car garages, which Dad organized as workshops for different purposes. The garage next door at 410 Welch Avenue was for tool storage, 426's garage contained reclaimed lumber stacked neatly by type and length, and 535's ancient garage, which had once been a carriage house, stored used furniture. Every item in every garage was absolutely tidy and organized, every tool meticulously oiled and maintained. Among our network of garages, Dad could locate anything from the right-size nail to a drop cloth within seconds.

Mom took the pitcher of milk and refilled the glasses of our three youngest brothers: eight-year-old twins Paul and Steve, and seven-year-old Mark. We older siblings referred to Paul, Steve, and Mark as a single unit. At first we called them the Three Little Boys. Over time, we shortened that to the Three Littles, then the Three Lids, and finally just the Lids. The Lids, like all of us, knew each of our houses' numbers by memory.

Dad reached over from the table to the built-in, extra-long kitchen desk and grabbed a pencil and our daily task list, which he'd drafted as usual the evening before. "Denise, you and Marla and Greg should be able to rip up that old carpet on the stairs to the second-story apartment within 2304 and bundle it out to the junk pile." Though we'd only been on this job a couple of weeks, we had already produced a sizeable junk pile in the driveway of 2304. "Ripping out that carpet won't take long," he said as he scribbled another item on The List. "Then join Clare and Cheryl cleaning out the basement."

Clare shuddered as she buttered her toast. "Not the basement! Imagine the spiders!"

I put down my fork and moaned. "No one's ever going to live down there! Why do we have to clean it at all? Why can't we just leave it?" I'd seen the cellar at 2304, a network of damp subterranean rooms crammed with ancient junk. Earlier, we'd lifted its slanted wooden access doors to reveal a short, uneven flight of cement stairs, which led down into that spider-webbed catacomb, filled to its low, raftered ceiling with broken furniture and wringer washers and molding sports equipment and antique canning jars—all left by previous owners. The space was barely lit by daylight struggling through panes of filthy glass in tiny basement windows.

Dad looked up from The List, perplexed. "It won't hurt you to clear that out. That's easy work. That part will be done by noon." Complaining mystified him. He approached every job, no matter how daunting, with gusto. He and Mom had both grown up on farms during the Depression, Dad in Ohio, Mom in Iowa. In his world, it was usual and expected that children work alongside adults in the family business. He didn't cotton to us holding jobs outside the family, where we might encounter bad influences or rough bosses, but working within the family was fine. He didn't care one whit that our peers spent their summer days riding bikes, lounging at Carr's Pool, or going to the movies. Such idleness in teens surely led to delinquency. Instead, in his view, we were getting real work experience and gaining life skills. Anyway, we'd be off duty by five o'clock and had our evenings free after supper. What could we have to complain about?

"Paul, Steve, Mark," Dad continued without stopping, cutting his single slice of bacon as he addressed the Lids. "You start picking up branches and twigs off the lawns at 410, 412, 420, 426, and 508," he rattled off. "The lawns need to be cleared before Greg can mow them tomorrow."

Dad took a bite of bacon, necessitating a millisecond pause for swallowing, before he carried on delivering instructions. "Mark, toss any twigs and sticks on the pile behind 420. Greg and I sharpened all the mower blades yesterday. When you three little boys are done with the twig pickup, move on to the pile of old lumber in front of 426 garage. That needs denailing."

Denailing was a constant job. Our ceaseless fixing up of houses generated a bottomless pile of cast-off lumber. Dad saw to it that not so much as a splinter was wasted. Using the claw end of a hammer, we'd dig into a two-by-four to wrench out old nails with a metallic screech. We pinged used nails into old coffee cans, sorting them by size. Then we'd stack the denailed lumber in the lumber garage, again sorting by size, leaving ample aisles among orderly stacks. Though tedious, denailing was easy, which meant the Lids did a lot of it. The Lids, who had finished their eggs and bacon and were filling up on whole wheat toast topped with peanut butter and honey, had mouths too full to complain.

Dad seized on the momentary lull to make the sign of the cross and lead our post-breakfast Morning Offering: "O Jesus, through the Immaculate Heart of Mary, we offer You our prayers, works, joys, and sufferings of this day." We shushed instantly, crossed ourselves, and joined, our voices as one, finishing "for all the intentions of the Holy Father, Amen."

Everyone jumped up, running to brush teeth and use the bathroom before loading our copper-colored '58 Chevy station wagon, known as Old Betsy, and driving to the work site. Today's job was barely two blocks away, but we needed the car to transport tools and haul material. We kids were meant to be working by eight o'clock, but on most days, the clock usually ticked close to eight twenty before we were swinging hammers or wielding paintbrushes. On the job, ten o'clock meant break time, and we returned home to demolish an entire watermelon. Then we were back to work until noon, home for lunch, and back to work again. Midafternoon, one of us would whip home to fetch food and drink for all of us siblings on the job, and bring the snacks back to our work site. We'd knock off for twenty minutes then, with homemade cookies and a pitcher of lemonade, kicking back under the dark green shade of the mature oaks and maples lining the street.

We were a motley crew of kids and teens, lithe and lean, tan by early June. Half of us wore glasses; at any given time three or four of us sported orthodontia. We'd dress every summer morning in old, worn work clothes: shorts made from cutoff jeans, with rough edges trailing a ragged fringe; a shapeless T-shirt not fit for anything else; handed-down tennis shoes without socks. We girls also kept a red or blue bandanna tied around our heads to keep long hair from swinging forward.

We wore the same uniform every workday, modifying it only on days when The List specified painting. Then our attire moved even more down-market, each of us donning our special Paint Clothes: spattered cutoffs, and one of Dad's old white dress shirts with its long sleeves hacked short and shirttails hanging low. We liked these shirts because they were loose and cool against summer's humidity. Several of us topped off the ensemble with a little paint store hat, which came free with a paint purchase. The hats protected our hair against thousands of specks of paint that flew freely during ceiling painting jobs, and were almost impossible to shampoo out.

Denise steered Old Betsy into 2304's driveway. Greg, Clare, and I, riding on the open tailgate, hung on as she made the curve. Denise took the responsibility of ramrodding her crew keenly and started in with instructions before she turned off the ignition. "Marla and Greg, bring all crowbars and hammers upstairs. We'll use what works best to rip off that foul carpet," she said as she handed out white dust masks, which we snapped over noses and mouths. "Clare-Cheryl, get a move on!" Denise waved us off. Our older siblings occasionally addressed Clare and me, two girls between boys in the family birth order, as one unit. "What are you sitting there for? Get to that basement!"

Denise, Marla, and Greg vanished around the house to the

front door as Clare and I heaved open the cellar door, glumly surveying the dank staircase festooned with cobwebs. We gingerly took a few steps down, trying not to breathe. A mountain range of junk lay before us: molding cardboard boxes, listing metal shelves packed full and covered with dust, broken riding toys, a rotting, empty trunk, and piles of newspaper. Broken furniture legs stuck out from the mountain's flank at odd angles.

"We'll never get all this cleared out," I groused. "This is insane! We can't do it, even if we work till the end of time, even if we work till the universe cools down! What's the point? No one's ever going to use this space for anything—it's too damp!" Overwhelmed at the sight of the job, I wailed into the soft summer morning.

Clare, work gloves on, grabbed a box of canning jars and handed them up to me. "Let's move what we can. We have to work anyway; we might as well work here." She carried a rusting broken trike up the stairs and tossed it in an arc atop the junk pile, already more than head high.

Resigned, I waded down into the mess and extricated a wood desk chair with wobbly legs. "Dad can fix this and sell it," I said, hoofing it up the stairs and placing the chair to the side, away from the junk.

"Help me carry this dresser," Clare said. "He'll fix this wonky drawer too." We squatted on either side, using our legs instead of our backs to lift, as Dad had taught. We maneuvered the bureau up and out, lowering it carefully onto the dry driveway. By midmorning, when Denise, Marla, and Greg joined us, we were making real progress.

Hours later, hands on hips, Denise paused to survey the former contents of the basement, now organized across the side yard into piles of Fix, Keep, Sell, and Throw Away. "Order from chaos," Denise said in a satisfied tone. By late afternoon, we had emptied the warren of little basement rooms. Sunlight streamed in shafts through newly Windexed windowpanes. Walls of concrete and brick had been broomed clean. Marla and Greg were sweeping the last dirt from rough concrete floors.

I knelt to hold the dustpan for Marla's broom, gritty cement pressing into my knees. Now that it's clean, it's actually kind of a nice space, I thought, though I wasn't going to admit it aloud after my rant. By summer's end, before students returned en masse, 2304, like all Stritzel properties, would be clean and neat and fixed, with fresh paint and proper curtains. Everything would work, fit, and shine. Everything would be ready for tenants. Everything would be orderly—even a cellar that no one would ever see but us.

Beat, we trooped up the uneven cellar stairs, circled around the growing junk pile on the wide gravel driveway, and piled into Old Betsy. Denise's watch was ticking toward five fifteen. We needed to be home, hands washed, seated in our places around the table, by five thirty. Denise hummed as she turned the ignition. An impromptu songwriter, Denise composed rhyming couplets when the mood struck her, and the day's work inspired her now.

"You've heard us speak of 2304; it's a name we often *use*," Denise began in a singsong tone.

Marla, in the front seat next to her, caught the spirit and continued the tune. "We pour our sweat and blood in there . . ."

We thought. Denise pulled the gearshift on the steering column toward her and shifted into reverse, looking over her shoulder, arm flung along the seat.

Musing, Clare took off the bandanna that had kept spiders out of her hair all day, and then yelled an ending line: "Congratulations we won't *refuse!*" She waved her bandanna out the window as if she were a parade queen atop a float.

Old Betsy was rolling home now, windows down, the passing air cooling our sweaty faces. "That's fun," Marla said as she shook her hair in the car's breeze, letting sweat evaporate. "Let's keep going."

"OK," Denise said. She was always game for a song. "Two blocks till home. More verses?"

"Yes!" Marla took up the challenge. "We ripped that house from stem to stern; not a single person *grieved*," she started.

"Plaster, lath, and the kitchen sink," Greg offered from the back seat.

And suddenly a rhyme popped into my head. "Out the window, it was *heaved*!"

One block to go. One more verse about 2304. A cool summer evening, off work, awaited.

Denise began a third verse: "We tried to keep it quiet, though we worked there every *day*," she sang, lifting her foot off the accelerator, slowing the creaking station wagon to give us time to contribute to the rhyme before we turned into our own driveway.

"People soon found out we owned it," Clare jumped in. Her line supplied Marla with an opening.

"The junk pile gave us *away*!" Marla was victorious.

"I like it," Denise said. "Let's write a whole song about us, like those three verses. We could call it 'The Baseball Team' because Dad calls us his Baseball Team. That'd be perfect." As the station wagon slowed, Denise's imagination gathered speed. "I know! We could each get our own verse. Maryanne would have to be pitcher, of course. Hmm, how about this for her: The pitcher's name is Maryanne, she's really on the *ball*."

Denise steered in silence for a moment as our brows furrowed in thought. Maryanne, with her generous hugs and cat-eye glasses, was our perfect big sister. Of the nine of us siblings, Maryanne was kindest, most capable, and—the ultimate compliment in our family— hardest working.

Marla nailed the ending line of the verse. "She helps the whole dang family, best worker of us *all!*"

That day, Old Betsy swung into our driveway and rolled to a stop, but the years, and we ourselves, did not. On that long-ago summer day, we were still Dad's Baseball Team, a single entity. We lived and worked as one. The years would roll on, and the world would change around us. We would change too, though we didn't know it then. That day, we were secure in our sense of ourselves, and our place in the universe.

More verses were to come, but we weren't thinking about the song anymore. We were done with the first verses. We were hot and sweaty and tired. We were done with the day's work on the Victorian Lady. We were home, and it was time for dinner.

Stritzel Family in backyard, 1963

JULY, 1971

above the fruited plain

Dad was a professor by trade, but a farmer at heart. Though we lived on a city street in Campustown for nearly thirty years, Dad and Mom always thought of themselves as farm folk. They saw the rich Iowa soil in the sixty-by-one-hundred backyard of 412 Welch Avenue as an opportunity to grow food.

The two-thirds of the backyard nearest the house was planted with grass for play and picnics and encircled with fruit trees, including peach, pear, plum, cherry, and apple. The remaining third of the yard, at the rear of the property, was given entirely to food production. Dad's masterful landscape design included an attractive fence to divide the lawn-and-fruit-tree area from the garden area. This fence bore swags of Concord grapes, dusky purple clusters hanging heavy among leaves bigger than the palm of your hand. The center of the fence featured an opening under a graceful arbor twined with more grapevines curling extravagantly up and over the top, inviting all comers to pass beneath and stroll the center grassy path into the garden. Inside, on both sides of the center path, were three rows of thick, productive red raspberry canes kept upright and in bounds between waist-high wood standards strung with thick wire, which was set so the canes would just nod over it, seeming to offer fruit to passersby. A single, lush rhubarb plant punctuated the end of each row of raspberries. Over the whole scene played a humming orchestra of industrious insects.

This single garden and the several fruit trees behind our house would have kept most gardeners busy, but we had three more gardens, each as big as or bigger than the first, in the yards of nearby rental houses. The long, skinny garden by 410 Welch grew luxuriant rows of bush-type green beans, green peppers, and sequential varieties of lettuce, which we picked daily. The little garden by 432 Welch was planted with masses of tomatoes. We'd pick the sweet little cherry tomatoes, warm from the sun, and pop them into our mouths on the spot. The big, heavy tomatoes were loaded into baskets and lugged to the kitchen. The huge square garden behind 426 Welch was given entirely to sweet corn. We'd hoe the corn early on, stepping ever so carefully between rows of baby green blades on the wide-open plot of black soil. Two months later, in the same spot, we'd push through shade created by a tight maze of stalks and leaves, well over head-high, topped by feathery yellow tassels.

The nine of us children didn't know we were living in Eden. We didn't know we were blessed with an abundant, fresh, local diet. We just knew that, every summer and autumn, we had to pick, snap, clean, husk, press, pit, put up, or otherwise process in some laborious manner, tons of garden produce. We thought it was hard labor.

The cherry trees in our own yard were the worst—or best, depending on your point of view. The pollinating pair of sour cherry trees behind our home was stunningly prolific. The peach, pear, plum, and apple trees that ringed our backyard were all good bearers, thanks to Dad's expertise, but it was these fifteen-foot Montmorency cherries that dominated the yard and, it seemed, our lives.

Their trunks were shiny, dark, and sturdy, with gilded horizontal rings. They burst into lavish bloom every spring, an explosion of pink-tinged white beauty that provided a handy photo background for each of us children as we made our First Communion. This Montmorency variety was uncannily reliable, laden with huge harvests year after year. Never, to our sorrow, did the trees suffer blight or disease or the slightest insect infestation. Not even flocks of descending birds, happily pecking themselves drunk in the upper reaches, could significantly dent their massive harvests. As June waxed warmer and drew to a close, we'd watch the cherries redden and swell, knowing what was coming.

And, sure as the Earth orbits the sun, early every July that day would arrive. Year after productive year, the dreaded Cherry Day unfolded in similar fashion.

"Cherry picking today!" Dad, who loved cherry pies, was cheerful as a cherry himself that day at breakfast. All of us were in our regular places, tucking into pancakes stacked double on our plates, each spread with butter and topped with honey, a single slice of bacon lying adjacent like a sidecar. The two casement windows flanking the big center picture window at the end of our colossal kitchen table were already cranked open, a whisper of breeze wafting through screens, shifting the printed curtains. The morning outside was summer soft, the temperature hovering on the line between cool and warm. Pairs of mourning doves hooted, sending low notes back and forth like avian Valentines. The rising sun backlit the early-morning haze, but the natural beauty of the abundant garden beyond our window was lost on us. All we saw when we looked outside was work.

"Both trees are at peak ripeness today," Dad said. He'd been checking the cherries every evening after his day of teaching. "Another great harvest ahead, thanks be to God. Maryanne and

Denise, Marla and Greg, Clare and Cheryl, and you three little boys, we'll need the whole Baseball Team picking and pitting today." Dad passed a little glass pitcher of honey down the table.

"I don't even like cherries," Greg said. He slathered his top pancake with butter before picking up the little pitcher and tipping a stream over his stack.

"Make sure you pick every ripe cherry before moving to another branch!" Dad, paying no attention to grumbling, passed one of a pair of tall, shiny aluminum pitchers filled with skim milk so cold the exterior sweated condensation. "You're picking for maximum efficiency. Strip one branch clean before moving to the next spot." Dad quickly wiped his mouth, mindful of the class he was due to teach within the hour. "Be methodical in your movement. You only go through the tree once. No going back to get what you missed, because you're not going to miss any! Think of it as cleaning the tree, not just picking cherries."

"We all pick together," Denise said. Our second-oldest sibling was so frequently in charge of our work crew that she often assumed a leadership role. Dad's view of her as "ramrod" was seeping into her psyche. "We clean both trees, and then come inside together to pit."

"Except for Maryanne," Dad said, fine-tuning the order of work and turning to our oldest sibling. "You pick with the crew for the first part of the morning, and then come inside to help Mom set up for indoor processing."

"The kitchen will be ready for mass pitting before everybody comes in," Maryanne said. Her dual role was important to streamline the process for everyone, and she took it seriously. "We'll be prepared, so every pitter can achieve maximum efficiency!"

Clare glanced up from her plate at Maryanne, and then at the wall behind Maryanne's seat, on which hung two framed linen prints. Each featured a cherry tree rendered in the one-dimensional style and muted avocado greens and blues of the late sixties. Incorporated into the artwork of one print was the saying *Patience is a tree whose root is bitter, but its fruit is very sweet.* We knew that saying especially appealed to our mother, though we couldn't imagine why. Incorporated into the other print was *In the hum of the market there is money, but under the cherry tree, rest.* This particular print got a lot of attention every July.

"Rest, my foot!" Clare scoffed under her breath. "Since when does anyone under a cherry tree *rest?*"

"It's inconceivable to link a cherry tree with leisure," Greg muttered.

"Who could even think up a saying like that?" I was bemused by the connection between markets, money, and cherries. Since the framed linen prints hung in their places beside our kitchen table for decades, I had years to ponder it.

"Quit your bellyaching!" Dad viewed cherry picking as a pleasant and easy way to spend a day. "You're outdoors in God's creation, it's a beautiful day, we're working for ourselves here! Get a job for a boss in a factory ten hours a day—then you'll know what real work is. Mark, finish your milk. You're lucky to *have* milk left in your glass." Dad shut down the grousing by launching into our after-meal prayer: "We give Thee thanks, Almighty God for all Thy benefits, Who lives and reigns for ever and ever, world without end, Amen."

We'd said Amen, but our prayer wasn't through. Mom and Dad thought it right that we honor those who had gone before us. No one budged. No hands unclasped. "Sacred Heart of Jesus," Dad continued without missing a beat, "may the souls of the faithful departed, through the mercy of God, rest in peace, Amen." We tacked this final sentence routinely onto lunch and dinner after-meal prayers, too. It would occasionally flummox a guest, who would break rank after the first Amen, only to have to clap his hands back together as we plowed on into "Sacred Heart of Jesus."

Decades later, Clare would muse, "What about the souls of the unfaithful departed? Do they get to rest in peace too?" But on this summer morning in the early 1970s, with the sun climbing higher and Dad vanishing out the side door on his way to teach a 400-level class on fertilizer manufacture and its agronomic use, no one was pondering existential questions. We weren't inclined to seriously challenge the order of our universe, and in any case, we didn't have time. Instead we all spilled out the side and back doors toward the garage, where the ladders and cherry-picking cans waited.

The summer morning was so lovely, it was infectious: once we were out of the house, our grouchiness evaporated like morning mist. Unbidden, a scrap of song from the musical *Oklahoma!* popped into my head and, since I lacked any filter of self-consciousness, out of my mouth. "Oh, what a beautiful morning," I sang as I ambled into the garage. "Oh, what a beautiful day," I warbled, grabbing the end of a wood six-foot stepladder.

Marla lifted the top of the ladder, joining in with "I've got a beautiful feeling, everything's going my way!" as we maneuvered it out the garage door, across the yard, and under the cherry tree, where we snapped it open.

"We've got all the cherry-picking cans," Denise said as she and Maryanne dropped all nine cans in the shade under the trees. These home-rigged picking receptacles were old metal coffee cans, six inches in diameter. On one side, at the top rim of the can, were punched two little holes an inch or so apart through which a length of twine was threaded. Mom and Dad had rigged the cans years before. Now they were familiar equipment, upside down on their garage shelf for most of the year, clean and awaiting fruit-picking time.

"It doesn't take much twine to go around your little waist," said Maryanne, passing the twine around Steve's middle, knotting the twine in back so the can hung conveniently in front. Paul and Mark, cans tied on securely, scrambled up one of the trees.

"All the cattle are standing like statues," I sang as I pulled a branch low and stripped fat, full cherries by the fistful and emptied them into the coffee can at my waist. Wearing a cherry can freed both hands for maximum picking efficiency: none of us would waste a free hand holding a receptacle. Occasionally, though, when we came across an especially big cherry, sweetly warmed from the sun, a picking hand might waste a moment as it detoured upward and flicked that cherry into a mouth. Then it was but a moment to expertly extract the pit with the tongue.

Now up in the tree, I spit a pit in an eight-foot arc, then swallowed the cherry before trilling again, "All the cattle are standing like statues."

"Any song but that!" Clare was up on a stepladder, surrounded by heavy branches laden with fruit, wrists flying between branch and can as she plucked gobs of cherries with both hands. "I'm sick of that song!" During an earlier year at elementary school, right after our class finished the Pledge of Allegiance, my classroom teacher would lead our class of twenty-five youngsters in singing "Oh, What a Beautiful Morning." Every single morning. And every morning, Clare's teacher next door would scold her class: "Hear that?" Clare's teacher would clap her hands. "The younger grade next door is ready to go! Let's get to work!"

"I detest that song," Clare continued. "I never want to hear it again." Her hands flew faster between branch and can.

Marla, pausing atop her ladder, placed one hand at her throat, flung the other hand wide as if she were a performer on stage, and belted the next lyrics even louder: "The corn is as high as an elephant's eye, and it looks like it's climbing clear up to the sky!"

"STOP!" Clare left off picking, jabbing one index finger at her own open mouth over and over, as if she were gagging. "No, Marla, don't stop *picking*! Stop singing that!" Clare grabbed a branch to steady herself and leaned over to look in Marla's can, two-thirds full.

"You're slow. I've filled my can twice already," Clare said as she climbed down the ladder carefully, the weight of her full can making the fraying twine tied around her waist dig into her midsection. Kneeling next to two huge aluminum dishpans on the grass in the shade and bending forward so she didn't have to untie her can, she gently tumbled cherries into one of them.

We filled the dishpans over and over, toting them into the house to empty them, as the morning ticked by and the heat index rose.

"Let's sing 'This Land Is Your Land,'" Marla suggested amiably.

"Even worse. No!" Greg grumbled from the other tree.

"He's right—that one's too singsongy. So unmusical." Denise, another fast picker, knelt on the grass to upend her full cherry can into a dishpan. She straightened up and surveyed the trees for a more auspicious picking spot.

Marla, picking again, burst into a soldier's marching song: "Drunk last night, drunk the night before."

"Gonna get drunk tonight like I've never got drunk before!" Every one of us joined in, singing full volume into the now-hot summer morning. "For when I'm drunk, I'm happy as can be."

The song had a contagious rhythm, and soon our hands were moving in unison, branch to can, branch to can, as we picked to the beat. "For I am a member of the Souse family!" None of us knew who the Souse family was, or how they came to be in this song. It didn't concern us. We enjoyed the song because of our own family story connected with it.

Years ago, when our oldest sister Maryanne was in a younger grade at Crawford Elementary School, the music teacher, a whiny, pleading sort of dry spinster, one day finished her planned curriculum before class time was up. Youngsters, tired of standing in rows on risers, began to fidget, pinch each other, giggle, and talk. Miss Riggenbach tapped her hands together in a weak attempt to corral attention and begged in a squeaky whimper, "Class, pleeassse . . ."

The clique of class troublemakers ramped up the volume. Hidden by rows of children, one boy's leg shot out and landed a solid kick on the rear of another.

"Ow!" The victim grabbed his backside and leapt off the riser.

"Children! Pleeeasse . . ." Miss Riggenbach entreated feebly. Distraught, casting her eyes desperately over the wriggling mass of diminutive humanity, she queried, "Would anyone sing a song for us?"

Maryanne, a gentle soul from birth and a perfect pupil who never did anything bad or wrong or even slightly unkind, felt sorry for the poor, reedy music teacher. Miss Riggenbach's misery distressed her. Plus, she knew a new song; Dad had taught her one just the night before!

"I'll sing!" she called out. Hands clasped in front of her plaid jumper, smiling above the Peter Pan collar of her pressed white blouse, Maryanne stepped confidently before the group, a performer sure of her material. The class, struck by her bravery, stopped gabbing, and into that moment of silence Maryanne's sweet soprano rang clearly: "Drunk last night, drunk the night before."

Mom got a call from school and, so family lore has it, lit into Dad the moment he got home from work. "How could you teach her that song?" She grabbed his shoulders. "That song you learned in the Air Corp barracks! What must they think of this family!" Mom and Dad rarely drank. Very occasionally, they would share a single, cold bottle of Pabst Blue Ribbon beer, poured into two little glasses, as they read the paper in the evening after the Lids were in bed. "And she sang it not just in front of one or two children," Mom said, beside herself, "but the entire class! Not to mention Miss Riggenbach! And now the principal too!"

We enjoyed the story partly because it was rare for Mom and Dad to argue or disagree, but mostly because Dad, who was always the one disciplining us, got dressed down himself.

Now, in the heat of late morning, the nine of us—festooned across two cherry trees, reaching deeper in, our arms and legs a map of scratches from twigs—carried on singing. "Glo-ri-ous! Glo-ri-ous! One keg o' beer for the four of us!" It seemed to us that no matter how much we picked, or how often we filled and refilled the huge twin aluminum dishpans, the trees remained resolutely loaded with fruit. We persevered, picking steadily as we soldiered on into the second verse: "Now the Souse family is the best family, That ever came over from old Germany."

This verse goes on "with the Highland Dutch, and the Lowland Dutch, and the Rotterdam Dutch," ending with "the goddamned Dutch," but we never sang or even heard it that way. Dad might have had a lapse in judgment, teaching a drinking song to a tot, but he never swore, no matter how provoked. The worst he ever said was "Son of a buck!" Whenever he rolled out that phrase, in extreme frustration or thunderous fury, it was as if the foundations of the Earth were shaking, and guilty or innocent, we'd scatter like dry leaves before a hurricane.

Today, pegged on ladders or wedged in crooks of the trees, as always we finished the song "the *other kind* of Dutch." But our voices were losing oomph. We'd been picking three hours. Maryanne had just gone inside to help Mom ready lunch for all. The day was hotter, the trees scratchier, and the remaining cherries seemingly as abundant as when we began.

"I'm tired! I'm hot! Any cherries left now are bird-bitten," I said, casting about for a reason to quit, trying to convince my siblings the job was done.

"Cheryl!" Clare shrieked in mock terror. "You're on the plains! Don't let yourself be on the plains!" Every one of us knew she was referring to another of Dad's sayings. He'd heard a 1950s-era politician named Adlai Stevenson use it and adapted it slightly for our benefit. It was long, but we knew it by heart, and once it was brought up, there was no escaping what came next. We had to recite it.

"On the plains of lethargy," Clare began the oration grandly, standing tall on her ladder.

"Lie the bones of countless millions . . ." Denise, on the ground, raised a dishpan full of cherries overhead and looked outward, as if beseeching a rapt congregation.

"Who, at the dawn of victory . . ." Marla, hanging in a tree with one hand while punching the other fist upward, intoned the words slowly, with heavy portent.

"Lay down to rest," Clare thundered from her ladder, in a tone that suggested anyone contemplating a moment of rest might as well contemplate murder.

"And in resting," the rest of us chorused, "died!"

But there was no rest for the weary, and certainly not for the merely lethargic. Maryanne opened the back screen door and called across the yard, "Bring in that last dishpan. That's all we're going to pick. We have to start pitting now!" We trooped toward the kitchen.

❧

After a quick lunch, we sponged off the kitchen table. The Lids wiped it dry with dishtowels, snapping each other's legs with the towels. Denise, Marla, and Greg spread layers of newspaper over the table. At the white enamel sink, Maryanne and Mom rinsed vast batches of cherries, one after another, in sink full after sink full of cool water. Clare and I plumbed the depths of every kitchen cupboard, extracting strainers, bowls, colanders, pots, and pans, and handing them up to Mom and Maryanne, who swished the steady stream of cleaned cherries out of the sink into them. We placed the containers, overflowing with shining cherries mounded high, down the newsprint-covered table's protracted length until its surface resembled cherry mountain ranges, ridge after ridge, crimson peak after crimson peak. As we all slid into place around the table, each of us covered neck to knee with an apron, we could barely see one another across red mountaintops.

"O beautiful for spacious skies," Marla sang, inspired by the tabletop landscape. Her elbows were perched on the table in front of her, her forearms levering up and down, up and down. With each dip, she'd pick up a single cherry. A quick jab with a thumbnail into the juicy globe freed its pit, which plopped into a pile on newsprint as the eviscerated fruit flew into a clean vessel.

"For amber waves of grain," sang Maryanne and Denise, who were speed-pitting at the rate of a cherry per second. Cherry juice began to soak through the newsprint under their elbows. Maryanne got up to fetch a stack of clean, folded rags from a drawer in the laundry room and passed two to each of us. We put a folded-rag pad under each elbow in an attempt to stanch the juice flow.

"For purple mountain majesties," the rest of us chimed in, one thumb digging into fruit, elbows in a fixed spot on rag pads atop newsprint, forearms in motion, dipping, plucking, pitting.

"Enough with the singing!" Greg yowled. "It's like living in *The Sound of Music*!" We all stopped, except for Steve. He was the only one of us nine who couldn't carry a tune, and so it was that he especially enjoyed singing, always joining in with gusto, his joie de vivre even more endearing because he was so thoroughly oblivious. "ABOVE THE FRUITED PLAIN!" Steve belted now, hugely off-key, into the sudden silence above the fruited plain of our table. He looked up, wide-eyed in surprise at becoming a soloist.

"Stevie, you go right ahead and sing." Mom, perennially upbeat, spoke through our indulgent laughter as she stirred a batch of cherry jam on the stove, glass canning jars lined up next to her. Though the cherries in this pot were being sugared for jam, most would be frozen whole, with no sugar. On the counter behind Mom awaited stacks and stacks of quart-size plastic freezer cartons ready to be filled with pitted cherries. The cartons were squat and square, so as to stack efficiently in our eight-foot-long chest freezer in the laundry room next to the kitchen.

By midafternoon around the pitting table, it looked as if a strip mining operation had come to the Appalachians. The mountain peaks before us were lowering, the valleys filling with pitted cherries. Eighteen forearms, ceaselessly pivoting in and out of containers, resembled construction cranes. Sticky, half-dried juice streaked our forearms. Overwhelming the now-soaked folded rags, rivulets of cherry juice wended their way over soggy newsprint bogs to the cliff edge of the table, falling in toothpick-thin waterfalls onto apron-covered laps, the bench beneath us, and finally to the floor. As we pitted, mountains became flat plains, only to rise again to groans as Mom or Maryanne swept more cherries out of the sink and into another colander on the table.

"My fingers are all pruney!" Mark held up his palms and wiggled his fingers in Paul's face.

"And the rims of our nails are turning black," Marla murmured and wondered aloud whether scrubbing them later with Bon Ami sink cleanser would get them clean.

"Honestly, are we going to pit till the end of time?" Clare asked, craning her neck in an attempt to see how many more cherries were waiting in the kitchen.

"No, just till my beard grows down to my knees," said Greg, who by generous estimate had three or four hairs on his chin. Greg stopped pitting for a moment to read a saturated page beneath his elbows.

"Never put comics or Ann Landers's advice column face up when we're working." Denise raised her eyebrows and frowned, making mental note for next summer. "That's a sure route to the plains of lethargy."

"OK, that's the last of them!" Maryanne placed the final jumbo container of washed cherries on the table, and all our forearm cranes picked up speed. Next to Mom at the stove, rows of jam jars, their delectable contents gleaming garnet, were cooling upside down on a rack on the counter. In the freezer in the laundry room, dozens of square plastic boxes full of cherries stacked into a neat igloo.

"I made plenty of piecrust this morning," Mom said. Thick disks of pastry, wrapped tight in plastic in the fridge, were ready to be rolled out, draped into pie tins, and crimped. Maryanne had already measured pitted cherries, sugar, and cornstarch into a voluminous pot on the stove. We Stritzels didn't fool around with small quantities; when we made pie, we made five at a stroke.

At the sink, Denise and Marla began to wash the dozens of kitchen containers. Clare and Greg and I rolled up sopping newsprint, stuffing it into the roll-out garbage bin. Our steps were quickening, our spirits rising. Paul and Steve mopped the sticky spots under the table.

I breathed in the fragrant scent of sweet cherry pie filling bubbling on the stove. This year's picking and pitting were behind us. Ahead were twelve months of pies, cobblers, and cherry sauce over ice cream. At the kitchen sink, nudging between siblings, I stretched sticky arms under the cool shower of the tap, rubbing dried juice off my forearms. I moved in closer, squishing between Clare and Greg, getting my elbows under the welcome flow of water. I flipped off the faucet and stepped back, rubbing a rough kitchen towel over my arms.

Somehow, dreaded Cherry Day had become delightful Cherry Day. I looked at the neat lineup of jam jars and, beyond them, the freezer, which hid cartons of cherries awaiting winter desserts. Maryanne stirred the bubbling pie filling with a wooden spoon. Maybe work was not the grumble-filled burden we perceived it to be. Maybe work was a blessing that brought its own gifts, like cherry pie.

Marcella and Joseph Stritzel at a dance, early 1960s

three

how they did it

"oodness!" the mother of a new friend clucked. "You have *four* sisters? How do your parents manage so many children?"

"That's not all of us," I corrected, as politely as possible. At age five, I knew to be respectful of adults. "I have four brothers, too."

"Did I hear you right?" The mother blanched. "Four sisters, four brothers, and you? *Nine?* I have enough trouble with two! How do your parents do it?"

Our parents managed nine children by setting up the house, and indeed our lives, so each of us could help ourselves as well as the group. This involved coming up with creative solutions to problems of volume or quantity. For example, rather than continually running to the store for milk, our parents bought a commercial refrigerated-milk dispenser, the kind you'd see in a dorm or fraternity, and had milk delivered to our back door in five-gallon metal cans. This was much more efficient, as well as cheaper. The milkman let himself in our back door, opened the stainless steel dispenser on the kitchen counter, removed two empties, and installed two full cans. As years went by, the metal cans were replaced with two five-gallon bags of milk in stout rectangular cardboard containers, but the system remained the same. Two white plastic tubes, each connected to a container of milk inside, protruded from the dispenser's lower half. Since the tubes looked like teats, and indeed dispensed milk, we called our shiny dispenser The Cow. Even the littlest kids could help themselves to a glass, or fill a milk pitcher for the family if they were setting the table for a meal.

Their first home addition, built in the mid-1960s onto the rear of our old frame house, gave Mom and Dad the opportunity to try more innovations, some of their own invention. This first-floor addition comprised a new kitchen, laundry room, and full bathroom. Mom designed the space. The bathroom featured two big sinks, with roll-out risers, built into the base of the sink cabinet, that shorter, younger kids could pull out and use to reach the sinks. When done, the child rolled the raised step smoothly back into its cabinet base, out of the way of taller siblings and adults who might use the sink next.

On the roll-out risers, the Lids could also reach our sink-mounted drinking fountain. The drinking fountain was Dad's idea. He couldn't bear the inefficiency of everyone using a new glass every time we needed a drink or the poor hygiene of cup sharing. The drinking fountain solved both problems, saving gallons of dishwashing water and hours of labor over the years. On hot days when we were thirsty from outdoor adventure, we'd line up in front of the sinks to use it. It was fun, and our friends thought it was cool, too.

The pullout garbage bin in the kitchen was another neat solution. Two plastic bins were hidden in a kitchen cabinet that slid smoothly out and returned to its home slot after use. (This design, common now, was virtually unheard of then.)

The kitchen "dust drop" was Mom's idea: upon opening a certain cabinet door, you'd see a twelve-inch-by-four-inch hole neatly cut in the linoleum-covered floor. Directly under the cutout, in the basement below, hung a small garbage can. In the kitchen, instead of wasting time with a dustpan, which would have to be lifted and emptied, you swept straight into the dust drop.

Openness to unconventional solutions was how we first came to take college student boarders into our home. Mom and Dad, married in 1950, had four children by 1955. Just before child number five, also known as Clare, was born in 1957, Mom told Dad she needed help. (Clare enjoys joking that she was the one who pushed Mom over the edge.) Mom and Dad brainstormed a solution: offer room and board to a college girl in exchange for a few hours of housework and childcare per week. Presto: Mom got help, and a girl who couldn't afford college suddenly could. It was a simple but brilliant answer to an ordinary problem. This idea, like their lives, wove threads of creativity and thrift into results that benefited everyone.

During the school year, we had anywhere from one to four college girls living and eating with us. In the very early years, before we built additions on the house, we converted the den on our first floor into a college girl's bedroom, since the three bedrooms upstairs were already packed with Stritzels.

The college girls who lived with us from 1956 through 1979 changed over time, mirroring changes at the university and indeed throughout the country and around the globe. The earliest college girls were sturdy and sensible midwestern farm girls with German or Scandinavian surnames. Already well experienced in the domestic arts, these were young women who could cloth-diaper a squirming baby in seconds flat without jabbing it with safety pins. They were not fazed by the daily spectacle of supper dishes for a dozen. Like more than half of Iowa State's female students in the late fifties, our college girls during this era majored in home economics. Our household provided a perfect laboratory for their studies.

In our fuzzy home movies, our college girls of the fifties and early sixties smile genially, sporting cat-eye glasses and happy demeanors. Their stiff-sprayed hair is inflated up top and tapers at temple and nape. They wear slim pedal pushers and sleeveless ironed blouses, as well as the perennial fashion accessory of those years, a Stritzel baby slung atop a hip.

As years rolled on, the students at the university, and within our house, evolved. We children grew older, and the college girls paid rent, rather than provided childcare, for their room and board. Midwestern farm girls in bouffant hairdos were replaced with West or East Coast hippies in flared jeans and long, iron-straightened hair. Young people came from around the world to attend Iowa State's flagship colleges of agriculture, veterinary medicine, and engineering. Africans in colorful tunics and Sikhs in turbans could be seen in Ames, our little city of fifty thousand, especially in Campustown. We began to get foreign boarders, from Venezuela and South Africa, Taiwan and Iran.

One of our earliest college girls was Norma Burshem. She left her family's farm in Minnesota at age eighteen to attend Iowa State, moving into our den-turned-bedroom. She wanted to try living with us for a semester and see how it worked out. She stayed several years, earning undergrad and graduate degrees, so apparently it worked out fine.

Norma excelled at her studies, though God knows how she got any studying done in our ebullient household. Her den-bedroom closed off from our living room by a heavy sliding pocket door that rolled open and closed on a track hidden within the top frame. On winter evenings in the early sixties, the living room next to her bedroom served as our play space. One favorite make-believe game was Pioneers Heading West.

"Norma, can we play with your animals?" Clare and I, six and five years old then, knocked on the dark-stained door of the den. Norma rolled it open. Her young, pretty face behind those fashionable cat-eye glasses was indulgent. Beyond her, we glimpsed her child-free sanctuary: an armoire and a tidy dresser, her desktop spread with papers, a desk lamp casting a cozy pool of yellow light. Past the desk, against the wall, stuffed animals decorated a neatly made bed.

"I mean, *may* we *please* play with your stuffed panda and tiger and bear?" Clare corrected herself, remembering Mom's drilling. "We'll be careful!" The plush animals Norma had brought from home were, to our eyes, colossal. We had none as grand.

Norma, endlessly patient, looked down at two little upturned faces. "Yes, all right. Here," she sighed, handing over the panda and tiger. "But my bear is special. He stays with me. Now quietly, OK? I have to study."

Clare and I were building a Wild West stagecoach in our living room, and we needed her animals to fill in as passengers. Huffing, we dragged our own Clip-Clop the Wonder Horse, a big, white rideable horse on springs, into position in front. We maneuvered the bench from our old upright piano, its finish dark and sticky with age, into place behind Clip-Clop. Then, having conscripted big brother Greg, who at age eight was strong and manly enough to lift anything, we hoisted a big upholstered chair atop the piano bench. This formed the driver's seat of the stagecoach. Clare and I, nattily attired in something approximating Wild West garb from the dress-up box, perched regally on the teetering chair. From high up, we had a grand view of the surrounding plains, and any Indians who might be hiding out. We'd smartly snap the reins, fashioned from jump ropes, across the fading paint on Clip-Clop's plastic back. Behind us, down below, were rows of kitchen chairs filled with Norma's mute plush passengers, as well as whichever little brother was handy.

Norma and the other early college girls fit into our household so well because they were farm kids, like our parents. Unlike our parents, they had not grown up in that fiery crucible of character molding known as the Great Depression. The decade of the 1930s shaped the adults our parents would become.

To understand our dad, Joseph Stritzel, you first have to meet his immigrant parents, starting with his father, Andrew Stritzel. Andrew was born in 1885 in a village in Austria. Like most children in his village, he did not go to school, and he never learned to read or write. At age twelve, he was apprenticed out to a shoemaker; that meant he moved out of his parents' home and into the cobbler's cottage, where the cobbler and his family lived and operated their business. It was customary for poor families to apprentice out their sons at this age, leaving fewer mouths to feed at home.

Apprenticing was a hard life. In the cobbler's house, though he sat with the family for meals and shared their daily potato soup, he was still a hired hand and would always be an outsider, an underling. He and the family members old enough to work toiled in near servitude, sunup to sundown. The first few weeks of his pay went entirely toward purchasing his own shoemaking tools. Even after that, the pay remained meager. Yet, hammering at the soles of shoes at his dusty little workbench day after day and year after year, as the nineteenth century rolled over into the twentieth, Andrew squirreled away part of that pay, hoping to emigrate someday to America.

Others from his village were already doing so. Many were settling in a Cleveland, Ohio, neighborhood centered around Holy Trinity Catholic Church on Woodland Avenue, near East 70th

Street. Andrew set his sights on joining that enclave of Austrian immigrants. By 1906, his savings were finally robust enough to purchase a ticket for a mid-price berth on a ship heading to America. No steerage for him! He was twenty-one years old and proud of being able to afford a berth that wasn't in the bottom of the boat. He left his shoemaking tools behind in Europe. He would never make shoes again.

In Cleveland, Andrew applied to work in a machine shop. The boss asked him if he knew how to operate the machine that made nuts and bolts. Having never seen any sort of machinery remotely like it, Andrew had no idea, but he nodded anyway and said, "Yah, yah, sure." He figured once he got on the job, other workmen would show him what to do. They did.

As time went on, Andrew eventually left the machine shop, joined a construction crew, and learned carpentry. He became such an expert craftsman that women customers began telling the foreman, "Make sure you have Andy build my kitchen cabinets." He began to do fine carpentry exclusively, finishing the elaborate molding, grand staircases, and banisters that swept up through stately new homes rising along the boulevards of Cleveland Heights and Shaker Heights. The city was flush with money, the economy was booming, and work was plentiful. Immigrants, mostly from eastern Europe, poured into the city, swelling Cleveland's population to the fifth largest in the nation by 1920. That same year, the Cleveland Indians beat the Brooklyn Robins, later known as the Brooklyn Dodgers, to clinch the World Series.

Andrew was not paying attention to baseball. For his first fifteen years in Cleveland, he kept his head down and his gaze focused on work, which was transforming his life from Old World poverty to New World possibility. Steadily employed, he labored long hours, six days a week. On Sundays, he went to Mass, walking along railroad tracks as a shortcut to Holy Trinity. One day he met a young woman, Regina Perz, taking the same shortcut to the same church.

Regina was an immigrant from the same region of Austria as Andrew, but she'd made the sea crossing with her family years earlier, when she was seven. At that time, Regina and her five-year-old sister had great fun roaming the massive ship, looked after by kindly friends as their pregnant mother lay moaning and tossing in her bunk with seasickness. (Their father had emigrated earlier and was waiting for them, job secured, in Cleveland.)

Growing up in the lively and expanding city, Regina was popular and friendly, as social and outgoing as Andrew was quiet and introverted. Regina was the oldest of nine children; upon her graduation from eighth grade, she did not continue to high school, but went to work to help support her younger siblings. At age fourteen, she worked six days a week in a hat factory in downtown Cleveland, making fashionable chapeaux for ladies. For laborers like Regina, this wasn't a creative, design-centric endeavor, but long, tedious toil. As was natural for that time, she turned over her pay to her parents, to be spent on the family.

Andrew and Regina married in 1921 and started their new life in a rented house in Cleveland. Their first child, Joseph, who would become our dad, was born in 1922, in a small upstairs bedroom, with immigrant midwives in attendance. A brother followed two years later. Subsequent births were not as successful. Over that decade of the 1920s, one daughter died at birth, and another daughter succumbed to whooping cough at six months of age.

During these years, Andrew left the construction crew and struck out on his own, thinking of becoming a contractor himself. His first project was a white clapboard frame house for his own family in a modest section of Cleveland Heights. While not grand, it showcased Andrew's signature quality. It was nearly finished on

October 29, 1929, when the stock market crashed. The Depression hit and construction work began to slow, but the family moved in anyway. Joseph was eight. Thomas was six.

By 1932, any possibility of construction work had vanished. Andrew and Regina decided that the only way to keep their nearly new home was to rent it out and move into something cheaper themselves. They rented it to a minister, one of the few professions still drawing regular pay, and moved into a farmhouse on a small farm outside the little town of Berea, twenty miles west of Cleveland. "On a farm, at least we can grow food for ourselves," Andrew told Regina.

Hard work and thrift had always served Andrew, but with the Depression tightening its grip, those qualities became paramount to survival. He planted fruit trees and grew vegetables for sale. He acquired a couple of dairy cows and began selling milk and growing the herd. Regina, the city girl, began raising chickens and started an egg route. Used to the sociability of Cleveland, where siblings and parents lived nearby, Regina found her new life in the country isolating. The egg route, with regular customers who looked forward to her cheerful weekly visit, helped somewhat.

The two sons worked alongside their parents. Any hours not spent in school were devoted to farming, gardening, building, and fixing. From their father, Andrew, they learned perfection in carpentry and gained a German and Austrian sense of order. From their mother, Regina, they absorbed social skills.

Joseph learned salesmanship selling home-raised vegetables door to door. Andrew would load up the trunk of their Model A Ford coupe with green beans or sweet corn, drive to the Cleveland suburbs, and park at one end of a street. Andrew would walk with a full basket down one side of the street, and his oldest son would take the other.

For the ten most formative years of his young life, Depression hardship forged Joseph into the man he would become. The concept of one's teenage years as a separate and selfish time of life would not emerge in America for another quarter of a century. For Joseph, being a teen did not mean bonding with friends or playing sports, but growing in achievement, both at school and on the farm. He learned to value order, structure, quality, and productivity. Life in rural America in the thirties, bolstered by his parents' immigrant experience, taught Joseph that the natural and normal role of children was to contribute real value to the household as soon as they could.

Andrew and Regina, proud of their new country, decided that their two sons would be good Americans and speak English only. This was important for Andrew. If the family spoke English, even at home, it would help him at work. Andrew eventually did learn to speak English well, though always with an accent. He never learned to read or write in German or English. (Regina, with her eighth-grade diploma, kept the household and farm accounts.) As years went by, Andrew and Regina's Austrian-inflected German receded into the past, with their sons hearing it only occasionally.

So it was that their first-generation American sons grew up in an Austrian-immigrant home speaking English entirely. Well, almost entirely. One of Andrew's German sayings survived, intact and robust, into his sons' generation and beyond: *Morgen, morgen, nur nicht heute, sagen alle faulen Leute!* Young Joseph heard his father toss off this phrase so frequently that he never forgot it. The phrase lay dormant within him for decades, until he became a father himself. When we were growing up, if Dad came upon us loafing instead of working, dreamily staring out a window at the summer day while our paintbrushes stiffened in cans of hardening paint, the German proverb would burst forth from him with Old Testament ferocity, shivering the rafters and rattling the windowpanes. When we heard Dad shout in German, we'd snatch up our brushes and rollers and hustle back to work. We didn't hang around and make scholarly inquiries as to the translation. We already knew it: *Not today, but tomorrow, say all the lazy people.*

Lazy, Joseph was not. He graduated from high school and business college and was working in the shipping office of a local chemical company in the early 1940s when he was drafted into the army and sent to Madison, Wisconsin, to become a radio technician. Within three months, he was teaching classes on radio mechanics to new recruits. "They didn't wait around," Dad told us later. "If they saw you had what it took, they made you a teacher." He served nearly four years. When the war ended, he took advantage of the GI Bill to enroll as a freshman at Iowa State College, which became Iowa State University.

The son of an illiterate immigrant, Joseph eventually earned his PhD in agronomy and became a member of the teaching faculty at Iowa State. He also worked as an extension field agronomist, traveling the length and breadth of Iowa to teach farmers about crop production, nutrient management, and soil conservation. His work, with others in agronomy, contributed to the development of agricultural practices that brought millions globally out of hunger. One of his favorite tasks remained teaching the undergraduate farm boys who could only afford enough time off from the farm to come to Iowa State during winter quarter. In those young men he saw himself as a youngster, thrilled to be in college.

Even with the GI Bill, it was unusual in the 1940s and 1950s to complete college, and only about 10 percent of Americans did. In this regard, Joseph was unusual, but our mother, Marcella Hill, a female college graduate, was more unusual still.

The Great Depression followed by world war rerouted the

course of millions of lives, including our mother's. Marcella was a slim, dark-eyed child of eleven years living with her older brother, sister, and parents in Waterloo, Iowa, when the stock market crashed in '29. Panic struck the financial world like an earthquake, with shockwaves radiating from its Wall Street epicenter out across the country. Marcella's father hung on to his job at the local creamery until it went out of business during the winter of 1932–33. All work, everywhere, was evaporating.

Marcella's parents decided to move to a farm, where at least they'd be able to grow food. Her father was a big man, six feet tall and capable of swinging a hundred-pound bag of feed up onto each shoulder and carrying them quite a distance. He'd always been a hard worker, which boded well for rural life.

They made a down payment and signed a contract to make payments on Beaver Creek Farm, near the town of New Hartford, Iowa, twenty miles west of Cedar Falls. A few weeks after they moved, their bank failed. The savings they were counting on to make the payments vanished.

The first years on the farm were incredibly difficult. Marcella's father was able to get a little money through the Federal Farm Loan Act of 1932. He bought a horse and walking plow, so he could put in crops. "He also bought two bred sows to begin raising pigs for market," Mom told us later. "A short time later both sows died of cholera. There was a lot of hog cholera on farms in those days. My father guessed the seller had cholera in his herd and simply sold them all off before they could die. After a great disinfectant job, my father did finally begin raising hogs for market."

Their family's savings may have evaporated when their bank failed, but they didn't lose their sense of themselves as upstanding members of the community. Our mom told us of her father's driving horse and wagon into town to get supplies for spring planting.

The family waited anxiously at home, not knowing whether the merchant would extend credit until harvest. "My father had always been an independent person, so he hated asking for credit, hated it with all his heart and soul. From our window, my brother and I watched the road, waiting for our dad to return. Then, in the distance, we saw bright new work gloves on my dad, holding the reins, so we knew he'd gotten credit for supplies, and we could get a crop in," she told us, pursing her lips and going quiet for a moment. "We paid that merchant back, you know. Not everyone did."

Shortly after this, the horse died. It was a devastating loss. "The horse had been old when we'd bought him," Mom remembered. "We were all sad to lose him. My father said, 'He was a horse! He wasn't a member of the family!'"

As a young teen, Marcella learned how to look fashionable without spending money. For years, as an adolescent and a young adult, she cut her own hair, using a three-sided tabletop vanity mirror strategically placed in front of a standing mirror, so she could see the back of her head. In her senior class picture, mid-length jet-black curls fall in perfect waves around her face. She had to borrow money from a friend to buy the photo. Decades later, we were glad she had: we enjoyed seeing our mother as a young beauty. But when she looked at that photo, she said only, "I had quite a time paying that back!" and shook her head.

Mom's youth wasn't all hardship. She liked telling us about Sunday picnics with relatives at the farm, down by Beaver Creek. She'd hike up her skirt to wade into the creek and catch crawdads with her brother, while the grown-ups set up a table of fried chicken and potato salad in the shade of the cottonwoods. Occasionally, the youngsters would catch a snapping turtle the size of a trash-can lid, and young Marcella would later make turtle soup from it. Among her relatives at those picnics were a female relative and her husband, who had been manager of the local bank and had known it was going to fail. Perhaps he hadn't known at that time that Marcella's parents were in the process of committing to make payments on a farm. Perhaps he was unable to warn other family members about the impending disaster—but he was able to whisk his own money out in time. Mom remembered: "They always had plenty of money and drove big new cars right through the Depression. It was hard to watch, knowing they'd known and hadn't told us." Then she'd dust off her hands philosophically. "Still, they were always welcome at our farm on Sunday picnics. They were the ones who arrived with the elegant picnic basket, all fitted out with plates and silverware and glasses that matched."

After graduating from high school in 1936, Marcella got a job as a teller at a different bank and, after a couple of years, gained a promotion to branch manager. Even so, living at home on the farm as she turned twenty, she felt her life was stalling. The rural area didn't offer many single men, and Marcella further narrowed the small pool by refusing to date any man who even suggested they go to a tavern. She too vividly remembered her father's stories of years before, when he'd been employed at the creamery. "When he'd go to work early in the morning at the dairy," she told us, "he'd occasionally see some of the neighborhood's drinking men coming home from the night before. Those men would be flat on their backs in their wagons, with their horses pulling the wagons home. Their wives had to take in washing to make some sort of living." The dating situation worsened after 1941, when America's entry into World War II plucked all eligible young men out of her town and surrounding farms.

Marcella knew she didn't want to make banking or the family farm her life; she wanted to go to college. She had no idea how she could ever afford it, but she knew that to accomplish anything you had to make a start, however small. Marcella gathered her funds and her courage, left the bank, moved twenty-plus miles east to Waterloo, Iowa, and enrolled at a business college that allowed students to pay as they went. She lodged with her aunt and favorite cousin, who lived in Waterloo.

While a student there, Marcella worked a series of part-time jobs. She filled in briefly for a dentist's receptionist, but once had to act as nurse during a wisdom tooth extraction. The dentist held a chisel against a patient's impacted tooth and instructed Marcella to tap his chisel with a metal hammer. She did—timidly. "Harder, please," the dentist instructed, holding his chisel steady. Marcella tapped a little more. The tooth did not budge. "Harder, please," the dentist said, louder. Marcella, shrinking, tapped at the chisel again. The tooth held fast. "Harder!" the dentist shouted, but before Marcella could swing her little metal hammer again, the patient fainted.

After that, still a student at the business college, Marcella got a job waitressing in the tearoom on the top floor of a grand department store, the James Black Company, which filled several stories of a landmark corner building in downtown Waterloo. "It was a nice tearoom, but I was not prepared for what went on behind the scenes," Mom remembered years later. "We were to go into the kitchen and yell out our orders, and the cooks would put it out on a high counter. Sometimes if I was out getting another order, some other waitress would snatch my order and make off with it." Store management could see that the genteel Marcella was not suited for the tearoom's cutthroat kitchen, and transferred her to the more tranquil position of cashier in the second-floor lunchroom.

Later, Marcella worked as a secretary at John Deere's Waterloo manufacturing facility. One day, the head of the department asked her to stay late and help him with orders that had to go out. He was older, professional, and married. When he gave her a ride home, he asked her for a date—to be kept secret, of course. Marcella was appalled. That proposition shone like a searchlight swinging wide across the night sky, illuminating a future she did not want.

Redoubling her efforts toward higher education, she quit John Deere, moved home to the farm, and enrolled at Iowa State Teachers College (now University of Northern Iowa) in Cedar Falls. It was a hopeful half step toward her dream of someday transferring to Iowa State in Ames. During her first quarter, she drove twenty-four miles round-trip daily from the farm to Cedar Falls, but she soon found a local family in town with whom to board. The family included a girl aged six, a boy aged two, and a baby on the way. "One evening," Mom remembered, "the family had chop suey for dinner. The mother remarked that though she didn't know her own ancestry, she liked Chinese food so much, she must have a little Chinese in her. The next day, the daughter went to school and announced, 'My mother's having a new baby. And it's going to be Chinese!'"

Working and taking a few classes at the teachers college, Marcella did not know how she would ever get to Iowa State. Her mother suggested she take a day off, and together they'd drive the couple of hours to Ames, to see what they could do. Iowa State's home economics department was among the best in the nation. With a college degree, careers in teaching or hospitality management could beckon.

The cost of room and board was the stumbling block for Marcella, as it was for so many other potential students. Their first stop on that visit was at the Office of Student Employment. Marcella was hired as a dining room hostess, which would pay for her dorm room and board, thus allowing her to enroll at Iowa State. She worked in the dining room of Oak Hall dorm. Each table, laid with white tablecloths and napkins, had its own designated hostess. As a hostess, Marcella needed to dress well, but even with limited funds, that was not a problem. An accomplished seamstress, she could look at a drawing in a fashion magazine and sew a similar outfit by recombining various pattern pieces she already had, using whatever fabric was available. Students entered the dining room as they would a restaurant, with Marcella and other hostesses seating them. White-jacketed male students, earning their own room and board, swirled in to wait on tables, bearing great trays of steaming plates on their shoulders. "The manager of dorm food service, Elsie Guthrie, was strict," Mom told us. "If one of the waiters so much as snatched a radish from one of the food trays, that was all his life was worth. He got blasted!" The dorm food was wonderful, she said, varied and delicious. "This was an education in elegant dining!"

One day, one of the waiters, a vet student, brought the jawbone of a horse to work and stored it in the cloakroom, where Miss Guthrie discovered it. "She was horrified to have a horse bone in her dining hall. She was a tornado on wheels, but good-hearted. I learned later she sometimes loaned money to some of her waiters so they could finish school."

Meanwhile, Marcella's own finances were precarious. She was never sure she'd be able to return for the next quarter. She loved everything about school: classes, dorm life, and her dining hall job. She was especially captivated by the sweeping beauty of Iowa State's verdant campus, with its expansive lawns, huge trees, and picture-book Lake LaVerne, where resident swans Lancelot and Elaine held court over lesser fowl. But over this idyllic scene hovered the near-constant specter of dropping out due to lack of funds.

Her grades were not a problem. They were high enough to catch the attention of President Emeritus Raymond Hughes, who called her into his office for a pep talk, encouraging her to stay the course. He exhorted her to keep studying, keep working the dining hall, and keep focused on finishing. After that, a couple of small scholarships came her way, and in the spring of 1950, she walked across the stage, diploma held high.

The head of Home Economics Extension offered Marcella a full-time job as extension home economist for Butler County, where she would disseminate best-practice information to homemakers, but Marcella turned it down. She had met Joseph, and could see a bright future ahead with him.

Perhaps it was the memory of her own student need for room and board that spurred Marcella several years later to think of other college girls. Perhaps she remembered needing just one more piece of the puzzle, a convenient job, to tumble open the lock on a university education. Others would have thought our house had no space for boarders, being already packed to the rafters with children, but Mom and Dad could make room. So began the thrifty solution of our family taking college girls and, eventually, a few college boys, into our home. They would live with us, weaving themselves into the fabric of our lives, from before most of us were born until after we left home ourselves. Nine children, apparently, were not enough. We would take in more, year after year after year, and from the midwestern farm girls of the fifties to the hippie protesters of the seventies, they would be a force that shaped our lives.

Stritzel Family at church, 1957

four

1964

hammer-shammus

rugality that summoned a constant stream of college-girl boarders was one force shaping our lives, but faith—in the form of mid-century, mid-American Roman Catholicism—was a stronger one. Church loomed large for us Stritzel children. We attended St. Thomas Aquinas Catholic Church, near campus, not far from our rambling frame house.

Our family didn't miss Mass. On Sunday or any holy day of obligation, you'd find, next to our parents, nine scrubbed Stritzel children lined up in a pew near the front, kneeling with clasped hands, the heights of our bowed heads stepping up and down because older, taller siblings sat next to and minded smaller ones. In nearby pews, you'd find similar up-and-down lines of similar families.

The parish's founding members, who included our parents, named their magnificent modern building for a medieval saint known as a philosopher and scholar, which was fitting for a university church. St. Thomas Aquinas, designed and built in the late fifties, was a testament to mid-century modern architecture. It had a raised altar anchored in the middle of the worship space rather than at the back wall, as in old churches, so the priest wouldn't be so far away. Large, double-glass doors swung wide to admit streams of worshippers through both back and front of the building. The interior space was grandly rectangular, the white ceiling soaring fifty feet, crisscrossed with giant, dark-stained beams. A modern Italian terrazzo floor, with flecks of gray and silver stone embedded in its polished surface, gleamed underfoot.

St. Thomas didn't have huge gothic-arch windows of fragile stained glass depicting biblical scenes. Instead, its architects brought light inside through narrow vertical slits filled in with thick slabs of varied glass, their random edges polished. The slabs glowed jewel-like with the morning sun, throwing slivers of reverential light into the space within. The long rectangular church, with balconies front and back, offered seating for nine hundred worshippers in polished blond wood pews. Modern in all things, St. Thomas had girl as well as boy altar servers by the 1960s, decades before other Catholic churches.

At Mass, we girls wore lace mantillas, draped over soft-brushed pin curls that had been set with bobby pins in damp hair the night before. Mantillas are large triangular pieces of lace that cover your head and cascade to your shoulders. Or, we could wear a little disk of lace, called a chapel cap, atop our heads. Either type of veil—long and flowing, or small and round—served to cover our heads. Mantillas and chapel caps were, and still are, a traditional sign of modesty and piety. The boys wore white shirts with clip-on ties and crease-pressed dark dress pants. As the fifties segued into the sixties and seventies, our clothes and hairstyles changed, with the girls' patent leather shoes and ankle socks giving way to above-the-knee A-line dresses with white crochet knee socks, and later, swingy bell-bottom pants.

But no matter the decade, we Stritzels were not the first parishioners out of the pew after Mass ended. As priest and altar servers processed out and the last strains of the closing hymn faded, other parishioners exited their pews, spilling into the aisles, greeting, smiling, talking. The crowd formed its own mass, one that flowed slowly, like a human glacier, toward the church foyer and basement stairs beyond. Dad felt it would be better for us to spend that seven or eight minutes on our knees in the pew. Why join the crowd in the aisles? We were already in church, and not going to get downstairs through that crowd anytime soon, so why not get more praying done? It was a perfect dovetail of his reverence for God and his respect for efficiency. So Dad and Mom taught us by example, after Mass finished, to kneel on the swing-down padded kneeler one more time, heads bowed. Our pew stayed full and quiet until the church was nearly empty, the aisles and basement stairs clear. Then we were free to join the last of the crowd, full of that getting-out-of-church bonhomie, and troop down the basement steps toward doughnuts.

The church basement, brightly lit with overhead fluorescent fixtures bouncing cool light off more polished terrazzo flooring, was furnished in a mod style with molded plastic chairs grouped congenially around circular white Formica tables. Like the worship space upstairs, the basement formed a spacious rectangle.

The doughnuts, or Spudnuts as they were known in Ames, were legendary. Opinions differed among citizens of Ames as to what made a Spudnut a Spudnut: Was it the addition of potatoes, potato flour, or just water in which potatoes had previously been boiled? What was agreed among all was that, no matter how fresh and delightful a doughnut is, a Spudnut is better. Comparing a doughnut to a Spudnut is like comparing a little wood clapboard country chapel to St. Peter's Basilica in Rome.

Yeast-raised, generously cut, with glossy tops reflecting a light sheen of sugar or a fresh frosting of chocolate, maple, or vanilla, Spudnuts were a heavenly treat. We were allowed two Spudnuts each, with a glass of milk or juice. Two! And they were big! To a child—to anyone—it was a magnificent portion.

The doughnuts were so fresh that parishioners would sometimes be downstairs waiting when the Spudnut deliveryman came swirling in the back way, bearing atop a shoulder an immense bakery tray laden with fragrant Spudnuts that minutes before had been bobbing in a bubbling vat in the shop across town.

The Spudnut man was hugely fat. He was the only fat man in town, but he was so fat, he made up for everyone else. We'd watch in wonder at his agility and balance as he swept into the room and spun around, placing the gigantic aluminum tray of Spudnuts on the serving table with a flourish. Then, wordless, he'd spin again, his ballooning belly seeming to hang still in space for a moment before it joined the rest of him as he sped down the corridor and up the back stairs to his truck.

That was Sunday morning, week after week, year after year. Saturday mornings were another matter. Saturdays, we children went to religious education class, or catechism as we called it. By the 1960s, with the number of nuns dwindling across the nation, our catechism was taught almost exclusively by laywomen.

Almost exclusively. There was one nun left in our parish, Sister Mary Patricita. Like the lone fat Spudnut man spinning his way through a town full of lean citizens, Sister Mary Patricita in her voluminous floor-length black habit was nun enough to make up for all the laywomen teachers in their beige double-knit polyester pantsuits. Sister Mary Patricita—even the name rolled grandly off the tongue—had a shiny, beneficent face rimmed by a tight wimple. We didn't know what other body parts she might have had, as her entire person was buried under layer after layer of black habit. Her sleeves reached to her wrists, and her skirts puffed out like a ballgown. Were there petticoats beneath? No child ever knew. Her waist was cinched snug with a belt, from which dangled a big circular string of wooden rosary beads. The beads clacked softly whenever Sister Mary Patricita moved, and we loved to hear the comforting *click, click, click* that told us she was near.

Other Catholic children have stories of strict nuns, but only kindness radiated from Sister Mary Patricita. As kids, we didn't register whether she was old or young, chubby or slender. We looked up at her, our eyes wide, our mouths open, and knew only that she cut an imposing figure in that burgeoning black habit. Surely such a personage had a direct line to God the Father, God the Son, and God the Holy Spirit. Sister Mary Patricita pulsed waves of love outward in concentric rings, and we felt them whenever we wandered into her orbit.

"Children," she said one Saturday morning in November 1964, as we gathered close around her skirts like beaux surrounding Scarlett O'Hara, "you must listen carefully tomorrow at Mass, as it will be said for the first time in English, not Latin."

Huh? I realized I'd never listened at all. As a kindergartner, I couldn't have told you if Mass had previously been said in pidgin Chinese. After the pope and Church hierarchy in Rome issued the documents of Vatican II, priests everywhere in the world would say Mass in the local language. Also, they would now turn their faces away from the altar and sacristy in the back of the church and toward the congregations in the pews. Both changes signaled increased participation of religion in modern life.

We children didn't understand the earthshaking changes coming from Rome, but we did understand that girls and women did not go to church without hats or veils. One Sunday, our third-oldest sibling Marla, who was ten, forgot her mantilla. Desperate, she scrabbled through her little-girl black patent leather purse. No mantilla. She was already out of line entering the church without it, but to go up to communion with her hair uncovered, she thought, would be even more deeply unholy. Ever ingenious, she slipped out of the pew, tiptoed down a side aisle, quietly exited into the foyer— and then dashed downstairs to the basement ladies' room, flung open a stall, and tore off a suitable length of toilet paper. She paused momentarily before the mirror, carefully affixing one end of the line of paper to her head with two bobby pins. Then she layered the rest of the toilet paper back and forth, back and forth on top, hiding the hairpins.

The effect was perfect. She walked slowly and carefully now back up to church, decorously joining the communion line, hands folded in prayer below an angelic face, bringing up the rear. As she progressed down the aisle, the toilet paper atop her pixie haircut began ever so slowly to unravel. Like a toilet paper waterfall in slow motion, it unfolded gracefully down her back in full view of the congregation, lapping gently against her black patent leather Mary Janes before finally brushing the terrazzo marble floor.

She received communion with covered head, and she felt her soul was safe. Other parishioners, save for an incredulous look and a muffled laugh or two, honored her childlike and ingenious solution.

In addition to not getting Vatican II, we kids didn't always understand the prayers we said. At home before and after every meal, our family routinely said prayers together. "BlessusOLordandtheseThygifts" was our familiar start, and we'd rattle on, gaining velocity like a freight train going down the track, fetching up at the end breathless before punctuating it with our hearty, unison Amen. Then we'd all pause for Dad to tack on another bit. He'd intone, "Sacred Heart of Jesus," and we nine, as one, would respond with confidence, "Hammer-shammus!" We figured it was some sort of Latin.

We were well into our teens before we realized it was actually "Have mercy on us."

five

1963

let them swim

"Duck your head!" Our teenage swim instructor, swaddled in sweatpants and sweatshirt, with a beach towel wrapped over that, stood on the concrete deck of Carr's Pool in Ames.

"Go ahead, duck and blow bubbles! It's fun!" She crossed her fists up under her chin, snugging her thick towel tighter. Overhead, a lofty tree threw solid shade across our end of the colossal oval pool, a breeze snapping through its branches. On this fifty-nine-degree morning in early June, the shade seemed to lower the temperature of the icy blue pool even further.

"I c . . . c . . . can't duck," I said through clenched teeth to Clare, who stood with me and a handful of other four- to six-year-olds, our arms wrapped around our chests, in arctic water in the shallow end. "I c . . . c . . . can't even move." My teeth were locked, my lips blue.

Clare dipped her knees an inch, gasping as numbing water lapped higher. Next to her, a boy unwrapped his arms from his chest. Keeping elbows tight against his body, he gingerly patted the surface of the water, causing a drop to splash up onto our instructor's flip-flop-clad foot. She jumped back and pulled her sweatshirt hood over her head.

"Duck and blow bubbles!" Forced cheer emanated from deep within the hood.

Our flesh goose-pimpled, eyes squeezed shut, we in Carr's Pool's Tiny Tots swim lessons bent knees and dropped our shoulders beneath the glacial melt. Pausing there for a moment, summoning courage I didn't know I had, I quickly pinched my nose and submerged, then instantly leapt up, shaking wet hair.

"Good! Again, under you go!" Our teenage drill sergeant was not placated, only encouraged.

Mom enrolled all of us, from tender ages, in swim lessons at Carr's Pool. A strong swimmer herself, she held it nonnegotiable that we learn. Carr's offered Tiny Tots lessons for ages two to six, plus lessons for older children. Mom saw to it that we participated.

Her determination sprang partly from the fact that Dad couldn't swim. His childhood had held no time or place for such a luxury as swimming lessons. After Mom and Dad married, Mom tried to remedy the situation by signing him up for adult beginner lessons at the indoor pool in the venerable men's gym on campus. The lessons didn't take. At all. Eventually, Mom accepted that defeat and turned her considerable energy and resolve to the nine of us.

In the early years of our family, even on those June mornings when the temperature hovered near sixty degrees and clouds scudded low across the sky, Mom bundled those of us of appropriate age into Old Betsy and drove across town toward Carr's Pool. During those early summers, Dad was often out of town during the week. At that time, his job as an extension agronomist for the university involved traveling to speak to farmers and agricultural firms, disseminating the latest agricultural research. Maryanne and Denise, who had graduated swim lessons, stayed home to watch the Lids, who were toddlers, while Mom drove us middle kids to the pool.

On these days, sitting on the vinyl middle bench seat of Old Betsy with Marla, Greg, and Clare, I clutched a threadbare towel miserably around my four-year-old, swimsuit-clad self. Mom, hands on the wheel, smiled as she looked out the car windows at the breezy beginnings of the day. Her short curly haircut looked pert and pretty, her plaid Bermuda shorts reached not quite to her knees, her short-sleeved white blouse was crisp, and a cardigan draped her shoulders. Early morning sun winked in and out behind clouds. The wind whipped a flag straight out from its flagpole in a front yard. Mom hummed a little tune, pressing the accelerator to climb the hill.

Carr's Pool was built in the 1920s down by the Skunk River, so you reached it by driving over a hill and then descending into the river valley. Central Iowa is flat, so any hill is unusual. This one commanded our attention.

As the station wagon trundled up, gut-twisting anxiety built like an orchestral crescendo in our stomachs—then Old Betsy crested the hill. In tandem with the car's lurching over that rise, our stomachs lurched with dread as we caught sight of the glittering aquamarine jewel of Carr's Pool spread far below us, its icewater surface shimmering and glassy, lying in wait for small bodies to submerge beneath its depths.

That sickening lurch over the rise was so indelibly linked to our first glimpse of the pool that years later in adulthood, even if we weren't going swimming, we'd feel a stab in our stomachs when we drove that hill.

At Tiny Tots, we knew there was no dodging swim lessons, no

running from the freezing blue. Like prisoners who realize resistance is futile, Clare and I gathered with other four- to six-year-olds on the deck by the snack counter. Our teen instructor organized us into line, and we trotted off behind her. She led us each through a large tray of warm water on our way into the pool area. We stepped through it, one by one. Though it was intended to clean feet, I saw the footbath as a deceptive trick: the warmer the footbath, the colder the pool.

Now our swaddled instructor, up on the deck, exhorted her small charges standing waist-deep in ice water below her. "Duck!" she encouraged from her warm, dry cocoon. "You can do it!"

Gasping, my flesh blue, I dipped my shoulders. Finally, one child ducked fully, then another, and then all of us. We jumped up and down, flush with accomplishment, wet hair plastered to our faces.

"Now paddle! It's fun!" Our instructor smiled from deep within her wrap, her hairdo protected from the wind. She could not be satisfied!

Why doesn't she try it herself? I thought. *She knows it can't be done. Anyone can see things sink in water.*

Mom returned midday to drive us home. Though the day had warmed considerably, we never did. Still purple from cold, we piled into the station wagon. Mom rolled up the windows and turned on the heat, never mentioning that the sun was now downright hot and she herself was sweltering in the closed car.

I never learned to swim at Carr's Pool. Stomach-knotting fear is not conducive to mastery. Besides, as a Tiny Tot, I believed deep in my soul that if I weren't standing on the blue-chipped-paint bottom, I would go under.

At the end of the two-week session, some Tiny Tots triumphantly swam from one edge of the pool's shallow end to the other. I "swam" too, hopping along the concrete bottom on one foot while kicking up the water's surface with the other. This turbulence obscured any view of my cheating foot, safely in touch with the pool bottom.

The instructor didn't notice. Neither did anyone else. As the sixth child out of nine, I could get away with fake swimming, since no one was really paying attention. I realized for the first time as a Tiny Tot at Carr's Pool that my place as one child among many allowed me to hide a little from parental scrutiny.

Eventually, inexplicably, my older siblings learned to swim. In our family, swimming unassisted across Carr's Pool earned you the ultimate reward: your own fishing rod with a black-and-white Zebco reel, which Dad awarded with ceremony in the living room. One by one, as years passed, Maryanne, Denise, and Marla earned their rods, then Greg, then Clare. I wanted Dad to bestow the prized Zebco on me, too, in the living room in front of everyone. But I wanted even more not to drown in Carr's Pool. Internally weighing my horror of that hypothermic blue water against the glamour of a Zebco fishing rod, I chose to be content with flying low under parental radar. I stayed mum. No one noticed I still couldn't swim.

Until Mom did. A few years later, she took a hard look at the inadequate swimming skills of the four of us at the bottom of the family. No Carr's Pool this time. Without inquiry or discussion, Mom signed the Lids and me up for group swim lessons at the big indoor pool in Beyer Hall, the new gym on campus, where members of the Iowa State men's swim team taught kids in the summer.

The first day in Beyer Hall, under cold blue light from fluorescent tubes high overhead, I edged onto the grouted tile surface of the deck as the heavy metal door of the women's locker room clanged shut behind me. This pool was all business, with no shallow end whatsoever, just six long lanes for laps. A still deeper end, off to

one side of the lanes, featured high and low diving boards for com-
petitions. But even in the swim lanes, the water was deep enough
that none of the twenty-four kids milling around on the deck would
be tall enough to keep head above water.

I paid no attention to the other kids, none of whom I knew, or
to my three little brothers emerging from the men's locker room.
My focus locked on four young male instructors lounging around
the deck joking with each other. One held a clipboard. All wore
whistles on lanyards, which lay against trim, tan chests above
washboard abs and next to impeccable pecs. All were pretty much
naked except for itty-bitty, second-skin Speedos. I knew these
muscled gods of Neptune wouldn't fool around cajoling kids to
"duck, it's fun." I looked in silence, trepidation rising: it would
never occur to these college men—lean, strong, confident, relaxed—that a present pupil couldn't actually swim yet. Dread,
worse than any occasioned by Old Betsy cresting the hill on the
way to Carr's Pool, flooded my gut.

"Line up!" Clipboard blasted his whistle and turned back to his
teammates. Children jostled themselves into groups of four and
lined up behind six blocks fronting six lanes. The block raised the
swimmer a foot or so above the water to give a stronger start. At the
bottom of each lane, a line of dark tile showed edges made wiggly
beneath the shimmering surface. Sick, I realized we were meant to
keep our eyes open *under water*, to stay straight in our lane.

"Five laps' warm-up!" Clipboard turned to us and whistled a
single blast. The first line of children, crouched with toes hanging
ten over blocks' edges, sprang forward over the water, arms out,
headfirst.

Tweet! Another blast, and seconds-in-line followed like lemmings
off a cliff.

I couldn't protest, I couldn't run, I couldn't extricate myself from line. I couldn't see the Lids but couldn't have helped them anyway. I couldn't help myself.

Tweet! Thirds-in-line, their sleek small bodies stretching forward toward watery oblivion, sprang off blocks and knifed into the pool.

Last in my line, I mounted the block as a prisoner mounts a gallows. Clipboard and his posse weren't really watching. They'd swum before they could walk. They'd grown up in pools. They swam miles every day before breakfast.

Tweet!

No other choice. I flung myself wildly into the drink, flailing toward the opposite edge, pretty sure I'd go under long before I reached it. I couldn't cheat because, for the first time in my life, I couldn't touch bottom. With primal instinct, I stroked and kicked, rotating my face to the side to suck in air. Stroke, kick, gasp in a lungful of air—I was swimming! I could do it!

It was a miracle. Confidence carried me across, but not my own confidence. Clipboard and his trio of acolytes carried me with nothing more than their casual certainty. They'd virtually tossed me in to sink or swim, and I'd swum.

The Lids and I carried on with lessons in the Beyer Hall pool on campus for a couple of weeks, biking there every afternoon in our swimsuits, threadbare towels draped behind our necks, until we achieved superior swimming skills.

Now I wanted to return to Carr's Pool, to show Mom and Dad I could swim across unassisted, but enough time had passed that they had forgotten about the black-and-white Zebco fishing reels awarded with ceremony in the living room. Or maybe they felt our household owned enough fishing rods. Anyway, I never got my own. But I did learn to swim.

six

1971

summertime,

but the livin' ain't easy

My camouflage technique of evading scrutiny by melting into a mass of noisy siblings could sometimes play to my advantage. Where it would not work at all, ever, was when we kids were on the job. Our family culture was such that none of us, not even I who knew how to hide in the middle, could imagine skipping out of work. On summer workdays, our team identity held strong—even when The List specified scraping off old wallpaper.

Like denailing, scraping off ancient wallpaper was a near-constant task for us. Floral, patterned, striped and trellised, dotted or swirled, every wall in every room in every old house we bought came thickly adorned with layer upon layer of wallpaper and paste, calcified over decades into a surface hard as tooth enamel. The worst cases also had wallpapered ceilings.

"Wallpaper must've been the height of fashion for ages," said Maryanne, panting as she climbed stairs. Maryanne was ramrodding the crew of older kids today. She plunked down a five-gallon plastic bucket filled with tools and rags in the upper hallway of 535

Welch Avenue, a once-stylish two-story frame house with a capacious third-floor attic, rambling basement, and carriage house out back. She surveyed The List through thick-lensed, cat-eye glasses. Several of us, whether through our proclivity to spend every free moment with our noses in library books or just due to the genetic roll of the dice, were myopic as moles.

"Four upstairs bedrooms and the hallway, every one of them floral!" Denise said, her arms loaded with drop cloths, as she reached the top of the stairs and looked over Maryanne's shoulder at The List. "You figure the house was built in 1900. Even if they wallpapered only every decade, we can still expect seven layers!" She dropped her dusty load with a thud on the worn hardwood floor.

"At least we don't have to scrape the bathroom," Marla said as she put down her bucket of putty knives, scraping tools, and steel brushes. Marla could find sunshine in a hailstorm. Investigating the bathroom, she hopped up on the rolled edge of the claw-footed tub, balancing in her holey tennis shoes. Days before, Denise and Greg had knocked all the plaster off the walls of the little room with crowbar and hammer. Now pipes were exposed, awaiting plumber and electrician. Dad would later enlarge the window, add storage, and complete the bathroom remodel.

"This is kinda cool. In here we can see the guts of the house," Marla said as she walked atop the tub's edge, a graceful gymnast with arms curved elegantly upward. She approached the end, turned with a flourish, and started back. "Now the plaster's off, you can see the old narrow strips of wood lath nailed to those big two-by-fours, and all those dirty white clumps of loose insulation behind."

"Come on, let's get to it!" Clare exclaimed. "All these walls need to be scraped free of wallpaper, wiped clean, spackled, sanded, and painted." Clare knew, as we all did, that this job had to be finished before students returned in late August. "The house has to be perfect, not that they'll appreciate it," Clare said as she elbowed past Marla to position the metal cylinder of a fruit-tree sprayer under the tub spout, and turned on the hot water faucet. She grabbed a plastic bottle of dishwashing detergent and squeezed a steady jet of the liquid into the rapidly filling cylinder.

We employed the old sprayer to mist wallpapered walls. First, we'd use the sharp edges of our flat scrapers to scratch, or score, through layers of wallpaper. Then one of us would pump up pressure in the sprayer, sling the strap of the big old dented cylinder over a shoulder, and aim the sprayer's wand up and down the walls. Moisture, with its added touch of detergent making it slimy, eventually permeated the iron-hard paper and paste, turning it to a mass of sopping goo, which theoretically could be scraped off.

I laid drop cloths throughout the rooms. We six would spread out around the upstairs, misting and remisting, scoring and scraping, moving to any place wallpaper would come off. In the hallway, Marla turned cartwheels, landing one after another precisely on a straight line of hardwood.

I dropped the last cloth on the floor and tucked my shapeless T-shirt into my cutoffs. "Let's have a handstand contest," I said, placing my palms on the hardwood and kicking my feet up quickly, ankles together, toes inside tennis shoes pointing toward the ceiling.

"Let's see who can stay up longest." Marla was now upside down also, with perfect form, moving her palms to keep balance.

"Enough!" Maryanne had had it. "The rest of us are doing all the setup while you two lollygag." She tapped us and we came down, landing lightly upright. Maryanne handed out scrapers. "Marla and Clare, southeast bedroom! Greg, start in the hall. Cheryl, you're with Denise, northwest bedroom. I'll spray everything again and join Greg." Denise slapped a scraper into my hand and bent down to turn on our old work radio, which she'd propped in an open window against the screen. We carried this black plastic, paint-freckled old soldier of a radio to every job, summer after summer, groovin' to the sounds of sixties and seventies America.

"Ugh! That southwest bedroom has a wallpapered ceiling. I'll spray it over and over, and we'll do that last." Maryanne, like the rest of us, hated scraping ceilings.

"At least on a wall the slop falls at your feet," said Greg, who was already loosening great rips of wet paper from the hall walls. "From a ceiling, this slimy muck lands in your face."

"I see three patterns already," Clare said as she wielded her scraper, digging into the softening mass of gluey paper layer by layer. "Let's count and see how many layers. Is this yoo-glee or what?" Clare held up a tear of saturated floral that resembled nothing in nature. Yoo-glee was her word that summer for especially ugly.

"Let's lay out pieces of the different papers on the hall drop cloth; then we can count." Denise contributed a strip.

"Here's a different one." I dug deeper into a wall. "I'm up to seven different layers!"

The radio played as we worked our scrapers up and across walls, singing along. Maryanne knew all the words, and Denise led harmony. We loved to sing—pop songs and folk ballads, hymns and anthems and show tunes—and our voices blended well. We warmed up our voices and warmed to our work, hitting a rhythm, working steadily now, all of us moving in our ragtag ballet of score–spray–scrape played out on a stage of steaming second-floor rooms. Outside wide-open windows, a canopy of shifting green leaves dappled the sunlight, and the slightest of summer breezes wafted through the rooms. We turned off the radio and sang from memory, our crew working room to room like gears of a well-oiled machine. We sang Peter, Paul and Mary, every hymn we could think of, then worked our way back through the sixties and fifties to the Kingston Trio, and Herb Alpert and the Tijuana Brass. Marla upturned her five-gallon plastic bucket, dumping out tools, and leapt atop it, dancing; I beat a rhythm on the side of another bucket with my scraper. We were back to the current decade and John Denver, bellowing "Leavin' on a JET PLANE" a cappella, when Maryanne judged the southwest bedroom ceiling wallpaper saturated enough for scraping.

"Let me get the ladders in there." Greg paused his work in the hall to heft one of our old wood stepladders up from the first floor and snapped it open under the offending ceiling. Denise followed him with another ladder; Maryanne toted up a third.

On the upstairs hall drop cloth, I squatted to inspect our row of strips of different wallpaper, laid newest to oldest, a straggly history of interior décor. "How did anyone ever think this was pretty?" I murmured, imagining the decorators of these rooms: women in turn-of-the-century pompadours and fine-pleated shirtwaists, flappers with bobbed hair and dropped-waist beaded dresses, women of the forties with nipped-waist jackets and below-knee straight skirts.

Denise joined me and bent down. "Twenty-two layers in the northwest room alone. It's a record!" she crowed. "That's more than in any of our other houses."

Maryanne, Denise, and Marla, balanced on ladders, now attacked the ancient wallpaper on the southwest room ceiling with gusto, wielding scrapers with determination. It wasn't enough. Dry, the layers had been thicker than a quarter inch. Now sodden, they were even thicker, but still stuck to the old plaster ceiling as if they'd been soldered. After half an hour, the girls had made little headway.

"We'll tackle this after lunch." Maryanne, as ramrod of the crew that day, made the decision and climbed down off her ladder. In the other room, Greg, Clare, and I wiped scrapers clean, and drifted toward our older sisters, remarking on their lack of progress. Maryanne had bits of wallpaper stuck to her glasses. Denise and Marla wore flecks of sticky goo on sweaty arms and aching shoulders. A little wet flag of 1930s wallpaper flew from one of Denise's decrepit sneakers. Across the ancient plaster overhead, moisture hung in heavy droplets. The drops were bigger, more numerous, ominous. The ceiling was starting to resemble a midwestern sky before a thunderstorm.

"I'll soak it one more time before we leave." Maryanne pumped the sprayer, picked up the wand, and delivered yet another soaking of sudsy water to the recalcitrant wallpaper. Like five highway workers standing around watching one guy work, we watched her spray, and so were all in the room when the ceiling dropped at once without warning. The overweight plaster fell like the wrath of God, as though a great fist had smashed it from above. Cracks snaked across the rest of the ceiling instantly, and a massive sheet of it broke and crashed down in pieces two and four feet long, pelting us, showering us with white plaster dust from decades past.

"It's all falling!"

"Run! Run for it!"

"Get out!"

Denise and Marla scrambled off their ladders and dashed for the door, where Greg and Clare and I, tangled in a Gordian knot of arms and legs, jostled to get out.

"Anybody—anybody hurt?" Maryanne gasped, tumbling out into the hallway with the rest of us, unaware that she was still clutching the heavy metal sprayer and wand. Her glasses had taken a hit from a falling chunk of plaster and jammed into her nose, drawing blood. Denise and Greg had goose eggs rising on their heads, and Marla had a splinter in her palm from her ladder. All of us were scratched and bruised, but nothing worse.

Silent and shaken, we surveyed the Armageddon of the southwest bedroom. "Whoa, you can see how they used to build in the old days," Clare said, looking up in awe. The ceiling showed dozens of thin strips of wood lath nailed three-eighths of an inch apart onto hefty two-by-fours. Plaster had been swirled onto and in between the lath to form the finished ceiling surface. The ceiling had stayed up because the long-ago workman had squished fresh plaster between lath, forming thick ribs of mortar above that held the whole. Moisture from our spraying had made the plaster too heavy for its own ribs.

Clare, still looking up, her mouth an *O*, had plaster dust in her nostrils. We looked at her and at each other. We were covered with white dust. Marla started to laugh. Denise joined in, hooting, and soon we were guffawing like hyenas. Clare, inspired by whiteface, puckered her lips and made like the French mime Marcel Marceau, arms out, hands twirling.

Greg edged into the tumbled debris within the room and gripped a jagged sheet of plaster, flipping it over. He scraped at its wet wallpaper with a fingernail, then picked up a steel-blade scraper and attacked the wet floral paper with that. It still didn't budge.

"Nothing on Earth will get that wallpaper off! We've proved it." Marla dug at the splinter in her palm. "Hey!" She looked up, eyes alight. "Maybe we can get the rest of the day off!"

Denise raised her eyebrows, causing white dust to sprinkle down her face. "Not likely." But Marla's unfounded optimism inspired her. Denise tilted her head, thinking. She started humming the tune of our own song, "The Baseball Team."

"Summer is vacation time, a time to laze and *shirk*." Denise began a new verse as we moved down the stairwell and out the front door, Greg feeling the goose egg on his head, Maryanne gingerly dabbing her nose.

"Extra sleep and fun for some," Denise continued singing, "but at Stritzels it means *work*!"

Marla caught the tune and thought up the next line. "Yes, work at stripping wallpaper, in a wet and steaming *room*."

"The sticky glue is reborn again," Maryanne contributed, right on key.

Denise's brow furrowed.

"The general mood is . . . breaktime!" Denise sang the spontaneous verse triumphantly, refusing to end with the rhyme *gloom*.

We piled into Old Betsy and headed home for lunch. Around the table, lobbying for the afternoon off, we made much of the supposed danger at the work site and of our little bruises. Since the plaster had already fallen, any danger had passed. Dad, who often came home from the university for lunch, wasn't buying our bid for an afternoon off.

"Work needs to be done before students return, and we'll alter today's List so you all can spread out on other jobs, in other houses," he quickly decreed.

"No." Mom dropped the single word like a stone into the river of chatter. We snapped into silence, surprised. We paused, forks raised, mouths full, a glass half lifted.

"No," Mom repeated. Everyone looked at her, her head tilted, mouth set, face calm. "These children are *not* going back to work anywhere this afternoon. And that house will be ascertained safe by you and me"—she looked at Dad—"before any of them go back in."

We dropped our chins to our chests to hide our grins, already thinking of biking, swimming, or stretching out on a blanket with a library book under the shade of fruit trees in the backyard.

Dad paused, but only for a single beat. He liked pleasing Mom. He trusted her judgment. He would never contradict her. "OK, Mother." He smiled. "OK." And he meant it.

Usually, we kids marveled at the power of Dad, but this noon we marveled instead at the power of Mom, who could change Dad's mind with a single word.

seven

AUTUMN, LATE 1960s

scavenging

The horse, more than five feet tall from hoof to shoulder, swayed above us. We had maneuvered one front hoof up into our Radio Flyer pull-behind wagon. The other front hoof dangled free in space, fourteen inches above the pitted concrete sidewalk. The horse's rear end, towering over us, listed to one side as we coaxed one back hoof up and into our worn wheelbarrow. Swaying, with two of its four legs now on wheels and two hanging free, the nag achieved a momentary, precarious balance.

Marla, age twelve, gripped the black metal handle at the front of the wagon. Greg, eleven, reached up to hold the beast in place, both hands flat against the brown painted canvas of the horse's withers. Clare, ten, on the other side to the rear, likewise reached to press small palms against paint-stiff cloth, stretched tight and tacked snug over the horse's lumber skeleton. Behind one rear hoof, I grasped the wood handles of the old wheelbarrow and crouched, ready to hoist and push forward. Paul and Steve, age seven, and Mark, six, orbited the contraption, keeping the beast balanced on its shaky foundation of wagon and wheelbarrow.

"All together now." Marla, wiry and strong, gave the order. "Ready, set . . . *go!*" She pulled the wagon in front, I pushed the wheelbarrow in back, and Greg and Clare and the Lids held the critter upright on its uneven wheels and pushed. It moved not an inch. We were seven Lilliputians trying to shift an equine Gulliver.

"We'll never get this home!" I was sweaty and discouraged. It was a warm autumn Sunday afternoon two weeks after Iowa State's big homecoming weekend, and we were already hot from lifting and maneuvering the awkward lumber-and-canvas mare onto our makeshift conveyance.

"Move." Big brother Greg ordered me off the wheelbarrow, taking over the handles at the rear. I skipped up front, pushing the teetering horse back into position before it could topple. "Let's try again."

"One . . . two . . . three!" Marla shouted. With mighty effort, the seven of us heaved forward. For a moment nothing budged, but we strained like soldiers pushing and pulling a creaking, swaying, painted Trojan horse—and the beast rolled forward six inches.

"Keep going! Push! Pull! Everybody together! Don't let it fall! Keep 'er rolling!" we yelled, jubilant, trundling forward another three feet. We had six blocks to go.

Every autumn before the university's big homecoming football game, fraternities and sororities throughout our Campustown neighborhood paired up to build, in the fraternities' front yards, giant three-dimensional displays illustrating the dominance of the Iowa State Cyclones over the rival team. These lawn exhibits, two and three stories high, remain unmatched by any other university. The tradition began around 1910 as simple signs on fraternity lawns proclaiming Cyclone football superiority. Engineering students electrified one early sign, making it blink on and off, but that marvel was topped the next year. As decades passed, the signs grew into mammoth scenes featuring enormous renditions of both teams' mascots; usually Iowa State's muscly cardinal was pummeling the other team's hapless mascot into the dirt. Competition among fraternities inspired ever more elaborate scenes, and by the 1960s, the lawn displays were the size of small houses. Each fraternity's gargantuan diorama, enhanced by floodlights and music, included several bigger-than-life characters constructed from lumber, fleshed out with molded chicken wire, and covered with a skin of crepe paper tufts or heavy canvas.

After homecoming, with the party over, the frats would slowly dismantle their creations, salvaging what they could and throwing away the rest. This particular year, homecoming had a Wild West theme. The painted-canvas-and-lumber horse, standing forlorn among the detritus in the front yard of a frat six blocks from home, had caught our eye. One Sunday afternoon, we seven younger Stritzels gathered our resources and pulled wagon and wheelbarrow through the neighborhood to the grand brick-and-stone front entrance of a big Tudor fraternity house on Lincoln Way, the main street through Campustown. We assembled on the broad front steps, suddenly nervous.

"You knock," Greg whispered to Marla, pointing to the large carved knocker on the massive oak double door. "You're the oldest one here. Besides, this was your idea."

"Come on! That horse is great! We can ride it in our backyard." Clare, from our vantage point on the stoop, had gotten her first up-close look at the horse. Previously, we'd seen it only from the public sidewalk in front of the frat. It was majestic. "Don't lose nerve now."

"I never lose nerve. I'm just planning what to say." Marla

stalled a moment longer. She closed her eyes, paused, took a deep breath, then lifted and let fall the weighty brass knocker, one, two, three times. We waited. Marla was reaching to lift it again when the door swung open. A fraternity brother looked out and then swung the door wide.

"Hi!" Marla turned on the full wattage of her smile. "May we," she asked, careful to use proper English, "take the horse from your homecoming display? We see you haven't taken it apart yet."

The student crossed his arms over his chest, biceps bulging through his T-shirt. He leaned against the doorframe, surveying the seven serious faces turned up to his. He flipped long brown hair out of his eyes and flicked ash from his cigarette out toward concrete steps. "You kids think you can move that thing? It's heavier than it looks."

"We can do it," Greg said, confident, tipping his chin up and nodding in the direction of our wagon and wheelbarrow.

"We can do it," the Lids echoed, tipping their chins and nodding.

"Well, hell yes, then," the college man said quickly, before we could change our minds. "We need to clear out what's left." He surveyed the deteriorating display. "Take any of that sh—" His gaze returned to us. "Any of that stuff you want."

Now we rolled our prize slowly, laboriously homeward over city sidewalks, sweating and heaving, switching positions as we tired. Neighborhood kids gawked and ran to join us, walking alongside, pushing, pulling, or just holding the lurching lumber-and-canvas beast upright. Our group grew larger, like a comet with a lengthening tail, as more kids joined in. With more hands holding the horse in place on its shaky wheels and more kids powering the wagon and wheelbarrow, we creaked and swayed forward a little faster. As we crossed streets, traffic was obliged to stop to let the impromptu parade pass by. Windows rolled down, and heads popped out of car windows. The mare—her painted eyes wide as if she were perpetually frightened by her precarious perch—rolled along, one hoof in a red wagon, another in a wheelbarrow. By the time we approached Welch Avenue, we resembled a medieval religious procession following an equine icon through the streets. Once in our backyard, we managed to hoist the critter up and out of its transport and maneuver it onto the lawn near the cherry trees.

All that autumn and winter, Mom never seemed to mind that the view out of our rear picture window was dominated by a large, fading horse with perennially frightened eyes. Dad, who did not tolerate junk of any kind around our house or any of our rental houses, accepted our acquisition immediately. He nailed two long flat boards under its feet so it wouldn't topple. We quickly figured out that if we pushed our picnic table close enough, we could take a running start, leap up on the table, and from there launch ourselves high enough to land atop Old Paint. On sunny autumn afternoons, Dad got out the Super 8 movie camera to take movies of us, lined up five at a time, bouncing up and down along its sturdy back.

The attraction lasted a few months, but the long Iowa winter was not kind to our creature. In early spring, with the paint completely gone and the canvas thin enough to show its lumber skeleton, we dismantled Old Paint. Any shred of canvas that had survived the snow, ice, and rain was bundled into the trash. The chicken wire was removed, rolled, and stored with other fencing in one of Dad's well-organized garages. The lumber became another stack of two-by-fours awaiting denailing.

❧

Iowa State's fraternities and sororities were rich sources of another treasure that appealed mightily to us: pop bottles. In the sixties, all pop came in glass bottles, friendly to hand and mouth, that
tapered up into a long neck topped with a crimped metal cap. The
bottles were returnable, for two cents apiece! Two cents! Such riches
were the stuff of dreams. It took only a few bottles to beat the penny-
per-paper each of us kids earned on Wednesdays delivering the
Ames Advertiser, our town's weekly classified ad circular.

After weekend parties, the back stoops of the Greek houses
throughout Campustown were littered with these discarded trea-
sures. Environmental awareness was decades off, and most people,
including college students, couldn't be bothered to return pop bottles to the store. That left the bottles, tossed in weeds near the alleys
behind frat houses, fair game for kids.

One spring Saturday morning in the 1960s, as we gathered on
our front porch for a bottle-hunting expedition, Marla held an
imaginary carrot peeler near her eyes. "Here, take this peeler, and
peel your eyes so you can find pop bottles." Slowly, she arced the
"peeler" over one wide-open eye, then the other. "Whew!" She
shook her head and blinked wide. "I see everything now." She
handed the peeler to Greg and waited as he too carefully peeled
both eyes. Clare dropped the metal handle of our red wagon on the
deteriorating concrete of the narrow alleyway, solemnly took the
imaginary peeler from Greg, and likewise peeled one eye, then the
other. I waited my turn after Clare, while Marla pretended to extract a second carrot peeler from her pocket and cradled each of
the Lids' heads in the crook of her elbow, in turn, peeling their eyes.

Blinking rapidly after my session, it seemed I actually could see
better. Call it the placebo effect if you like, but all seven of us were
now fully alert to finding hidden treasure. Clare pulled our empty
wagon slowly as we progressed up the alley, seven heads swiveling

to back stoops of Greek houses and aluminum garbage cans on either side, eyes darting toward open cardboard boxes that might hold wealth in the form of empty bottles.

"Look here!" Greg crowed, finding a stash of a dozen near the rear service entrance of the industrial-sized kitchen of the Pi Kappa Phi house. He scooped up deep-green 7-Up bottles with their "You Like It, It Likes You" slogan printed on the front, Pepsi-Cola bottles of swirled clear glass, and a couple of Mae West–curvy Coca-Cola bottles tinted lightest green. We laid them neatly in the wagon, end to end.

"More here!" Paul gloated, flipping open a rain-dampened cardboard box filled with a tumble of bottles: Hires Root Beer, Royal Crown Cola, and Orange Crush with its pebbly clear surface.

"Ya-hooo! Mountain Dew!" Mark read. He and Steve picked three dark-green bottles out of long grass by another fraternity's back stoop and laid them in the wagon.

Clare parked the wagon in the middle of the alley as we scampered to the back porches of the Greek houses—each sheltering forty to sixty still-sleeping young men—scanning for tossed bottles from the previous night's parties. We progressed through our neighborhood: Pi Kappa Phi, Theta Xi, and Adelante on Welch Avenue; Alpha Kappa Lambda on Knapp Street; Delta Upsilon, FarmHouse, and Tau Kappa Epsilon (nicknamed the Teke house) on Ash Avenue. By the time we got to Alpha Tau Omega on Lincoln Way, our wagon was nearing capacity.

"Here's a couple of Dr. Peppers." I balanced two clear bottles on the top of the pile, puzzling over the odd clock face printed on the bottle front. The logo showed the hours of ten and two in the right place, but a four where six should have been. Apparently, the makers of Dr. Pepper felt you should refresh yourself with their cola three times a day, at ten, two, and four o'clock. Why the four was out of place, none of us could guess. The only number that really mattered to us was two, for the two pennies each bottle would fetch at the little neighborhood store. With Greg and Marla taking turns pulling the now-full wagon, we navigated toward it.

The little store was a neighborhood institution situated conveniently near Crawford Elementary School, which all neighborhood children attended. The store, though impossibly tiny by today's standards, offered fresh produce, canned goods, household necessities, and fresh meats. Neighborhood housewives depended on the store for last-minute needs. If Mom found herself without an ingredient in the midst of dinner preparation, she'd send one of us kids to the little store for it. One late afternoon weekday when I was in second grade, she sent me around the corner from our house to buy two cans of sauerkraut to accompany link sausage frying in the skillet for supper. In the store, sauerkraut cans in hand, headed down an aisle toward the cash register up front, I suddenly encountered my teacher. Stunned that she existed outside the classroom and surprised to find her doing something as pedestrian as grocery shopping, I was struck mute.

"Hello, Cheryl." She paused her little cart and smiled down kindly. "What are you buying?"

I shifted from one foot to the other on floorboards so worn from shoppers' feet that the middle of the aisle was noticeably lower than the sides. Embarrassed to be purchasing something so ethnic, I dropped my head and mumbled into my chest, "Sauerkraut."

"Ah." My teacher nodded her head. Her beehive hairdo, stiff with hairspray, didn't budge. "Ah," she said again, at a momentary loss for words, unable on such short notice to call up any sort of casual remark about sauerkraut. She pushed her cat-eye glasses up her nose, caught sight of the candy-filled glass display case that supported the cash register, and then seized on the only comment she could think of: "It's always fun to go to the store when there's money left over!" She smiled at me again.

Money left over? Each can cost twenty-nine cents, and Mom had given me a dollar. In our house, it went without saying that money left over was brought back home, immediately and in full. None of us would think of spending it on ourselves. For the first time, the thought exploded in my head that not all families were like mine. Imagine being entrusted with family money and spending it on yourself! Not to mention eating candy before dinner.

I looked up again at my young teacher. Her blonde 'do still hadn't moved. Her generous eyeliner was magnified behind her perky glasses. I could see thick beige makeup on her face. She suddenly seemed like an alien from another planet, a carefree planet where a child could spend a leftover forty cents whooping it up in wild living.

"Yes, Miss Sheldon," I said as I paid for the sauerkraut and put the change in a safe pocket. "Yes, that would be fun."

But I was just agreeing to be polite. I knew my family was right.

Our family's culture of thrift made our pop-bottle refund money all the more precious. This was our money, fairly earned, and we headed directly to that abundantly stocked candy display case in the little store. Clare held open the battered screen door of the clapboard-front store as Greg pulled in our loaded wagon. Marla and I helped lift its rear wheels over the lip of the threshold, worn low and smooth from years of foot traffic; the Lids trailed in behind. Flushed from our labors, we felt exuberant, like sailors looking to collect their pay and go on shore leave.

"Well, lookee here!" Mrs. Shaw, stout, jolly, and short, was behind the single register as usual. "If it ain't the Stritzel clan!" She placed sweaty palms on the glass countertop and leaned over to peer down at our wagon. Her diminutive stature and generous girth made the move difficult, but with an extra heave, she could lean over just enough to see. "That's quite a haul! Been cleaning up behind the fraternities again?" A smile creased her worn chubby face, showing a row of teeth with some gaps. She turned to the back of the store and bellowed, making us jump. "Little Kenny!" She sucked in a deep breath, and bawled louder, "Little Kenny! The Stritzel boys are here!"

The Shaw family owned the store and lived in a close-by apartment. Their home wasn't like the single-family frame houses on neighboring streets, which were set back from the street with mature shade trees and a stretch of front lawn. Instead, this short stretch of Knapp Street along the tracks of the Fort Dodge, Des Moines, and Southern Railroad was zoned commercial for the store and, next to it, a one-up, one-down, white clapboard duplex apartment building. The Shaws lived in the upstairs unit. They had a rear, covered balcony that overlooked the rest of the neighborhood. On hot summer evenings after the store closed, Mrs. Shaw would often sit on that balcony, on a couch with shot springs, fanning herself with a piece of cardboard. The Shaws had three children about our ages: Lisa, Debbie, and Little Kenny. Little Kenny was a few months younger than our Lids. Mrs. Shaw was given to summoning her children home for dinner by standing on the balcony and hollering. She'd suck in a deep breath, haul back her head, puff out her ample chest, and call them by name, starting with the oldest, Lisa, who was Greg's age. "LEEEsah!" she'd shriek from her lofty perch, sending a stunning number of decibels ricocheting around the neighborhood.

Years later, when Greg was in his early teens, he'd entertain himself by adopting a falsetto tone and shouting back, from several houses away, "Whhaaat?"

"Diiinnnerrrtiiime!" Mrs. Shaw's shout would drift back over the neighborhood. "Cooome home!"

"Coming, Ma!" Greg would shift his voice higher, ramping up the volume, throwing everything he had into it.

"Make it quick!" With this shout, Mrs. Shaw mentally checked her eldest off the list. "Debbie!" she'd roar next, moving down the line of her offspring, and Greg was more than happy to carry on replying.

But such gentle mischief was years into the future. Today, Mrs. Shaw was behind the counter, smiling over it at us, ready to sell candy.

"Greg, take that wagon right on down the main aisle to the back door," Mrs. Shaw instructed. Greg and I pulled the wagon to the dim rear of the store, past a humming refrigerator case and a pock-marked chest freezer, and lifted a fly-specked drape to enter the stocking area. Mr. Shaw was on his knees unpacking a crate, his constant cigarette dangling from his lips. Ken Shaw Sr. coughed frequently. Skinny and barely taller than his wife, he had deeply tanned arms showing wiry muscle. Gray stubble adorned his sunken cheeks. His pleated work pants, shiny in the seat and thin in the knees, hung loose on his slight frame, his belt pulled snug to gather the waist. He stopped his work to smile at us, showing a few blackened teeth among the whites, and straightened up slowly, like a carpenter's articulated ruler unfolding length by length. He placed one hand on his lower back as he stretched, pinching his cigarette between thumb and forefinger. A man of few words, he left all the talking to his voluble wife.

A nursery rhyme popped unbidden into my head. *Jack Sprat could eat no fat, his wife could eat no lean.* The rail-like Mr. Shaw rapidly shifted bottles from our wagon into a plastic crate on the floor, his mouth moving as he counted silently. Every time I saw the Shaws, the rhyme played in my head. *And so, betwixt the two of them, they licked the platter clean.* I imagined the Shaws at dinner, skinny Mr. Shaw chain-smoking, corpulent Mrs. Shaw licking a platter.

"That's good—an even four dozen," Mr. Shaw rasped to Greg, then lifted the drape to shout down the aisle to his wife, "Ninety-six cents!"

It was enough, it was more than enough, it was an abundance of plenty. The Lids were already pressing against the glass case, trying to decide among Pixy Stix (striped straws full of sugar powder); packs of red or black licorice; handfuls of Bazooka bubblegum; or the sweet, red, chewy candy pellets called Boston Baked Beans. Little Kenny, finally summoned by the deafening shouts of his mother, shot like a barefooted streak down from their upper apartment next door, across the train tracks, through the back of the store, and down the aisle. He joined the Lids, choosing a box of SweetTarts, which his mother handed over free.

"Where you been?" Mrs. Shaw bawled at Little Kenny, her flowered housedress stretched across her voluminous bosom, front buttons straining to close the gap. "Watching Captain Kangaroo," Little Kenny snuffled, drawing a bare forearm across his runny nose. He was the youngest member of the Shaw family, the only one whose teeth were still all present and all white.

We clustered around the Lids and Little Kenny, craning to glimpse the bounty in the case. Clare chose a caramel Sugar Daddy on a stick and a strip of garish Candy Buttons stuck to paper; I got a handful of individual Root Beer Barrels, each in crinkly cellophane, and a roll of Lifesavers; Marla picked black licorice and a box of Good & Plenty; Greg chose a couple of jawbreakers and a Hershey bar.

Little Kenny joined us as we pulled the now-light wagon around the corner onto Welch Avenue and home. Marla bit off lengths of licorice, smacking her lips and turning her teeth as black as the Shaws'. We parked the wagon neatly in our driveway next to the side door stoop. Dad had painted small, individual parking spaces on the concrete driveway for our wagon, bikes, and trikes. Each piece of gear had its spot, so no outdoor gear would be left lying about. We trailed into the house, dropping wrappers in our pullout garbage bin, finishing our candy, licking lips and fingers. Mom, sitting amid flowing fabric at her sewing machine in the laundry room off the kitchen, raised her head from her work.

"All of you! Wash your hands!" She pointed to our first-floor bathroom. "And brush your teeth. This minute." We laughed and chattered and tumbled, still gleeful from our bottle hunt, into the bathroom. The quickest got to the drinking fountain and two sinks first, with the lollygaggers forming two lines behind them. Little Kenny, last in line, trailed out the bathroom door. He looked at Mom.

"Little Kenny," Mom said, her voice softening, her eyes smiling at the youngest Shaw child. "You can have one of the new toothbrushes from the drawer. I'll get it for you." She stood up, fabric rippling off her lap. "Stay and play with our boys today if you want. It's fine if you want to have lunch with us, too. Just make sure to run home and ask your mother first."

1965

don't run in the building

ag! You're It!" Marla bounded up the stairs, rounded a corner, and spied Greg in the second-floor corridor in the agronomy building on campus. Greg took off running.

"I see you, so now you're It!!" Marla's shout echoed down the vast, empty, tiled hallway. "You know the rules: if I see you, you're It!"

Greg was nine and fast. Marla was eleven and faster. Marla sprinted after Greg, both children forgetting Dad's stricture to not run in the building. Dad reminded us regularly, but this building was irresistible. Its long, broad hallways on two floors, linked by big, open staircases at both ends, made a perfect running loop. Only when we passed the open door of Dad's office on the first floor did we remember to walk. On this gray March Sunday afternoon, Dad was at his desk catching up on paperwork. He often took some of us with him to the agronomy building on Sunday afternoons while Mom and Maryanne stayed home with the Lids.

Today, Denise, Clare, and I, like Greg upstairs, were hiding from Marla. We three on the first floor wedged ourselves into the nook of a water fountain or behind the door of an open classroom.

In hiding, we couldn't see Greg pelting down the far staircase. Though quiet and still, we couldn't hear Marla's shouts as she gained on him because a pair of heavy swinging doors, meant to muffle noise from the staircase, separated the first-floor corridor from the staircase. Dad, though his office door was open, couldn't hear Greg's feet hammering down the staircase. He couldn't hear Marla's feet pattering after Greg. He couldn't see Greg race toward the heavy right-hand glass door, arms out to push it open. He didn't know, as Greg didn't know, that the right-hand door was locked.

An hour before, on this Sunday at the ragged end of winter, Dad had held open the main, front entrance door of the agronomy building for us five middle kids. We could come with him in the agronomy building, as in all buildings on campus, if we were quiet and respectful.

"Don't run in the building," Dad said as we wiped our feet on the mat. Our shoes had picked up slush even on the short walk from the curb, where Dad had parked Old Betsy against a rut of crusty snow.

Dad headed toward his office. He entered, leaving his door open, hung his coat on a hook, and sat down on his polished wood swivel chair. He picked up a round-barreled ink-cartridge pen, rolled the heavy chair forward to his desk, and started in on a stack of papers awaiting grading.

Out in the polished, echoey hallway, we five looked at each other with anticipation. "Auditorium first!" Denise breathed. She was, at twelve, the oldest sibling along, and we followed her lead. We five walked—fast—to the magnificent lecture hall. Today, as on previous visits, we tried to behave; we didn't want Dad to stop taking us. We loved going with him on Sunday afternoons, and we loved this building. Built in 1952, the agronomy building had mid-century rounded lines, spacious hallways, broad stairways, and modern classrooms. It was contemporary and curved, sleek with brick outside and gleaming with tile inside. Long and low, at three stories, with a curvaceous entry, the building didn't so much sit on its lengthy lot as recline on it. But the crowning jewel, especially to us kids, was the auditorium with its soaring ceiling. You could enter this indoor amphitheater on the first floor, run up the aisles toward the ceiling, and exit on the second floor. Rows of blond wood seats, with swing-up, click-in-place paddles on one arm for note taking, curved gracefully around the focal point in the center down below, where a professor—our dad!—would lecture students on some aspect of agronomy that would help feed a hungry planet.

"I'll be professor. You be students," Denise said. She stood down in the center of the auditorium, in front of the long blackboard, as Greg, Clare, and I scattered among the rising rows of seats. Denise pushed her glasses down her nose and looked stern. I discovered I could scoot under a seat, fold myself up, and hide entirely; I filed this information away for future games of hide-and-seek. Denise picked up a stick of chalk encased in a little aluminum holder, which she twisted to push more chalk out. In the agronomy building, even chalk was fun.

"Verily, I say unto you, fertilize!" Denise strode and gestured, chalk in one hand, long wood pointer in the other. She was quoting the saying from a cartoon poster of Dad that students had created as a gag gift for him a couple of years before. That poster, propped in his office, constituted our entire knowledge of agronomy.

"Here comes the screen," Marla called from the upper back of the auditorium. Her voice sounded different floating down from above. In the agronomy building, even talking was fun.

Up near the rear ceiling, Marla stood behind a flat console of knobs, levers, toggles, and lights. She pressed a button and, down behind Denise, a vast white screen descended with a soft electric purr. "Wow!" Marla pressed another button and the majestic screen ascended, rolling itself neatly up into its metal casing. "Let's see what these other buttons do." With Marla as conductor at the console, house lights dimmed and brightened, strips of stair lighting flicked on and off, and a floodlight illuminated Denise below. In the agronomy building, even turning on lights was fun.

We wandered out of the auditorium and down the halls, fascinated by locked display cases that held soil samples, thick little glass jars of field corn and soybeans, framed black-and-white photographs of students, all male, standing in cornfields. We gazed at treats in a vending machine without longing; we knew our family didn't waste money. Clare dipped her fingers into the little metal cubby of the change receptacle.

"A dime!" Clare was jubilant. In the agronomy building, even a vending machine we'd never use was fun.

We meandered into an open chemistry classroom, running our palms along smooth black lab tabletops, perching on stools. Each station had a little sink built in, and we turned the water faucets on and off.

"Don't touch those other handles!" Denise nodded at two chrome jets shaped like whorled seashells. "One's air, but the other's gas." The year before, Greg had inquisitively flipped the gas jet open and shut. When Dad had come to check on us, he had paused, sniffed, thrown open the windows, and laid down the law: no jets.

"Let's play tag," Greg said, and we scattered out the chemistry lab door into the hallway, like so many loose atoms.

"One, two, three." Marla stood against the wall in the first-floor corridor, her eyes covered. Greg sprinted toward the far staircase.

He flew up the stairs, taking steps two at a time, searching for a hiding spot among the open second-floor classrooms.

"Thirteen, fourteen, fifteen." Marla's voice was muffled, her mouth buried in the crook of her arm. Denise, Clare, and I scurried to find hiding places on the first floor.

"Eighteen, nineteen, twenty!" Marla crowed. She lifted her head. The first-floor corridor was silent, still, abandoned. Dust motes floated serenely in weak, late-winter light at the far end. Denise, Clare, and I, folded and tucked into hiding places not far from Marla, barely breathed. Marla deliberated a second, then spun around and darted up the staircase behind her. Loping over the topmost step, she rounded a corner, and at the end of the second-floor corridor, spied Greg, who ran toward the far staircase.

"You know the rules!" Marla repeated her shout, now edged with frustration. "If I see you, you're It!"

Greg gained velocity down the stairs, turned toward the first-floor corridor, and cannoned full speed toward the right-hand door, arms out. The locked door did not swing open. His left arm punched through the center of beveled glass, his momentum carrying his neck and head into the jagged hole. Glass smashed and flew, skittering like broken ice along the highly polished floor. Greg gave a heart-stopping cry, caught his toe on the bottom frame of the door, and jerked back. As he did, a serrated spike of glass sticking up from the wood frame carved an eight-inch hook-shaped gash deep into the inside of his left arm. Another dagger of glass, smaller, punched into his neck.

Screaming, crying, blood spurting and spattering. Glass everywhere, slivers of it sticking in the mess of Greg's inner arm. Slipping in blood on the floor. Greg, in an odd moment when time stopped, looking inside his arm at the strange whiteness of tendon and bone. Dad running faster than we'd ever seen him, scooping up

Greg, grabbing and holding the wreck of his arm, sprinting toward Old Betsy. Dad shouting at Denise to get Greg's coat and put it over him. Greg noticing, again with time stopped, gray clouds overhead and crusty gray snow around the station wagon. The rest of us in the back seat, crying with jagged breaths. Denise, in the front seat next to Dad, cradling Greg in his rough wool coat on her lap. Dad being firm with Denise, telling her to use both hands to clutch Greg's arm above the wound, tourniquet-fashion. Dad laser-focused on driving, gripping the wheel on turns, pressing the accelerator to the floor on straight streets, speeding to Mary Greeley Hospital in downtown Ames. Marla, Clare, and I, snuffling, shaking, looking over the seat at Greg's gaping arm. Marla thinking Denise was awfully calm, holding that horror-movie arm, keeping her tourniquet-of-hands tight.

At the ER, medical staff leapt into action, lifting Greg onto a gurney, tending his neck, running alongside the gurney as they whisked him to surgery. One nurse wound an elastic bandage, layers of it, around and around Greg's arm. Brilliant beads of blood oozed up between the elastic fibers. Another nurse began to cut Greg's shirt off.

Greg, his eyes serious, his brow wrinkling, frowned up at the nurse. "Mom won't like that!"

"Your mama won't be caring about your shirt," she promised, her eyes smiling above her mask, and Greg slipped under anesthesia.

The minute medical staff took over, Dad sequestered himself in a little phone booth off the waiting room to phone Mom. We kids waited and waited in that waiting room that seemed entirely washed with gray like the pitted, ragged snow outside. After what seemed a long time, Dad took the rest of us home. He pulled the station wagon into our driveway, and Mom came out our side door onto the concrete stoop, apron on, hands covering her face. Dad went to her and she melted into him, sobbing. It was the only time we saw her cry.

The more children you have, the more chances you have of meeting with catastrophe, but Greg's punch through the locked glass door in the agronomy building was our family's only serious accident. Greg stayed in the hospital a few days and returned to fourth grade a week later, something of a celebrity in his hard, white cast. Beneath the cast, layers of flesh in his arm, stitched with gold metal thread, gradually mended. When doctors removed the stitches, they missed one. Eventually Greg pressed on it, curious, and the tiny lump of gold emerged, he later said, looking like a parasite of precious metal. His neck healed completely; the glass shard that had stabbed into it had narrowly missed his carotid artery.

The only lasting effect of Greg's accident, besides the hook-shaped scar, is his tendency to pick things up using his thumb and third finger, instead of his thumb and index finger. The nerves responsible for that fine motion never healed.

"Don't run in the building," Dad had said. As years rolled past, we understood he meant behave: respect others, respect property, and remember you've been raised right, so act like it.

We never ran in a building again.

nine

1970

honeybunch and honeybees

ad knew how to do everything: build a house, close a sale, grow a fruit tree, teach a class, milk a cow, pour a concrete driveway, train a horse, or plumb a bathroom. On the summer day a rogue swarm of honeybees settled on one of the fruit trees in our backyard, we found out Dad knew how to keep bees.

They seemed to come from nowhere, materializing as a dark little cloud against soft blue sky. The Lids saw them first.

"Hey! What's that?" one of the Lids yelled. We children began to gather in the yard, puzzled and then intrigued by the cloud buzzing pianissimo in the distance. The dark, shifting cloud grew and shrank, changing shape, inflating and deflating as it ballooned at one end and contracted at the other. We ranged around the yard, sprinting here and there to keep an eye on it but always looking up. It was Saturday; we'd just done the breakfast dishes and were dressed in our regular motley collection of scruffy work clothes, ready for a summer day's work on our rental houses, yards, and gardens. Milling around the yard now, staring up with wide eyes, we looked like a crowd of yokels watching a barnstormer trying to land.

The little billowing mass tacked this way and that over neighboring backyards. It looked as if it were being squeezed into varying shapes by a giant, unseen hand. The buzzing grew louder, more ominous, and, it seemed to us, more hostile.

"It's coming this way," Paul said, fascinated.

"It does seem to be homing in on our yard," Denise murmured, not taking her eyes off it. The buzzing grew from pianissimo to pianoforte. Neighbor kids, their own antennae perpetually alert for any local excitement, saw the odd little cloud too and began to swarm to our backyard, following the droning cloud as if it were the Pied Piper. Like the shape-shifting mass above us, the shape-shifting mass of kids in our backyard was getting louder and more excited.

"What *is* it?" I hopped up and down on a bare patch of our lawn. Every summer, the grass back here lost its struggle to grow, surrendering to the constant traffic of kid feet. Every spring, under Dad's careful application of fertilizer, the lawn gained hope, thrusting up valiant blades of green, only to be battered down again as summer wore on.

Clare stood still. "Better get Dad."

"He's in the basement of 426 tinting paint," Denise supplied, not moving, watching the cloud.

As with many of the early 1900s-era houses on the street, the cellar of 426 was accessed from outside, through a wood-plank door laid at a forty-five-degree angle over half a dozen cement steps leading down into the dank, cool interior. Dad had outfitted this cellar as Paint Headquarters. We painted constantly: walls, cabinetry, plaster, drywall, basements, stairwells, ceilings. Some summers, festooned across scaffolding, we scraped and painted the exteriors of entire houses. We painted so much and so often that Dad finally purchased a paint-tinting apparatus so he could buy base paint in bulk and tint it himself. He set up this equipment in 426's basement because he could access it without disturbing student tenants in the house. Plus, this particular cellar with its cracked concrete walls couldn't be used for anything else.

Clare and I dashed through the backyards to 426. The cellar doors were opened and laid back. "Dad, a ball of insects, a bunch of bugs, or *something* is coming in our yard!" I yelled into the depths.

"What's that, honeybunch?" Dad appeared at the base of the stairwell. "Insects? All massed together?" He held an unopened can of paint in one hand, a little shiny steel opener in the other. "Bees." His eyes lit up. "It could be bees!" He put down the paint and sprinted up the stairs.

Over our backyard, the cloud was now a loose, amorphous aggregation of insects. It seemed to be homing in on one of our apple trees. The buzzing grew louder. The mass, as if it were a single organism, alighted on a limb and formed itself into a tighter, shape-shifting ball. To us children, the deafening spectacle of thousands of bees, crawling and droning and swarming over and over themselves into a hideous hanging clump that attached itself to the apple tree limb even as we watched, was the stuff of nightmares. The clump looked like a gargantuan, misshapen alien brain, writhing as it formed and reformed, constantly crawling, in continuous motion from its core to its outer edges.

We were fascinated and horrified at the same time. Dad, in contrast, was jubilant; he could hardly believe our luck. He immediately abandoned the planned work agenda for the day and called all hands on deck.

"OK, Baseball Team! We're going to capture the swarm and set up our own colony."

Efficient as always, Dad rapidly organized the pack of milling kids. "Greg, get the movie camera and start filming. Maryanne and

Denise, bring the big stepladder. Marla, honeybunch, get that card-board box, the big one, from the garage." We middle and younger kids, including neighborhood hangers-on, were to stay on the scene, keeping back but ready to help when needed.

"Clare-Cheryl,"—Dad's eye alighted on us—"run up into our attic and open the green trunk. You'll find an old bee-screen bonnet in there. Bring it down, and also the beekeeper's gloves." Dad knew something about bees from his childhood on the farm in Ohio; his father had kept bees at one time, and Dad had some of Grandpa's old beekeeping clothing.

We ran into the house, up through the second floor, and then clattered up another flight of stairs to our third-floor attic. We threw open the dusty trunk and saw what we were seeking. The bee bonnet was a hat with a cylindrical screen that came down from its brim to the wearer's chest. The bee gloves were leather gauntlets reaching nearly to the elbow, their yellow fingers stiff and mottled with petrified specks of a natural glue, called propolis, that bees produce. We grabbed the gloves and one bonnet and clattered back down the attic steps and through the house.

In the yard, Dad was using rubber bands to secure his pant legs tight around his work boots. Once he got the bee bonnet and gloves on, he looked secure, or nearly secure, against bees. He wasn't too concerned about stings, since he knew swarming bees first gorged themselves on honey before leaving their original hive. He told us that swarming is the bee way of multiplying. Bees swarm when their original home becomes too crowded. He said these bees were in a good mood, well fed and looking forward to a new home.

"This buzzing is not angry buzzing," Dad told us children, who ourselves were buzzing with excitement and not capable, in the moment, of making fine distinctions. "Stinging only occurs if bees feel they're being invaded, threatened, or attacked."

Dad, always the professor, warmed to his subject as the older girls organized the stepladder and cardboard box and Greg set up the movie camera. We middle and younger kids plus neighborhood children were swarming about the yard. Soon Dad had an informal, impromptu lecture class going.

"Once outside their old home, bees cluster on a tree branch or other structure until they're sure their queen is with them," he continued, setting up the stepladder. "If she's not, they return to the old hive. If she is, they wait in their temporary cluster until the scout bees come back to communicate they've found a new cavity somewhere else in which to make a new home."

These bees were in the waiting period, which could last anywhere from a few minutes to a day, depending on the scouts. "If we want bees," Dad said, rapidly passing his hands over the cardboard box to inspect its soundness, "we have to move fast!" We weren't at all sure we did want bees, but Dad's question was rhetorical. Want them or not, we were soon going to be sharing our yard with them.

"No need to worry about the bees left behind in the old hive with no queen," Dad continued as he pulled on the stiff gloves, though none of us was worried in the slightest about the welfare of the bees, queenless or otherwise. The only worries we had about bees involved their stingers and our own hides. "Before swarming, the bees remaining in the old hive will have begun raising a number of new queens, by separating and enlarging certain cells in the hives and feeding those hatched larvae a special mix of pollen and honey called royal jelly. One new queen will survive, and life in the old hive will carry on."

Soon all was ready. We kids stayed close enough to see, but far enough away to be out of stinging range should these bees' well-fed, happy mood suddenly turn dark. Greg switched on the movie camera as Dad placed the ladder under the apple tree and climbed up under the chaotically churning cluster, now the size of a watermelon. The droning of the swarm drowned out conversation, as well as any aircraft passing overhead. We children were finally silent, still and watching intently.

Dad neither hesitated nor rushed, but stayed slow and steady on the ladder as he brought the cardboard box up under the crawling, creeping, humming mass of bees. He calculated—then with one swift, decisive motion, like a guillotine blade suddenly untethered, he brought his fist down smartly on the apple branch.

The swarm let loose from the limb and dropped into the box, the bees on the outside roaring up in a cloud of surprise and commotion. Most of the swarm landed in the box with a surprising amount of weight; it tipped for an instant, some of the bees spilling out. A split second of insect mayhem ensued before, lightning fast, Dad recovered and slapped the cardboard box flaps over most of the swarm inside. Jolly bees or not, he may have gotten a sting or two, but that didn't faze him. None of us kids had a bee so much as lay a leg on us.

And just like that, we were beekeepers. Immediately, Dad perused the *Ames Advertiser* for used beehives and beekeeping equipment. He purchased new only what he couldn't find used and within two days had transferred the bees into a neat, well-organized beekeeping operation in the far corner of the backyard. He sited it behind a bank of tall daylilies, knowing that the natural obstacle would direct the bees' flight above the height of humans.

For a few days, we kids stayed well away from the bees, but we soon relaxed, realizing they weren't interested in us. The creatures were so benign, going about their nectar-gathering, honey-producing business, we nearly forgot they were there. They were too far from the house for us even to hear their industrious hum. The two short stacks of hives looked like a couple of miniature white apartment buildings. From a distance of ten feet, we liked watching our tiniest tenants, dressed in their fuzzy black-and-yellow striped suits, pause on the lip of an open hive to decide on a path before launching their commute. We knew they plumbed flowers, ordinary blossoms, for nectar and transformed it into honey. We appreciated this astonishing alchemy while suspecting that more tenants, even such small ones, would eventually mean more work.

We kids imagined that we were overworked already. Anytime any of us voiced this complaint, our Depression-era, farm-reared parents laughed out loud. Compared to their childhoods, ours was one of abundance and affluence.

But now, in addition to painting, scrubbing, and fixing the houses; pruning, raking, and clearing their yards of brush; picking seemingly endless rows of green beans and tomatoes; and husking what seemed like acres of sweet corn from our gardens, our family had another ongoing job: harvesting honey.

"Clare-Cheryl, you'll start with me outside at the hives this morning." Dad organized the day's work as usual while we were around the breakfast table. A good project manager, Dad allocated resources of time and labor judiciously. "Marla and Greg, bring in the honey centrifuge from our garage, plus that wood stand, and set it up in the kitchen. Tote up all the wide-mouth glass gallon jars from the basement and help Mom prepare them for the honey. Maryanne and Denise, we don't need everybody for honey extraction this morning, so you can clean the kitchen in 410 basement apartment."

Any of the rest of us would've groaned at this assignment, but our two oldest sisters just looked resigned, then determined. The pocket-sized kitchen in this particular subterranean apartment had just been vacated by a group of college boys who rented individual rooms in the basement but shared the kitchen. The young men had been laissez-faire, to put it kindly, about housekeeping.

"The grease will be an inch thick around that icky stove." Maryanne was not complaining, just stating the case. "And I shudder to think of the inside of the fridge."

"Why don't students clean up after themselves?" Denise knew no one would answer her question.

"Take all the cleaning gear we have. You'll need it," was all Marla could offer.

Dad glanced at the clock. "Paul, Steve, and Mark"—he spoke swiftly—"you're all three picking up sticks and other debris from all rental houses' lawns this morning, so Greg can mow tomorrow. We give Thee thanks for all Thy benefits, Almighty God." His leap into our after-meal prayer meant breakfast was over.

Dad pulled on a bee bonnet and gloves and headed out to the hives. Clare and I quickly changed into long-sleeved shirts and long pants, snapping rubber bands around our pant legs to keep errant bees out. We lifted the remaining two bee bonnets from the top shelf of the back-door closet.

"These look like something from olden days," Clare said as she examined one creased, sweat-stained hat with its circular fall of netting.

I examined the other. "Well, they were Grandpa's in Ohio, so they are really old, maybe from the thirties." New bee bonnets attached via zipper to a purpose-made beekeeper's coverall, but these ancient bonnets instead fit against the shoulders and chest of our regular clothes with nothing more than long tapes that tied under your armpits, looped around your back, and tied again in front. Using a series of complicated knots, Clare and I tied the tapes of each other's bonnets around our chests before running outside.

Dad was already working around our two white-painted hives

in the far corner of our backyard. Before starting to help, we watched for a few minutes as he extricated and lifted the honey-combed frames, full of honey, that fit in the hive's supers. Supers are wood boxes that form the hive. They stack up, one on another, indeed like floors in an apartment building. Within each super, honey-filled frames hang like files in a file drawer. We began to see why bees were some of Dad's favorite creatures. They worked efficiently, each to its assigned task, never lazing or shirking or whining about getting tired. And their individual efforts coalesced into a beautiful end product: honey. The hives were a microcosm of work and productivity at its finest.

"Do you know why we've chosen a bright, warm day to work with bees?" Dad spoke softly as he started the handheld smoker. We didn't. "Because the field bees are out today gathering nectar," Dad said, gently activating the smoker. "And this smoke will distract the house bees. We work gently around an open hive to provide a minimum of disturbance." Dad spoke just loudly enough to be heard over the hum.

Usually, we kids stayed away from the hives and out of the bees' flight path. Now, close up, Clare and I were silent, careful, slow-moving. The bees buzzed around us. I could hear my breath, loud and rapid. My heart was beating fast. We watched bees alight on the super's landing pad and crawl into the hive and bees exit the hive to take flight. It was like watching diminutive aircraft on an especially busy aircraft carrier.

"So, honeybunch," Dad concluded his lecture, using his favorite term of endearment for any of us, "stinging is not a problem if bees don't feel threatened, if a minimum of smoke is used, and especially if both bees and beekeeper are genetically of a calm and gentle nature."

A bee alighted on my chest. Perhaps it merely wanted to investigate the floral fabric of my shirt, but I didn't give it the chance. If I had, perhaps everything would have been fine. Instead, I smashed it. And my smashed bee loosed pheromones that instructed the rest of the hive to find and murder us. Even then, if Clare and I had stayed calm as Dad said, if we'd heeded his prudent lecture on how to behave around an open hive, everything might have been fine. But we did neither of those things. We were not of a calm and gentle nature, but preteen, flighty, and spooked.

From out of the hive, straight at Clare and me, came a dark, airborne river of bees, looking like enemy fighter planes out of a Saturday morning cartoon. The bees, supposed to be distracted by smoke and calmed by their gentle beekeeper, instead mobilized like a battalion and came roaring out en masse, bent on avenging their downed comrade. The bees hit on our bonnets and clothing, attacking again and again, their now-furious buzzing roaring in our ears. Calmly, gently, we ran in circles like whirling dervishes, shrieking and dodging to get away from the living nightmare zooming around our heads. Dad, who was not getting stung—or if he was, was not reacting—tried to calm us, but we could no longer see or even hear him. Our senses registered only the bees dive-bombing against the screening around our faces and the sound of high, thin screaming. I couldn't tell where the screaming was coming from. Then I felt the brush-crawl of insects against my cheek, on my neck, in my ear. The bees had breached our netting and were crawling inside Clare's and my bee bonnets. I screamed afresh, realizing the screaming had been coming from us all along.

Bees batted against our necks and faces. We felt them tangle in our hair and tried to smash them by smacking ourselves in the head through our bonnets.

"GET THEM OFF! GET THEM OFF!" We couldn't know which of us was screaming. Certainly neither of us could summon the mental acumen to get those long, complicated series of tapes on our bee bonnets untied. And Dad couldn't catch us to try. We galloped around and around the yard, and when that didn't faze the swarm of bees following us, we sped bellowing through the back door into the kitchen, howling at Marla and Greg to get our bee bonnets off. As we and our angry pursuers came careering in the back, Marla and Greg scattered out the front, vanishing a full second before the back screen door even fell shut behind us. Mom wasn't in the kitchen at that moment, having descended to the basement to fetch jars.

Dad, shouting at both of us to stop, caught up with us in the kitchen and extricated us from our well-tied, well-knotted bonnets. Mom made a paste of baking soda and water and tended our stings, which after all were few. Marla and Greg ventured back in, got fly swatters, and started swatting the handful of bees that had come indoors.

Dad was madder than a hornet at both Clare and me. It was our acting like fools that had caused the ruckus, he said. The bees were just innocent creatures reacting to our hysteria. Had we not absorbed his quiet words about beekeepers requiring calm and gentle natures? Had we heard one word of his lecture? We had not. Instead, we'd panicked at the first hint of trouble. Panic-stricken ninnies do not good beekeepers make. He'd expected better of us. Disgusted, he left to do the outdoor work at the hives by himself and put Clare and me on centrifuge duty in the kitchen.

We weren't sorry to leave the bees to Dad. Of course, we hadn't intended to foment trouble and strife out at the hives, but now that we had, I realized it was somewhat useful: Clare and I were unlikely to be called out for bee duty again anytime soon. As we settled down, we started to realize Dad was right. We'd deserved the dressing down. But there wasn't much time for reflection; our kitchen had become a honey-extraction factory and was gearing up for full-bore production.

I knelt on the kitchen linoleum next to the stainless steel centrifuge, a drum-shaped cylinder about three feet tall and fifteen inches in diameter, and gripped the hand crank that extended from the side. The big silvery cylinder had a spigot near the bottom. Mom, Marla, and Greg had placed the centrifuge on end on the little wood stand Dad had made from short lengths of denailed lumber; the stand lifted the device just high enough off the floor that we could easily place a gallon glass jar under its low spigot.

"This is fun!" I started to crank. The frame-like interior structure spun easily and pretty soon was whirling.

"Stop now," Mom said. "You see how it works, but it's empty. We need to wait for the frames with honey in them."

Dad, his bonnet and coverall bee-free, carried in two frames laden with honey. He held one of them on end over a flat pan. He picked up another beekeeping tool, a hot electric knife, in his right hand. Carefully, he moved the sizzling knife down the waxy face of the frame, slicing off just the top layer of the comb, called cappings, which dropped in thick ribbons into the pan. Quickly, he flipped the frame over and did the same to the other side. He loaded this frame into the cylinder, then repeated the process with the second frame and slid it too into our little cylinder.

"Now you can spin." Mom smiled at me.

I gripped and cranked. Loaded, the centrifuge was heavy and resistant.

"You're too slow. Let me." Greg reached toward the crank.

"She'll get it!" Mom held a gentle arm against Greg. "Clare will take the next turn, then you, then Marla."

Pushing at the crank, I could feel the inner structure start to move, weighted and slow.

"Come on, you can do better than that!" Greg was itching to get at the crank.

I pushed harder on the crank, which responded with an almost imperceptible increase in speed. Encouraged, my few bee stings forgotten, I threw my arm and back into it, building momentum. The inner structure began to spin like a merry-go-round overloaded with fairgoers who have eaten too many corndogs. I laughed in delight, whipping the crank around now. Inside the drum, centrifugal force began to fling honey out of each frame's thousands of tiny octagonal chambers against the interior wall. The honey dripped down and gathered at the bottom of the drum behind the spigot.

Mom had sterilized glass gallon jars ready; a couple dozen were lined up on the counter. As I spun the centrifuge, Clare placed a jar beneath the spigot and flipped the spigot open, loosing sweet golden honey in a stream. It was like turning on a kitchen faucet. The river of honey, thick as a thumb, flowed into the jar. We watched, fascinated.

"Wow. Cool." Greg was ready behind Clare with a second jar, and Marla was behind him with a third. We filled jar after jar, switching places at the crank, stopping only when Dad came in with more frames. Swoosh! His hot electric knife sliced off the cappings. Slide! He placed frames down into the centrifuge. Crank! Clare started the interior structure rotating. Flip! Greg opened the spigot, and we all paused for a moment, fascinated, watching it fill. The viscous liquid folded over and over itself in the jar, like a coiling rope whose shape melted into smoothness. Flip! Greg closed the spigot. Whisk! I swept one filled jar away and Marla put an empty into its place. Twist! Mom turned metal lids onto the jars.

Along the counter, the line of gleaming golden gallon jars grew longer. Sunlight streaming in the window behind the jars made the honey lustrous. Soon all jars were full. The contents of the golden jars looked celestial, like abundant blessings come down from heaven.

It was time for lunch. Dad came in the back door and hung up his bee bonnet. Mom put water on to boil for corn. Marla and Greg went out to 426's back garden to pick and husk a dozen ears. Clare started slicing tomatoes. I sponged honey off the sink, counter, and floor. Paul, Steve, and Mark came in from working on the lawns, loud and sweaty, flecks of grass sticking to arms and legs, running to be first at the drinking fountain. I set the table. Marla and Greg came in and tumbled armloads of clean, husked ears into the boiling pots.

Maryanne and Denise flung open the side door and lugged in a tote of cleaning products and a vacuum cleaner, parking the vacuum cleaner by the door. Maryanne straightened up and rubbed her lower back with her palm. "That basement kitchen at 410 was just as greasy and foul as expected," she reported cheerfully.

"But it's clean now," Denise finished, "ready for the next tenants. We could eat off the floor over there."

"How about we eat off our own table, right now? Hurry up!" Greg, like all of us, was waiting for the two older girls to wash their hands.

"Oh, hold your horses." Denise slid into place on the bench.

"Bless us, O Lord." Dad cut off further bickering by starting our before-meal prayer. I looked down at my folded hands, re-inspecting my now-swollen bee stings. I glanced up at the golden jars lining the counter. Blessings from heaven? I touched a sting and winced, then relaxed as I looked around the table at my siblings and parents. Yes, blessings from heaven.

We had bread slathered with honey for dessert.

ten

1968

weekend at the lake

Yum." Marla, fourteen, held a steaming ear of corn with both hands and munched it typewriter-style. She was wedged between siblings on a picnic table bench; the evening sun streamed sideways, glinting off her knife as she reached for a pat of butter.

"Can you imagine people actually buy sweet corn from grocery stores?" Maryanne, seventeen, picked up a salt shaker. "Poor things. They think it's fresh!"

Lined up at two tables in the front yard of a lakeside cabin, we nodded our heads up and down in a sort of gustatory rhythm as we crunched our homegrown corn. Maryanne sprinkled salt on hers, rolling it on her melamine plate, and wiggled her bare toes under the table, luxuriating in the cool short grass. The movement roused a hum of mosquitos, but all eleven of us had sprayed ourselves with repellent, so the insects' song was an empty threat.

"And this fish!" Dad cut into a whole perch, fresh caught that afternoon, then rolled in cornmeal and crisp-sizzled in bacon fat. "What a meal, thanks be to God."

"Nothing better than fish right out of the lake." Mom smiled.

The smell of hot bacon fat mingled with those of buttered corn and tangy Italian dressing on sliced tomatoes, and a lingering aroma of bug spray. Slanting rays filled the sky above us with light that ombréd into dusk at the horizon. Under our feet—all except Mom and Dad were barefoot—green lawn swept down to a flat, grassy lakeshore of cattails and smartweed. Before us lay Beaver Lake, ninety-four acres of water, now glass-calm and reflecting the evening's lavender sky. Behind us on the lawn sat our accommodations for the weekend, a humble brown cabin.

The cabin was one in a line of properties, interspersed among trees, entirely ringing Beaver Lake. Our college girl boarder Norma Burshem, who embraced our unwieldy family during the several years she lived with us, had invited us to use her family's fishing cabin for this long summer weekend, and Mom and Dad had happily accepted. They liked to fish, indeed had spent their honeymoon fishing on a Michigan lake, but now rarely got the chance.

Norma's cabin, near the town of Ellendale in southern Minnesota, with its compact bathroom and tiny kitchen, was built for a family of four. We eleven Stritzels were packed in like anchovies in a tin, but who cared? We weren't inside that much, anyway. The sun shone during our three long summer days there. We ate meals outdoors, scooped up minnows in a bucket, and caught fish with bamboo poles off the splintery dock. Greg, a gangly twelve-year-old, had managed to fall off that dock into the drink within minutes of our arrival. We played catch and volleyball on the lawn and headed off for three-hour hikes on the dusty one-lane gravel road that circled the lake.

Now, on our last evening here, the light fading, Mom and Dad held hands as they strolled toward lawn chairs on the dock. We nine cleared plates, forks, and glasses off the picnic tables and toted everything inside. The little countertop in the dark kitchen was already crammed with two big electric skillets of fishy cornmeal crumbs in solidifying bacon fat, two deep pots of water, and cutting boards coated with drying tomato juice and speckled with seeds. We pushed cookware aside to dump our dishes, making a towering pile of plates, as we split for the outdoors.

Maryanne did not join us. She surveyed the kitchen, hands on hips. As oldest, she felt obliged to always do the right thing, to always set an example for eight younger siblings. As oldest, she was perennially caught between behavior expected of an adult and mischief inherent in children. As oldest, Maryanne took the high road in a lifelong attempt to lead us on the right path. In return for her efforts, we early on pegged her with the nickname Big Pah-Blah, which meant Boss. Now, standing alone in front of congealing bacon fat in the claustrophobic wood-paneled kitchen, Maryanne was suddenly fed up with picking up the slack.

"Marla, you know it's your turn!" Maryanne shouted with uncharacteristic pique at the vanishing back of Marla, who with the rest of us was disappearing out the screen door. At home, we relied on a posted chore schedule for divvying up chores. Here, our schedule had gotten out of whack. No one wanted to stay in the hot, cramped kitchen, when outdoors the cool summer evening beckoned and the rowboat rocked gently against the dock. Maryanne raised her volume. "Marla! Get in here and do the supper dishes. There's no dishwasher here, and I'm not doing it this time! *Get back here!*"

"It is NOT my turn, and you're not in charge of me!" Marla flung back furiously over her shoulder, quickening her pace toward the dock. Skipping faster, she snatched her library copy of *The Witch of Blackbird Pond* off the webbed seat of a lawn chair and sprinted toward the boat.

Maryanne—ever responsible, always compliant, never complaining—snapped. She shot out the screen door, flew down the path, and with one headlong leap tackled Marla to the ground. Marla, whip-thin and strong, wily and gymnastic, wriggled free and scrambled two steps, only to fall again when Maryanne, desperately scrabbling along the ground, clutched her ankle. In a flash, Marla squirmed free once more and sprinted around back of the cabin, heading for the gravel road that led to escape. Maryanne, calling on hidden reserves of speed and strength, caught the miscreant and tackled her again.

"You WILL do those dishes! You ARE NOT getting out of them!" Maryanne yelled, planting herself on Marla's trunk, pinning her shoulders to grassy earth.

"Those dishes aren't mine! I DO THEM WHEN IT'S MY TURN!" Marla twisted and kicked, but the fight was trickling out of her. Maryanne had the upper hand, as well as truth, on her side.

By this time, the rest of us had encircled the combatants and were hooting and cheering, enjoying the rare spectacle of two older sisters tussling in the dust.

"Two-four-six-eight." Clare stuck both arms straight out like a cheerleader, fists waving imaginary pom-poms.

"Who-do-we-appreciate?" I joined Clare's chant as we waved arms overhead, and swung hips left and right in unison. "Two-four-six-eight!" We turned up the volume, picked up the pace, and swung arms and hips further.

"We-see-Maryanne-showing-an-arm-crossbar-move-to-gain-the-superior-position." Greg knelt in the scrawny grass by the combatants and rapid-fired into the imaginary microphone of his left fist. "But now here comes Marla! She's fighting back! She's trying the deadly scissor squeeze. If she gets those gymnastic thighs scissored around her opponent's middle and squeezes shut, it's all over!"

"Maryanne, don't get stuck in the scissor squeeze!" Denise coached, kneeling on the nearly bald earth between cabin and road, eyes wide in feigned distress, pounding her fists into the dirt.

"We've got the ring drawn." Paul dragged a stick in the dirt around our scuffling sisters. Mark and Steve clapped and whooped.

"It's the Big Pah-Blah against the Gymnastic Queen!" Greg yelled into his fist.

"Go Pah-Blah! Go Gym Queen!" I found a rhythm.

"Go Pah-Blah! Go Gym Queen!" The rest joined the chant. "Go Pah-Blah! Go Gym Queen!"

From the dusty cloud at our feet, Marla and Maryanne looked up at the circle of hilarity surrounding them. Marla relaxed her scissored thighs from around Maryanne's trunk and Maryanne gasped in relief.

"We didn't miss anything, did we?" Dad rounded the corner of the cabin, Super 8 camera held aloft. He raised it to his eye.

Mom was right behind him. "We heard the excitement and didn't want to miss out. I imagine the entire lake, if not the whole county, heard you."

The Big Pah-Blah scrambled to her feet, looking sheepish. The Gym Queen jumped up and pretended to put a hammerlock around her opponent's neck. Maryanne made a mock-fierce face and put up her dukes as Marla hammed it up, sparring, jabbing punches into the air as the Super 8 whirred.

"Make a movie of us! Take us!" Paul tackled Steve to the ground, falling in front of the camera. "Are we in the picture yet?" Mark took a flying leap and landed on top of Paul and Steve. "We want to get in it!" Steve rolled so the Lids' dogpile was up front, and Dad panned out to get them in the frame.

Marla and Maryanne beat dust off their clothes, picked grass out of their hair, called a truce, and did the dishes together.

Later that evening, as lavender twilight deepened and bats darted overhead, we built a campfire on the shore, on a cleared spot encircled with weathered logs. Now virtually bathed in bug spray, we perched on the logs. Denise tuned her guitar. The campfire crackled to life, its core of newspaper and tinder suddenly flaming, throwing orange light onto our circle of faces.

"If I had a hammer . . ." Denise started the Peter, Paul and Mary song. Mom came down the slope of dark lawn carrying a tray of marshmallows, graham crackers, and Hershey bars. Dad followed with an armload of old metal extendable roasting sticks he'd found in the cabin.

"I'd hammer in the morning . . ." Maryanne, Marla, and Clare took up the tune, nodding and raising eyebrows at Dad. "I'd hammer in the evening, all over this land." The song is about justice and freedom, but it was also about Dad, who indeed often hammered on the rental houses morning until night.

"Keep it coming—you sound great!" Dad helped the Lids extend the roasting sticks, which had jammed in the short position. Dad and Mom didn't sing with us, but they enjoyed listening. "You should be on TV."

We knew Dad was wildly biased, but we puffed a little with pride and pleasure anyway as we built volume. "I'd hammer out love between my brothers and my sisters, all over this land."

Steve speared a marshmallow on metal prongs and thrust it into the flames. Paul and Mark kept theirs nearer the glowing edge. I saw a cubbyhole of white heat within the fire and edged my marshmallow into it.

"Let's make up a verse about us, right here, right now, to add to 'The Baseball Team.'" Denise was inspired.

"OK." Marla was game. She started, "One summer while at Norma's cabin . . ."

"A vacation that was great to *take*," Maryanne supplied.

Denise paused mid-strum, thinking back over the weekend to our arrival. Her brow furrowed, then her face lit up. "Greg, he stepped right off the dock . . ." Denise paused. She had planned the obvious rhyme, but waited so someone else could have the pleasure of filling it in.

"And fell into the *lake*!" Clare and I finished with a flourish.

"That's fun. Let's keep going." I picked toasted marshmallow off metal prongs and transferred the blob of crackly caramelized sugar into my mouth.

Marla began another verse, "Our huge and horrendous family was in that cabin *packed*."

"We had most things we needed," Denise carried on. We paused to think.

"Space was all we *lacked*!" Marla nailed it.

"Let's sing 'Blowin' in the Wind.'" Maryanne wanted to get back to Peter, Paul and Mary before the evening ended, so Denise started the familiar chords. We harmonized through "Lemon Tree" and "500 Miles" as the fire dwindled to a flat circle of glowing coals, chill started to emanate from the water, and mosquitos began breaching our insect repellent.

"Enough. Let's wrap it up!" Denise took the capo off her guitar and laid the guitar in its case. Greg slapped a mosquito. Clare gathered roasting sticks.

"You kids go on ahead." Mom was somehow not bothered by the mosquitos. "Dad and I will see the fire out."

We straggled up the slope to the little cabin. At its door, we paused: we heard Mom and Dad singing. Our parents, who never sang with us, once in a rare while sang together. We turned around. We didn't know the song. We imagined it was from an era before we nine existed, from a time when Mom and Dad weren't Mom and Dad, but Marcella and Joe. We saw Dad shift closer to Mom, and their heads drifted together.

"Goodnight Irene, Goodnight Irene, I'll see you in my dreams."

We could just make out their silhouette against moonlight reflecting off the lake.

At the dinner table, early 1960s.
From left: Cheryl, Clare, Greg, Denise, Marla, Maryanne.
Note laundry and aluminum "cow" on pass-through
behind them.

1968

details make perfection

*F*rozen, black, and bone-cracking cold. In the midst of deep winter in Iowa, as the northern hemisphere wheels its face from the sun and looks outward to the far reaches of the universe, we got a taste of what deep space might feel like. We felt it waiting for us on those frigid, pitch-black mornings after heavy snowfall when Dad roused us from the nests of our rumpled beds at five o'clock.

"Many hands make light work!" Of all Dad's sayings, every one extolling the healthful, morally uplifting power of hard work, this one got the most use. As always, Dad infused the phrase with genuine, effortless cheer. Slowly, it permeated our sleepy consciousness. This early on a winter school morning, Dad's ebullient invocation could mean only one thing: it was time to shovel.

Each of our dozen rental houses had a front porch, a back stoop, concrete paths along the sides, and driveways. Some had backyard parking lots. Parking lots! Each house, of course, also had a long public sidewalk. Corner houses had two. After the night's storm, all this hardscape was buried under ten inches of heavy snow, and it was our job to remove it. Before breakfast. Before school. Before any of the sleeping college students inside our houses, cozily snuggled in their beds, awoke and ventured to class. Foot traffic over unshoveled walks—Dad never allowed this to happen, but if it did—would compact snow into icy patches and ruts that would freeze solid to the sidewalk until spring.

Buried under covers, barely awake, I resisted for a minute, burrowing deeper into bed. But weak overhead lights were snapping on in our upstairs bedrooms, and in those pools of illumination, I saw, through squinted eye, siblings pulling on long johns and searching for extra socks. I could hear Dad and Mom downstairs. I knew they were already dressed. Mom was making her coffee, its aroma wafting through the house. I lay still for another half minute until the thought fired in my brain that I was going to be scorned by my siblings as a slacker, the ultimate dishonor in our house. I threw off sleep along with quilted covers and jumped toward my warm clothes.

I pulled on long johns first, then one pair of pants, and yanked up another pair of pants over the first. The layer of air between two pairs of pants forms a surprisingly effective barrier against cold.

"Where's my long-underwear shirt?" I mumbled. Clare, rubbing sleep from one eye, silently lifted the waffle-woven top off a closet hook and held it out. I popped it over my head. Moving faster, I pulled on a pair of cotton socks, then a thick pair of wool ones over those.

My siblings were trickling downstairs and out the door. I did not want to be the last one outside. I grabbed an old sweater and sprinted out of the bedroom and down to the first floor, toward the overfull closet by the side door. Tangling with a last, lagging sibling or two in the small space, I jostled my winter coat off its hanger, then zzzipped! zzzipped! up boots, wound a crocheted scarf around my face, reached both arms behind my head to knot it, and pushed on mittens. Finally out the door with a tumble of siblings, I snatched up a snow shovel from several of them leaning against the metal railing of the concrete stoop.

We were in another world. A black dome of night sky, like the inside of a giant overturned cup, was lit by sparkling stars, spilled and flung across vast dark heavens. Underfoot, crystalline snow caught and reflected a million points of starshine. The deep snow transformed our ordinary neighborhood into a Christmas card: old frame houses hunkered under the thick, soft blanket, and arching tree branches traced deeper black outlines under their burden of white frosting. Windless, shining, sparkling, it was a still and silent universe—but only for a moment.

"Stop lollygagging! Get moving!" Clare's words were muffled by her scarf and drowned out by the scrape of her shovel against concrete. Our own sidewalks, plus side and back stoops and broad front porch, were shoveled already. Dad had been out minutes before us, and he shoveled fast. He was the usual blur of efficient motion.

To the back and side of our house, hidden behind a trellis that bloomed with bittersweet in warmer months, Maryanne jockeyed big aluminum garbage cans out of the way so Denise could shovel the concrete pad beneath them. In our driveway, Dad and Greg fired up our little gasoline hand-driven snowplow for the parking lots and driveways. The instant it sputtered to life, Dad left it in Greg's hands, snatched up his shovel again, and vanished off down the street toward another property. Greg, his impossibly skinny teenage legs still skinny even under two pairs of pants, wore a stocking hat with a tail that trailed halfway down his back. Hands on the muttering, growling plow, he maneuvered the little machine back and forth, back and forth, stocking hat tail flipped over one shoulder, methodically clearing our spacious driveway.

Marla flung her shovel aside into a drift, stretched out her arms, and dropped flat on her back, sinking five inches down in a perfect, untouched rectangle of pristine snow. Her arms and legs wind-milling, she pressed a deep snow angel into the white blanket. Her laughter bubbled up from below.

I heaved shovelful after shovelful up and off the front sidewalk. Panting, I scolded her through my scarf: "Get moving! Come on! You'll make us all late!"

That she might be slacking never occurred to Marla. Seeing her having fun, twins Paul and Steve likewise flung shovels aside and fell backward into their own rectangles of perfectly snow-covered yard.

"Ah-ha!" In an instant Mark chucked a shovel-load of soft snow onto their faces before sprinting, shovel in hand, toward the safety of a rental house down the street.

"OK, OK, enough, we have nine houses to go and I want to get to school early for my project," grumbled Denise, a perfect student. She shoveled steadily as Marla leapt toward another section of yard and fell flat again into its cushion, making another angel. We heard the city snowplow rumbling three streets over. Stars were fading in the navy sky. The ribbon of eastern horizon, broken by the line of houses with lights winking on here and there, showed an edge of pink and orange.

"Oh, what's your problem? The work'll get done!" Marla twirled up out of the snow, slapping it from pant legs and shaking it off her hat. "It always gets done!"

"That's because we do it," Clare and I muttered in unison, shoveling in tandem. We were starting to sweat under our layers of clothing. I finished one extra-long sidewalk and surveyed several more down the street.

"Why can't the students shovel their own dang walks?" I added.

"Because they won't do it, and then someone'll slip, and they might sue us." Denise didn't break stride as she kept her head down, steadily shoveling.

Push, lift, toss. Dad was still a house or two ahead of us, his shovel a study in efficient motion. We pushed our shovels along concrete, filling the metal faceplates with heavy snow. Lift! We bent knees, breathing hard under the weight of loaded shovels. Toss! We flung the shovel loads off to the left. Push, lift, toss. We were waking up, warming up, working faster. We nine, led by Dad, were a snow-removal team, moving from property to property, methodically clearing driveways, sidewalks, wood porches, parking lots, concrete stoops. The corner houses were the worst; 2603 Knapp Avenue in particular had vast expanses of hardscape, and we caught up with Dad here, working on 2603's extra-long sidewalks.

"Details make perfection," Dad said cheerfully as he shoveled. "But perfection is no detail!" Dad preached perfection no matter what job we were doing. Order, quality, and structure were not optional. He never did any job halfway, so we didn't either. We cleared every walk neat and square to the edges. No matter the volume of blizzard, our properties never showed a sidewalk with a single, lazy, wiggly shovel-width cleared down the center. We scorned such sidewalks.

Pausing to look at our work, I saw every walk shoveled right down to gray concrete, plenty of room for two to walk abreast between straight canyon sides of vertical snow. Sweat dripped under my thermal long-john top, and hunger started to gnaw, but I looked back with satisfaction at the snow-cleared properties. Just three houses to go—not much longer now. Dad had moved ahead of us again, out of sight. I thought of Mom at home making breakfast. She'd be heating hot chocolate in a pot on the stove and frying bacon in electric skillets, with eggs waiting to sizzle in bacon fat to sunny-side-up perfection.

"Finally!" Clare exulted as we finished neatening the edges of the parking lot behind another corner property, the last one. The sky was fully bright now, clear and baby blue. The early rays of the sun sparkled so brilliantly on fresh snow, it hurt our eyes.

"We're outta here!" Denise hoisted her shovel, and we fell in step behind her.

"Ah!" Mark yelped as a snowball pegged him square on the back of his head. "That's freezing! You beast!" Mark dug what was. left of Paul's well-aimed throw out of his collar and wrestled him into a drift. Steve dog-piled on top. We were on our way home.

"Told you it'd all get done." Marla skipped up our side stoop steps. Greg jockeyed the plow into a corner of our garage. The rest of us lined up our shovels against the stoop railing and pushed inside the side door, tangling again in the little entryway, dropping snowy scarves and mittens, peeling outer layers of pants. We were loud and warm and happy that the work was behind us. With the smell of frying bacon urging us on, we sprinted upstairs to bedrooms and changed into school clothes. I took an extra moment to run a brush through my hair, hustled downstairs, and hurriedly slid into my seat on the long bench behind our vast kitchen table. This morning, I was last to the table. Everyone else, including the current batch of college girls living in our house, who didn't shovel with us, was already seated.

"Bless us, O Lord, and these Thy gifts," Dad intoned, and silence descended as completely and suddenly as if a radio playing a dozen stations at once had been snapped off. Hands folded together and heads dipped until we finished in unison, "InthenameoftheFatherSonandHolyGhost," and made the sign of the cross with a flourish. Instantly the sound ratcheted back up.

Greg sat at the corner of our table, near enough to the kitchen cabinet behind him to access its specially built swing-out shelf—set at low height to be accessed from the table—which held a four-slice toaster and a long loaf of whole wheat bread. Mom and Dad had designed the toasting operation for maximum convenience. We called Greg's corner the Toast Seat. This morning, he kept the appliance loaded, managing to eat egg and bacon while simultaneously emptying the toaster, passing a plate piled with hot toast, and refilling the toaster with fresh slices. *Snap!* Greg pressed down the lever. *Tick, tick, tick,* Greg had a moment to transport fork to mouth once, twice, three times. Then *zap!* The mechanism popped up, and four toasty-dark slices jumped from their slots. With perfection born of practice, Greg suspended an egg-laden fork with one hand, caught toast with the other, and as if he were dealing cards from a deck, flipped warm slices sideways onto a waiting plate to be handed around the table. Years passed before Greg relinquished the Toast Seat to youngest brother Mark, who crowed with delight when he inherited the job.

Mom served from two big electric skillets, one of scrambled eggs, one of bacon, now taken off the stove area and placed on the table. She used a metal serving spatula to trace a grid in the eggs, dividing them into equal portions. She filled each plate with an exact amount of egg, placed a single slice of bacon atop, and passed it along.

Years later, when people said, "Oh, if you grew up in a large family, you must've learned to eat fast, to get any food!" we reacted with puzzlement. Our mealtimes may have been boisterous, but they were reasonably well-mannered. Our parents just didn't do disorder.

We also didn't do large portions. At breakfast, our places were set with one small glass of juice or half a grapefruit. That single serving of fruit was it. It didn't occur to us to ask for more. We were into our twenties before we realized there were people who ate more than one slice of bacon or consumed meat bigger than a deck of cards.

It was good that our portions were small because Dad conscripted us at tender ages into the Clean Plate Club. We were taught to leave no crumb or speck behind. Usually, this was no problem. Snacking hadn't been invented yet, so whether for breakfast, lunch, or dinner, we arrived at the table hungry. Dinner, served at five thirty on the dot, punctuated every evening of our lives. We generally ate everything in front of us, with gusto.

Generally. One exception, at the dinner table, was beets: two or three horrible, blood-red slices of beets, leaking tiny streams of icky crimson juice across the demilitarized zone of plate into little heaps of meat or potatoes on the other side. I hated beets. In a household where no one threw away food, those beets were meant to go nowhere but down my gullet. Incapable of swallowing beets, but unable to leave them, I'd be forced to take desperate action.

The go-to tactic, which all of us kids employed at one time or another, involved the large pass-through cut in the wall between kitchen table and laundry room. This Formica-topped ledge behind our bench and table was four feet high, six feet long, and deep enough to fold laundry on; it nearly always held nine tidy, stacked piles of clean clothes, laid out in order from Maryanne's to Mark's, awaiting pickup. Each of us always knew which pin-neat, short stack was our own because they were always in the same place. My stack was sixth in the lineup.

On frigid winter days, our golden retriever, Bridget, came in the back door to warm up in the laundry room. To a kid like me, with beets on my plate and insurrection in my heart, our gentle mama dog Bridget, sitting damply in melting snow on the linoleum on the other side of the pass-through, was a godsend.

"Look!" I'd raise my voice above the din of our dinner table, gesturing out the big picture window at the snowy vista of our backyard. "A cardinal!" Any Stritzel child employing this option had to have perfect timing, swift reflexes, decent aim, and luck. In the split second when everyone's head swung in unison toward the picture window, I'd set my loaded fork in one hand and pull the tip of it down with the other, then let go of the fork's tip. The payload of offensive vegetable would launch in a perfect arc off the tines, over the neat piles of clean laundry stacked on the pass-through, and into Bridget's grateful mouth on the other side. Our agreeable canine learned, à la Pavlov, to stay ready in case a snack should come flying over.

This move didn't always require a fork. You could use just your hand to scoop the morsel from your plate and chuck it backward over your shoulder. Without the fork, you had to release the bit of comestible from your fingertips as precisely as a tennis player tosses a ball for a serve. Whether by hand or by fork, the reverse-catapult food toss was an advanced move and required a circus acrobat's sense of timing. The ploy worked because we often did view cardinals, blue jays, and other birds out our window, which looked out onto Dad's tidy backyard of fruit trees and grape arbor.

"What cardinal? Where? Which tree?" Silverware rattled against melamine plates as siblings craned toward the window, searching for brilliant red plumage.

"You missed it. It flew away!" I'd fork up the remaining smidgen of potatoes and beef, smug about my good standing in the Clean Plate Club.

The cardinal ploy also worked when dinner included something especially tasty, like French fries. Mom used tongs to lift a small portion of those hot, fragrant, salty fries onto your plate, and that was all you got. Unless, that is, you were lucky enough to sit next to one of the Lids. Younger brother Steve, with his gentle nature and innocent, liquid eyes, was an especially easy mark.

"Look! A cardinal!" Heads swung toward the picture window as the paw of the conniving sibling snaked lightning fast toward Steve's plate, latched onto a fry or two, and popped the hot potatoes into his or her own thieving mouth. Those fries were seasoned with guilt, made worse because Steve would never see the swipe, or blame you if he did. He was so little, so sweet, so cherubic, so vulnerable. The guilt wasn't enough to stop us, though. In public, we'd stick up for each other, but at our own table, a French fry was fair game. Eventually, Steve, Paul, and Mark grew big enough—despite the pilfering of their portions—to wise up and lock a fist down on the forearm of an offending sibling before it could make off with a morsel of their food.

Though the Clean Plate Club is long out of fashion—indeed is now liability rather than virtue—the phrase "Look! A cardinal!" has reverberated through the decades among us siblings and can still make us dissolve in laughter. It reaffirms that, whether life throws obstacles such as beets or temptations such as French fries our way, we'll remain in good standing with each other in our own club, where plates are clean and details make perfection.

twelve

1969 AND 1972
for i have sinned

*I*n the upper Midwest, winter hangs on well past its welcome, delivering bitter winds and frigid temperatures right into April. Oh, sure, we might get a day or two of warmth and sun before mid-March, but that was just part of winter's diabolical plan to tease us with a hint of spring before slapping down another month of blizzards. Those last weeks of winter, when the season should already have grabbed its coat and hat and said goodbye, were bad enough. Then Lent arrived to add to the misery.

Every Ash Wednesday, a line of nine clean but empty Skippy jars sprouted on our kitchen counter. Each jar sported a strip of masking tape with a name written in black grease pencil. Our Lenten Skippy jars, unknown in any doctrine of Catholicism or Christianity, were our own idea. We gave up eating candy during the forty days of Lent, which in the Church calendar is a time of self-restraint and charity. But—thrift having been drummed into our souls—we couldn't throw candy away. If candy came into our lives during Lent, say from a birthday party, we could save it in a Skippy jar until Easter morning. Our childlike solution hit the sweet spot of holy and frugal.

"It's fun to see candy in my jar." Clare gazed at the Skippy jars on the counter by the window, their colorful contents of jawbreakers and gum and suckers backlit by weak February sun. "It'll be great on Easter to dump this whole jarful on top of the candy that will already be in our Easter baskets!"

"I have some in my jar already too." Denise tossed in a wrapped candy bar she'd accepted at a party the evening before.

"Here's a Slo Poke I got with my nickel for delivering the *Ames Advertiser*," Mark said as he dragged a chair to the counter and climbed up to reach the jars. "That's five pieces of candy in mine, same as Paul's and Steve's." With glass jars showing clear progress, even the Lids seemed able to practice self-discipline.

Levels in the nine jars varied, but only one, thirteen-year-old Greg's, was dead empty. "What's the big deal?" he asked, dismissing the whole endeavor as he pulled on boots to go outdoors. "We'll get candy at Easter. Why save now?" He looked again at his empty jar and plucked it from the lineup, pulling off his masking-tape name and returning the jar to a storage shelf. "I've changed my mind. I'm doing good deeds for Lent instead of giving up candy. That's for little kids. These days, the priest says you're supposed to do something positive for mankind, not negative like giving up stuff," he added on his way out the door.

"So where are these good deeds you've done lately?" Clare called after him. She turned to me. "Never mind. Cher, let's dump out our Skippy jars and count our candy."

"Seven, eight, nine." I sat cross-legged on the linoleum with Clare, candy spread on the floor. "And the gum makes ten." I dropped a fat rectangle of wrapped pink bubblegum back into my jar, thinking of the Bazooka Joe comic inside that would languish unread until Easter.

"I've got twelve pieces." Clare swept them back into her jar.

"We give up candy every year." Denise was thoughtful. "We're old enough to do more now. We could go to daily Mass with Mom or Dad."

Daily Mass? I looked up from the floor in alarm. Daily Mass was held ungodly early, before school even, with no organ, no piano, no singing, and only a handful of elderly parishioners scattered among empty pews, heads bowed, muttering responses into their chests. At age ten, I thought daily Mass was beyond grim. Daily Mass, on a dark winter weekday before sunrise, made Sunday Mass seem like a picnic.

"Forget it!" Marla's response was rapid, but Denise had planted the suggestion. Marla, like Denise, knew it was time for the older kids to do more than forgo sweets. Already during Lent we did not have dessert. On Lenten Fridays, we kept meals small and without meat. But we'd gotten used to all that. What would be a challenge?

Mulling the question over, Marla tried to block out the noise of our black-and-white television in the front room, where the Lids were watching *Leave It to Beaver*. "I could give up TV for Lent this year. That would be hard. Anybody willing to join me?"

Denise, Clare, and I looked at each other. Marla had thrown down the gauntlet.

"I'm in." Denise was quick.

I stayed quiet for a moment, thinking about *The Andy Griffith Show*, *The Flintstones*, *The Jetsons*, *I Dream of Jeannie*, and *My Three Sons*. I thought about *Bonanza* and Little Joe, the youngest and handsomest brother on the Old West ranch. Since not all nine children would be in on this, the television would still be on occasionally, and we four middle girls would have to leave the room. Maryanne, at seventeen, wasn't always part of our schemes now. Greg flat out wasn't interested, and the Lids were too little.

"I can give up TV for Lent!" Clare wasn't going to let Marla and Denise achieve a higher level of Lenten sacrifice than she did.

With that, I was in. Whatever my sisters did, I did. In my eyes, they knew everything. Their influence trumped even my crush on Little Joe.

The early weeks were hard, but as days ticked by, we found other things to do. We survived that first Lent without TV. As years passed, it became a Lenten tradition for a few of us to give up TV.

The most grueling aspect of the endeavor came in my junior high years, when I was about thirteen years old and spent TV-less Lenten nights babysitting for various families around town. Late at night, strange houses became extra scary without television to cover up creepy sounds.

Worst of all was the Grahams' house. Mr. Graham was an anthropology professor at the university. Painted wood masks, handmade by native peoples in Africa, Borneo, Outer Mongolia, and God knows where else, each lavishly embellished with hair, feather, bone, and tooth, hung decoratively on walls in their living room. The artistic masks featured leering painted eyes, sharp noses, and fierce, gaping mouths rimmed in red. Artifacts that couldn't be hung lay on shelves around the room. The three Graham children, who lived surrounded by anthropological items of all kinds, were unbothered by their home's décor.

At the Grahams', I lingered upstairs putting the children to bed, letting them drag out bedtime with extra stories, to put off the moment when I had to descend alone to a living room bordered with savage faces made of wood or hide. When I finally did go down, I sat stiffly on the couch, my library book unread on my lap, primitive weapons of war hanging behind and over my head. The masks, designed to scare opponents in battle, were artistically interspersed with spears and tomahawks.

The radiator wheezed and gurgled. Winds whistled outside, rattling old windows. The mask opposite me seemed to sway on its nail in the wall. Could its stretched-taut dried surface be actual skin? Did its eyes move?

Rumble, rumble, crash! I jumped and yelped, my scream strangled into silence by the need to not wake kids. The icemaker in the refrigerator-freezer in the kitchen behind me had tumbled ice into its receptacle.

I sank back into the couch. A mask of clay drooped long cheeks and thrust out a mouth spiked with fangs. Another of wood bulged green eyeballs; its permanent grimace showed real teeth driven into wooden gums. A mask of animal hide sprouted stalks of hair flopping over a prominent forehead. A skull glazed to shiny brown, eye sockets empty and shadowed, rested on a shelf. Was that a real human skull or ceramic?

I longed for the canned, cheerful babble of Mary Tyler Moore, Bob Newhart, Carol Burnett, and *M*A*S*H*. But the television stayed silent and dark, much like Lent itself.

Before Lent ended, we made sure to get to Confession, as is customary among Catholics preparing for Easter. On a blustery, freezing, late-winter Saturday afternoon, we'd hustle into the dark, quiet church and kneel among other silent penitents in the pews, mentally reviewing our shortcomings as we waited our turn to enter the confessional. We understood the purpose of Confession: examine your conscience, so you notice bad habits and little sins, and change before they get big. Confession was like washing hands; you left dirt behind and emerged as your better self. It was a do-over, another try, a chance to have mistakes forgiven and get it right next time.

A couple of weeks into Lent, we all had at least a few failed Lenten promises to confess. At age thirteen, I'd hardly committed murder, but I had a list of transgressions. First among them was my falling off the wagon about no TV.

"Bless me, Father, for I have sinned," I murmured while kneeling on a padded kneeler in the dark little booth of paneled wood and crimson velvet drapes, head bowed against clasped hands. I could hear but not really see the priest in the similar booth on the other side of the latticed screen. I could just barely make out a halo of light shining dimly behind his shadowy figure. I breathed in that familiar, comforting church smell of smoky incense with an undercurrent of industrial-strength floor cleaner, and shifted on the kneeler. The booth was close, womblike. It was just me and my conscience now.

"I'm giving up TV for Lent," I explained rapidly. "I was doing OK, but the other day I was with friends at someone else's house, and I just didn't want to get into the whole explanation of Lent," I rattled on. "They think it's weird and freaky. So I went along with the crowd, flopped on the floor in their family room, and watched TV." I took a breath, the better to recite my other transgressions, but for the first time in memory, I didn't get the chance.

"Ho ho!" the priest chortled from behind the screen. "In this day and age, it's not possible to give up TV. It's the seventies! How will you know what's going on in the world if you don't watch TV?"

"Huh?" Nonplussed, I looked up from my clasped hands at the screen, forgetting the rest of my sins. Our university parish tended to get young, modern priests. No doubt, one of them was behind this screen. But since when did a priest exhort a sinner to keep on sinning? I'd never encountered this. But I wasn't too flummoxed to take advantage of it.

"Um"—my mind raced—"does that mean I don't have any penance this time?"

But the countercultural cleric slipped back into priestly mode as he delivered absolution: "Child, say ten Hail Marys for your penance, but rethink your Lenten sacrifice in light of what it means to live in the modern world."

I stood up, stunned. I exited the confessional and then the church, dipping my fingers in the little vessel of holy water to bless myself on the way out. This time I would wait for my siblings outside. I stood on the broad gray stone front terrace, the big glass doors and soaring stained-glass front wall of our beautifully modern church behind me. I watched the traffic slapping through slush on Lincoln Way, spraying frigid, dirty water in a steady arc nearly to the church steps. The late-winter, late-afternoon sun hitting my face might as well have been a lightning flash of insight.

Might this priest, behind this screen, on this day, be wrong? Abstaining from TV was an appropriate if challenging sacrifice, and I would do it! Whether he pooh-poohed it or not. True, this was hardly the fulcrum upon which the entire faith turned, but in this tiny detail, I was right and he was wrong. And if he could be wrong, so could all in authority, including parents, teachers, principals, even the president.

Yet I knew that God, by definition, was right. How could right and wrong exist in the same place? How could both come through the same channel? Perhaps God's perfect love and perfect laws were delivered through flawed humans.

A sharp-fendered Buick swooshed past, throwing up a broad fan of brown slush, and I leapt away. I jammed my hands deeper in my wool coat pockets, discovering a hole in the satiny lining. I fingered the hole, careful not to enlarge it, and turned to look at the closed glass doors of the church behind me. I twirled my boot atop nuggets of ice-melting salt on the steps, grinding the chunks into crystal dust.

Hadn't I just acknowledged, moments before, my own human flaws? Could I blame adults for being flawed?

I was still alone on the church steps. No older sister was there to tell me the answer. What did I think? For the first time, I thought that adults could be wrong.

I kicked at clumps of dirty snow until my siblings joined me, and we walked home together.

thirteen

1969

easter magic

At long last, Lent culminated in Good Friday, when we got a day off school but couldn't do anything fun with it. But Good Friday's solemnity at least meant that the candy-less desert of Lent was nearly behind us. The next morning, Holy Saturday, we got to dye eggs.

"Careful with those." Mom opened more cardboard cartons as I placed the eggs in single layers on the bottoms of pots. I handed the pots to Clare and Marla, who filled them with cold water and placed them on the stove to boil. Once the water boiled, the pots were taken off the heat, and the eggs left to stand in hot water for twelve minutes. Then we drained the hot water down the sink, and covered the eggs with cold tap water to stop the cooking. Maryanne and Denise laid newspaper over the kitchen table and unfolded clean rags down the center. A dozen cups, each half-full of boiling water, with a spoon by its side, ringed the table. Walking around the table, Marla ladled a teaspoon of vinegar into each cup, refilling her teaspoon from the open bottle, and we breathed in the acrid smell that flooded the kitchen. Greg followed Marla, squeezing drops of food color into each cup.

"You can start." Mom delivered pots of cooled eggs to all of us at the table. "Lower one egg on a spoon into the dye bath. Leave it a short time for pastel or a long time for deep color. Lift the egg out with the spoon and tip it onto the rags to dry. I'll start writing name eggs." Mom found a white wax crayon and wrote each of our names on a white egg. When we dyed these, they emerged with the white name clearly readable.

We nine circled the table, dipping and spooning, until five dozen hardboiled eggs made a river of color down the center of the table. Mom and Maryanne poured a smidge of corn oil on their palms and rubbed each egg, making it gleam. Mom filled a couple of round shiny wood trays with finished eggs. Their beauty and abundance, glowing in the spring sunshine coming through the window behind our Skippy jars, promised that Lenten fasting indeed was nearly over, and feasting was coming.

"It's Easter! Get up, get up!" The Lids were up, running and jumping on beds, rousing the rest of us. In pajamas, we tumbled downstairs. Mom, in her chenille bathrobe and slippers, smiled over her coffee cup. Dad, also in bathrobe, reached into the back-door closet shelf for the square leather satchel that held his Super 8 movie camera.

"Wait till everyone's here before you start hunting for baskets," he reminded us.

"Who's missing? Maryanne and Denise! They're still in bed!" Our voices tangled as we ran back upstairs.

"Come on, it's time to hunt for baskets! You're holding everybody up! Oh for Pete's sake, you don't need to brush your hair!" Our cajoling spiraled into disbelief. How could our sisters care about hair when hidden Easter baskets awaited?

"Dad's going to take movies, and I want to look nice," Denise maneuvered a brush, coaxing long honey-brown hair into a flip. We left her and mobbed into Maryanne's room.

"Ahhh!" Maryanne croaked, awakening to the Lids' leaping on her bed and the rest of us piling on behind them. "Those baskets aren't going anywhere. Give me a minute." She shooed us out and headed to the bathroom to wash her face.

Finally—after taking longer than Lent itself—the older two joined us downstairs.

"All baskets are hidden in the house on the first floor, nothing in the garage or outside," Dad announced. "If you find a basket, be quiet until you read the name egg inside. If it's not your name egg, it's not your basket. In that case, shut the cabinet door and sneak away, so you don't give away the hiding place of someone else's basket. Everybody here? Everybody ready? Go!"

Pandemonium reigned as we dashed around the house, flinging open cupboards, crawling under stairs, looking in the washing machine, the dishwasher, the broom closet, the drawers, the closets. Dad's movie camera whirred softly amid the blur of pajamas.

"Here's mine!" Greg backed out on hands and knees, face flushed, from among the boots at the back of the side-door closet, holding his colored woven-straw basket high. No matter how cleverly Mom and Dad hid our baskets, Greg found his within fifteen seconds.

He surveyed the generous contents: big chocolate rabbit, plenty of jelly beans, speckled malted candy eggs, a chocolate crème egg, garish yellow marshmallow chick-shaped Peeps, and one real hard-boiled egg, dyed brilliant purple with "Greg" written on it in white. The name egg, glorious in its individually chosen color and personal identity, was the crowning centerpiece.

"Here's mine! Here's mine! Got mine!" A chorus arose as we backed out of various hiding places, each grasping a woven basket.

Seated around our massive kitchen table, we pawed through sweet booty. After forty days of self-restraint, we were free to eat anything we wanted. Occasionally we looked up, mouths full of jelly beans, to see little Steve still orbiting the kitchen. Steve was always last to find his basket. Since the rest of us had inadvertently encountered his in the hunt for our own, we directed him as he searched.

"Colder!" we yelled if he walked away from where we knew his basket to be. "Colder, colder, you're freezing!" So Steve would change course, tacking from broom closet to laundry room.

"Getting slightly warmer," we said as he faced the right direction, toward the basement.

"OK, you're hot now—hotter, hotter," we said as we swapped candy around the table, and Steve migrated toward the basement stairs.

"Now you're so hot, you're boiling!" Greg bit the ears off his chocolate rabbit with a snap. But then Steve turned in the wrong direction.

"Nope, colder." We lifted our chins to peer toward Greg's basket, investigating whether this year's rabbit was hollow or solid chocolate.

Steve finally opened the basement door and saw his basket tucked among various items crowding the far edge of the upper steps. "Got it!" he crowed, running to the table to join us, his basket aloft.

"Hey! Remember, we have our Skippy jars of Lent candy." Clare jumped up and scooted toward the line of jars on the counter. We scrambled to get our jars and upend the contents on top of the Easter candy already in our baskets.

"Finally," Denise exulted, unwrapping a chocolate that had taunted her from her Skippy jar for weeks.

"Excellent." Marla unwrapped a mint meltaway from her jar and popped it in her mouth with a smack.

"Ah, Happy Easter." Mark unwrapped a Slo Poke caramel-on-a-stick.

Dad kept the camera whirring as Mom readied the great clove-studded ham that would be the focal point of Easter brunch when we got back from Mass. Maryanne and Denise parked their baskets amid the detritus on our long kitchen desk and went to help Mom put finishing touches on our lamb cake. This homemade white cake, which Mom somehow fashioned into the shape of a lamb, rested in its woolly coat of white frosting and grated sweet coconut on a magnificent swirled-glass cake plate. Denise snipped a black jelly bean in two and placed the halves on its face for eyes. Maryanne positioned short lengths of black licorice to suggest its mouth. Mom scattered green-dyed coconut flakes around the plate, and the effect was complete: the lamb reclined in splendor on its bed of grass. Maryanne and Denise went upstairs to shower and dress for church. Marla, generous as always, gave Steve a couple of favorite treats from her own basket, then ran upstairs for her turn in the shower. Greg leapt up and danced around the kitchen, swinging his long-handled basket.

"Look at me, I'm magic!" Greg swung his basket overhead over and over in a graceful arc, fast enough that centrifugal force kept the loot firmly seated against its nest of green plastic grass.

"Wow," I said, eyes round. Greg really was magic. How else could he whip his basket upside down and have nothing fall out?

"Magic, magic." Greg circled his basket.

I was filled with wonder. I knew Jesus walked on water, and this Easter morning, I could see with my own eyes that big brother Greg could defy gravity. If he could do it, couldn't I too?

I swung my basket overhead, and—candy rained down around my head and shoulders, thudding onto linoleum. Plastic grass plummeted in a clump; a few strands landed on my head and static-clung to my face. My brilliant blue name egg, the ultimate symbol of Easter, hit the floor and cracked.

"Oh!" I looked in dismay at the wreck around my feet.

"It's OK, most stuff is fine," Greg said, feeling bad about his role in my small disaster. He knelt on the floor, swept plastic grass and candy back into my basket, and handed it to me. "You have to swing fast. Try it again."

I couldn't. Wouldn't it just fall again? Maybe Greg did have magic that I didn't.

"Fast." Greg looked at me. "Swing it fast."

I took a deep breath. Greg, an omnipotent older sibling, had told me to believe. He, like my older sisters, knew everything. I whipped my basket over my head, around and around. Everything stayed seated. "Got it!" I crowed.

For Easter Mass, we girls had readied spring dresses and patent leather shoes ahead of time (in the early years, we had hats and gloves as well). We understood and accepted that clothing was usually hand-me-downs. This wasn't a bad deal. To us, it seemed natural and right; we looked forward to growing into a favorite hand-me-down from an older sister. Who would buy new when nice things awaited you up the line?

Arrayed in spring finery, though it was buttoned under winter coats, we filled the station wagon: Mom and Dad in front, Maryanne between them, then Denise, Marla, Greg, and Clare on the middle bench, and finally, in the back cargo area with no seats, the Lids and me. I squatted on my haunches, keeping my dress off the floor, reaching out for balance as the wagon took the curves. If the '58 Chevy had seat belts, we weren't aware of them.

After Mass, we came home to our magnificent brunch of glazed ham, fresh horseradish, abundant eggs glowing in their trays, early spring vegetables, homemade sticky buns. Most memorable on the long, broad table were two little silver dishes filled with chunks of pure chocolate, Mom's acknowledgment of our candy-less, dessert-less Lent. We were allowed to eat it at will.

After Easter, life returned to normal. Most of us kept our Easter baskets around for a couple of weeks, making the candy last as long as possible. Greg was a reliable exception.

"Poor Greg," Clare said, four days after Easter, seeing his empty basket. "He's eaten all his candy already, just like last year." Her own basket was still nearly full and beautifully organized. The only thing in Greg's was a sprig of plastic grass snagged on the plaited bottom. Clare stood silent for a moment, remembering her own deprivation during Lent. Was this increased compassion she felt now due to those six candy-less weeks? Might this empathy with her brother be another sign of Easter magic?

"I wanted mine to last, but—aargh!—now I have to share." She plucked up a jelly bean and chewed, but it was no good. "I can't enjoy eating this when he doesn't have any." She took a deep breath, picked up her basket, and went to find Greg.

fourteen

1970
after midnight

Thumping music rocked the street as the clock ticked past midnight. Swirling lights swept Welch Avenue, penetrating the second-story windows of our house's front two bedrooms. In one bedroom, flashing lights illuminated the Lids, wide awake, kneeling on Paul's bed to see out the window. Their row of small faces showed red, then orange, then yellow as they stared at the bacchanalia in the front yard of the fraternity house across the street. Shouting and laughter rose and fell like waves that crested and troughed above the climbing decibel level. The crowd swelled, feeding off throngs of college students strolling Welch Avenue. *BOOM. BOOM. BOOM.* Bass thrumming from speakers in the yard across the street reverberated inside the Lids' chests.

BOOM. In the other front bedroom, Dad jumped out of bed and threw on his ancient blue-and-white-striped terrycloth bathrobe over his knit navy-blue JCPenney pajamas. Mom, lying next to him, opened her eyes but said nothing.

After midnight—somebody at the frat turned up the music—*we're gonna let it all hang down.*

Dad tied his bathrobe. He'd had a long day teaching, followed by a long evening working on a blocked toilet in a student rental house.

After midnight, Eric Clapton wailed louder, *we're gonna chug-a-lug and shout.*

Not owning slippers, Dad thrust bare feet into wingtips, turned the old metal knob of their bedroom door, and strode down the narrow staircase, shoes ringing with authority on bare wood.

After midnight—even louder now, throbbing—*we're gonna shake your tambourine.*

Dad flung open our heavy front door, crossed our old porch, and flew down three steps without noticing them. He crossed the street and within seconds was mounting the concrete steps of the frat house's veranda.

Throughout the 1950s and early sixties, Welch Avenue was quiet and friendly, a street mostly populated by families. We hosted the annual neighborhood potluck on our driveway. Ice cream socials in verdant backyards featured hand-cranked ice cream topped with homegrown peaches and cherries. Mom, youngest member of the informal Welch Avenue Ladies Club, would occasionally look in on old Mrs. Ruth or Mrs. Young, widows living alone, or send one of us kids down the street with a newspaper full of just-picked lettuce or green beans for them. The biggest drama in those years was when the Lids picked flowers from Mrs. Ruth's garden to present to Mom. Mom took the boys in hand down the street to knock on her door and apologize.

In those years, the fraternity across the street had curfews and a resident housemother. Social expectations of the time helped keep the young men in check.

But from 1968 and into the seventies, on our block as on campuses everywhere, calm waters began to roil. College men lost their crew-neck sweaters and nerd glasses—and found beards, long hair rippling past shoulders, and flared jeans that grew ragged where they dragged the ground. Shoes gave way to sandals, which gave way to bare feet. Buttoned-down and tucked-in went out. Loose-hanging and long-fringed came in. Curfews grew later and looser and finally vanished altogether. Housemothers, in many dorms and frats, were deemed an unnecessary expense belonging to an uptight past.

University enrollment at Iowa State and across the country spiraled up. Stampedes of incoming students, wave after wave in their increasing thousands, needed housing. The poultry farm at the far south end of Welch Avenue was torn down, and four massive dorms, each with ten floors, each floor housing sixty students, rose in place of the turkey coops. The huge, rectangular dorms were called The Towers. The name was apt, for indeed they towered over us, throwing monstrous shadows. It looked as if a giant had come to Welch Avenue, looked around, liked what he saw, and set down four colossal white suitcases.

The Towers, more than anything else, transformed our street. Hordes of students from The Towers streamed up and down Welch Avenue morning and evening, heading for central campus, overwhelming narrow old sidewalks, spilling onto the tree lawn and into the street. Like a trampling army, their feet beat the tree lawn—that strip of grass between sidewalk and street—into dust and then churned it into mud.

How to solve the problem? Concrete, the city decided. The massive, ancient shade trees lining the street would be cut down, and the tree lawn would be entirely paved over. We argued passionately for our trees—all Welch Avenue residents did—but lost. Two rows of venerable giants came down, and six-foot-wide concrete sidewalks were poured in their place. In one week, under the roar of chainsaws, the dappled shade of Welch Avenue vanished. Glaring sun replaced it. Families moved out. Students moved in.

Dad, who had chosen teaching as his life's work, liked students. He felt lucky to have received an education and wanted to share his abundance of excitement and knowledge with young people. He liked music too, especially the Big Band music of the World War II era, and understood the pleasure of sharing a beer with friends. But as the sixties boiled over into the seventies and student behavior grew drunker and wilder, he felt increasingly obliged to become a force of moral authority. "Nothing doing," meaning no way, not happening, became one of his sayings. It didn't occur to him not to stand up for what was right, and he never questioned that he *was* right.

Now, literally after midnight, the Lids, eyes agog, watched Dad take the broad steps of the fraternity's concrete veranda two at a time, his pounding feet somehow keeping time with the beat, his bathrobe billowing behind like a matador's cape.

We're gonna let it all hang down, Eric Clapton's wail reverberated— and at that moment, the stereo suddenly had competition.

"Nothing DOING!" Dad blazed onto the scene. His bare ankles rose out of his dress shoes as he waded into a mass of strobe-lit, booze-guzzling, pot-smoking, long-haired young men and halter-topped, barefoot, tangled-haired young women. The bald shiny middle of Dad's head caught the garish lights, reflecting the colors on, off, on, off like a stoplight. Dad whirled, bathrobe flying, toward the guy blasting the stereo. "Pipe down!" he thundered, and the DJ did! The music popped off, the screech of canned electric guitars snapping off mid-skreel.

"NOW YOU CAN TURN THIS DOWN AND MOVE IT INSIDE! I DON'T WANT TO HEAR ANOTHER PEEP FROM OVER HERE! IS THAT CLEAR?"

Partiers around the edges of the yard spooked, vanishing into the night. Carousers on the veranda scrambled toward the front door, blocking and bumping each other as they tried to get through. Others scampered after them, hurrying to get inside, dodging broken liquor bottles, spilled booze, and worse underfoot.

The Lids, frozen at their own upstairs bedroom window across the street, their three mouths forming identical *O*s, watched Dad spin around and stride toward home, the party behind him deflating like a wheezing balloon. The Lids jumped into their narrow, army surplus bunk beds, yanking covers over their heads, feigning sleep on the thin mattresses just in case Dad's powerful righteousness wasn't fully spent.

Dad opened their door, saw three motionless covered mounds, and went back to bed himself, the street outside blissfully quiet.

With the bedroom door safely shut, Paul whispered across his bunk to Steve and Mark: "Whoa, did you see them shoving over each other to get inside? Dad scares even a whole bunch of college guys!"

"They left bottles and ashtrays and clothes and junk all over their porch and just *split*," Steve whispered in awe.

"Did you see three of them trying to get that speaker through the window?" Mark, still quaking under the covers, marveled at the power of Dad, who could singlehandedly lick an entire frat party.

There is something compelling about the voice of moral authority when it is sure of its ground. Even if it is wearing wingtips and a bathrobe.

fifteen

1970

piano lessons

Mom never had the opportunity to take piano lessons as a child. She felt that was unfortunate. We thought it even more unfortunate, because Mom was therefore determined that all of us *would* have the opportunity. Whether we wanted it or not.

If Mom wanted something, Dad made it happen. Immediately. He perused the *Ames Advertiser* and for twenty-five dollars purchased a used upright piano with a bench seat, its black finish crackled with age, and had it placed against an inner wall in the den, which was no longer being used as a college girl's bedroom.

"The successful man knows a little about everything," Dad proclaimed when we whined about the tedium of practice. "It'll be good for you to know how to read music."

"You can't read music," one of us would point out, shifting on the hard bench, pausing mid-scale, hands lifted over yellowed ivory keys. "And you're successful."

"Never mind that." Dad paid as much attention to our objections as he did to comets whizzing past Earth in distant space. "I know good music when I hear it. More important, I know what's good for you. So quitcherbellyachin' and get back to practice."

We'd plod on, tinkling through "Teaching Little Fingers to Play," pounding our way up and down scales, sweating over John Thompson's "Modern Course for the Piano," toiling through classical arrangements, now and then earning the reward of a pop song by Simon and Garfunkel, The Mamas & the Papas, or Joni Mitchell. None of us liked to practice, but the boys were truly troublesome. Greg and the Lids approached the piano bench with mulish obstinacy, dragging their feet and scowling. Even Mom eventually conceded that paying for piano lessons for our brothers was akin to taking stacks of dollar bills into the backyard and setting them afire. She allowed the boys to drop piano lessons—Greg at least moved on to the guitar—and pinned her remaining hopes on us girls.

Even with the boys off the hook, the logistics of five girls, each attempting to get in a half hour of practice a day, meant that anytime our family was in the house, one of us was playing the piano. We banged on the old upright after school and before dinner. In the summer, after a full day of work on the rental houses, we practiced in the evening. Neighbors strolling down the street on warm nights grew accustomed to hearing piano music emanating from our open windows. During the school year—up through sixth grade we walked home at midday for lunch—we practiced before and after lunch. Sometimes, trying to fit in practice time before an upcoming lesson, two of us would play at the same time.

We practiced feverishly as a lesson approached because Mrs. Muller, piano teacher to every child in the neighborhood, terrified us. She petrified me, especially.

On Wednesday afternoons, my lesson day, I dragged my feet down Welch Avenue, turned left at Storm Street, and slowed further, pausing to examine cracks in the sidewalk or an ant crawling up a towering elm. Finally, despite my best efforts to stop time, I fetched up at her little white craftsman house on the corner of

Storm Street and Stanton Avenue. The pin-neat flower beds and razor-edged lawn outside hinted at the disciplined woman inside.

Mrs. Muller was on the graying side of forty-five, slim and tidy in pastel pedal pushers and a starched-and-ironed white blouse, with a hair-sprayed helmet of short, coiffed hair and half-lens glasses perched partway down her nose. She liked to wrinkle her brow, narrow her eyes, and peer over those glasses at a child on her piano bench, pinning the unfortunate youngster with her gaze, as one might pin an insect on a corkboard. Her glossy brown piano, a trim little upright, was somehow unnicked even after years of hosting fidgety students. Its ivory keys shone pure white, the sweet little carved fretwork of its music holder gleamed, and its brass pedals shone. I guessed it cost more than twenty-five dollars. It fit perfectly into her well-vacuumed living room, where tasteful light green wall-to-wall carpeting coordinated with framed art, fine furniture, and silver knickknacks. Everything about her home, like Mrs. Muller herself, exuded Germanic order.

One Wednesday afternoon when I was ten years old, I walked to her home after school as usual. I shuffled my shoes on the mat, careful to rub off any wayward dried mud that might be clinging to my soles. Once in the living room, I wiped my palms on my thighs, pulled the bench close to the keyboard, sat down, and looked up, an expression of the gallows in my face.

"Well, why don't we begin?" Mrs. Muller's thin, pressed smile told me she knew she was in for a trying half hour.

I placed my "White Christmas" sheet music on the dear little fretwork holder and plunged into the opening strains. It was only September, but Mrs. Muller had assigned "White Christmas" early, knowing I would need months to prepare this single piece for the December recital. Liquid notes floated through the room. I played confidently for the first few measures, since I'd practiced those over and over, but soon bogged down as I found myself in unfamiliar territory. By the time I turned the second page, I was slowing, backing up, trying again, then pausing entirely, trying to sight-read. By the third and fourth pages, which I had not even seen during the previous week, much less practiced, "White Christmas" was limping and struggling, stopping and starting, leaving huge chunks of silence here and there, falling down and leaping up again only to land with a fortissimo twang on the wrong octave entirely. "White Christmas" is not meant to be played fast, but I played it with way more ritardando than Irving Berlin ever intended. And more ritardando. And more ritardando yet, until it sounded as if the music were feeling its way down a long, dark hallway. I was not dreaming of a white Christmas, but living a nightmare in vivid color. I dared not think of Mrs. Muller, who I imagined was dreaming of a teaching studio devoid of Stritzel children.

Mrs. Muller raised no hand of mercy to stop the carnage. She sat silent, lips pursed, eyes narrowed to slits over those half lenses. During long, long seconds of silence, I sweated and wriggled on the hard bench, desperately trying to figure out chords. What were those bass clef notes anyway? Who could read such hieroglyphics? *E? C? Try something, anything—there's the G, try that!*

Mrs. Muller let the silence swell, leaving me to dangle and twist in a noose of my own making. My chords were questions, my notes unsure, my phrasing AWOL. Laboriously, I sight-read my way to the end, the music—if you could call it that—lurching as if on crutches. Finally, I dragged the carcass of "White Christmas" over the finish line, performing the last bit not with the triumphant flourish the composer had in mind, but with a tentative question mark that trailed upward and finally petered off into nothing. My butchering of Irving Berlin was complete.

Mrs. Muller let the last meager notes hang there for a full minute, so the ignominy could sink in. The clock ticked in the stillness.

"Cheryl." She made even my name sound damning. "Cheryl. Let's see your practice log for last week."

I produced the little book. She pushed her glasses up to read my entries. "Hmm, no practice whatsoever the first six days, then three hours of practice today, on Wednesday?" Her glasses slid down as she skewered me with her gaze. "It's Wednesday afternoon now. You've been in school all day. How was it possible to get in three hours of practice today?"

Miserable, I stared at the lint-free, light green carpet under shining brass pedals. "I got up early and practiced this morning."

It was true. Where piano was concerned, I was a master procrastinator. Right after the lesson, with my next lesson safely days away, I forgot all about practicing. Thursday, Friday, Saturday—the thought of piano practice never blipped across my radar. Sunday, Monday, Tuesday—how blithely the days sped by!—it was as if our big old upright had vanished into a crack in the den floor. Day after day, I'd wing past the hulking instrument without seeing it.

But in the dark, early hours every Wednesday, the piano seemed to grow. It loomed larger and larger, populating my dreams, inflating until it towered over me in bed, leering down close to my face, its horror-movie grin of eighty-eight teeth bared wide. I'd awake in a panic at four, sweating and gasping, picturing Mrs. Muller's narrowed eyes over those half lenses, feeling myself squirm beneath her aura of perpetual discipline. In my long flannel nightgown, full of dread, I'd feel my way down the cold, dark stairwell. By the ghostly glow of streetlights outside the front window, I'd tiptoe into the den, slide its two heavy doors closed, turn on the light, and practice with the soft pedal pressed to the floor, trying to learn a week's work all at once, hoping not to wake the household.

I was too foolish to practice day by day and too naïve to lie. My practice log told the ludicrous truth.

Whether or not Mrs. Muller believed the log, my six days of zero practice and one day of three hours of practice was clearly unproductive. I hung my head. I knew what was coming.

"Your poor parents," Mrs. Muller began, her pale thin hand pressed in distress to her clavicle. "Your father and mother, who never had luxuries themselves . . ." Of all Mrs. Muller's lecture themes, this was the worst. Wasting resources was the ultimate sin in our household, and Mrs. Muller's speech hit its target. "Your parents work like dogs so all of you—all nine of you!—can have opportunities they never had, yet you can't even be bothered to practice properly." Each word was a drop of acid splashing in an open wound. Mrs. Muller carried on, "They work day and night on those rental houses—all those rental houses!—to pay for this, and through your own sheer laziness you *waste* their honest toil."

I slumped lower on Mrs. Muller's polished bench. In my head, a fuzzy Super 8 movie started to unspool; it showed Mom and Dad struggling up the Swiss Alps, sweating and huffing, toting the dead weight of nine lazy, layabout, good-for-nothing children on their backs.

I was stricken. "I'll practice this week, really I will. I'll practice every day!" In the heat of my shame, I meant it.

But the moment I left her house, my heart lightened, my step quickened, and I sort of, kind of, really completely forgot about practicing until the next Wednesday, when I woke again in that four-in-the-morning panic.

Despite my ridiculous practice schedule, I did eventually, over the years, learn a few pieces. I could bash through a lively "Raindrops Keep Falling on My Head" by Burt Bacharach and even memorized one popular piece, "Abergavenny," by Marty Wilde. Denise and Clare, who were most disciplined at their schoolwork, were likewise most disciplined at the piano, and became proficient pianists and musicians in general. Denise performed beautiful

Schubert sonatas, and Clare could rip a perfect "Bridge Over Troubled Water." But even Clare, Mrs. Muller's favorite Stritzel child—which wasn't saying much—was capable of annoying her.

One day when Clare was fourteen, she arrived for her Tuesday afternoon lesson well prepared as usual, her sheet music and books neatly organized in a folder.

"Clare, delightful to see you. Come right in." Mrs. Muller greeted Clare with a genuine smile, not the pressed one she reserved for me. "I'll be with you shortly. I just have to run into the kitchen for a moment."

"Sure, Mrs. Muller. I'll get warmed up." Clare left her boots on the mat inside the door. She edged between the keyboard and the bench, and stood as she opened her piano music.

I can't wait to play "Für Elise" for her, Clare thought. *I've practiced, I'm really getting it right, and I can almost play the whole thing!* She confidently grabbed the top lid of the bench behind her to hitch the bench closer. As she did, she lost her balance and fell backward, her backside thumping down hard on the bench lid. Which closed, with all her fingers still under it.

"Ow. OW!" Clare jumped off the bench and screamed in a strangled whisper, not wanting Mrs. Muller in the kitchen to hear. "Aargh!" She held up her fingers. The top two joints of each swelled red and throbbed, ballooning instantly into cherry tomatoes. Her falling sit-down had neatly, consistently smashed each one.

Throb. Throb. Throb. Blood pulsed into the digits as Mrs. Muller swanned back into the living room.

"Now Clare," Mrs. Muller purred, "let's hear how you're doing with 'Für Elise.'" Mrs. Muller pulled her own chair alongside the bench and turned an indulgent smile on Clare. "I know you've practiced diligently."

Clare looked at Mrs. Muller, stricken, then turned back to "Für

Elise," and set her mouth with determination. She took a deep breath, placed her fingers on the keyboard, and launched into the familiar beginning. Only she didn't, because her fingers had become nerveless stumps.

"I . . . I can't." Clare held up her fingers. Throb. Throb. Throb. She could feel her fingertips pulsing like eight beating hearts. "I sat on my fingers!"

Mrs. Muller grabbed Clare's fingers and inspected them. Clare winced. Mrs. Muller sighed and looked skyward as if in need of divine assistance. None seemed forthcoming. She mentally flipped through her abundant lecture themes, but none fit this situation. Mrs. Muller was momentarily, uncharacteristically, at a loss for words.

"Well!" Mrs. Muller finally spoke. "Nothing we can do! You might as well go home."

Clare, with difficulty, repacked her music and slunk out the door.

Mrs. Muller, for all her annoyance at useless Stritzel pupils on her piano bench, once surprised me.

It was a warm spring Saturday afternoon in downtown Ames. I was with Dad, running an errand at the hardware store, unusually without any other siblings along, when we ran into Mrs. Muller. Dad, his white carpenter overalls hanging heavy on his lean frame, grasping three new paint rollers in one hand and their accompanying screw-on wood poles in the other, paused mid-aisle to chat.

"How's Cheryl doing on the piano?" Dad beamed at Mrs. Muller.

I froze in terror. My myopic brown eyes, always magnified behind my tortoiseshell glasses, grew larger as I stared at Mrs. Muller in alarm. I gulped, my tongue edging against the rough chain of silver braces on my teeth, as I blindly clutched four new metal scrapers in their cardboard wrappers.

I knew Mrs. Muller wouldn't lie. I knew what her answer would be. Abominably was how I was doing, and it wasn't the teacher's fault.

Mrs. Muller looked at me. I stood still on the worn, concave hardwood of the aisle, my two short brown braids motionless. She pushed her half-lens glasses up her nose.

"Well!" She stalled. She smiled and shifted her stiff, alligator-printed leather handbag with bronze clasp from one hand to the other. "Well," she repeated, and breathed deeply. "Cheryl, while she doesn't always have . . . ah . . . technical proficiency, under-stands the emotion and feeling within a piece of music, and that shines through!"

"Emotion? Feeling?" Dad cocked his head at Mrs. Muller. "I understand. Thank you. Thanks for all your good work."

Dad, who couldn't read music or play the piano, understood perfectly. You can't express the emotion of a piece of music until you learn the notes.

He didn't say anything, but his shoulders sagged lower under the weight of his overalls as we pushed through the double swinging glass doors into the bright sun of the day. Dad was not interested in shelling out good money so we could understand emotion. He was paying for us to progress in mastery of the instrument, and appar-ently I wasn't.

That would have been reason enough to let me stop taking lessons. Or maybe Mom and Dad finally got tired of my four-in-the-morning Wednesday practice sessions. Anyway, next time I asked to quit, Mom and Dad surprised me by acquiescing. Mom, with typical restraint, even refrained from telling me one last time that I'd regret the decision.

Mom was right. I was sorry later. But I can still pound out "Abergavenny" from memory. Ask me sometime. I'll play it for you.

Stritzel children painting, about 1970.
From left: Cheryl, Mark, Steve, Paul, and Clare on scaffold

1970

built for the ages

*I*n summer, our hardest workday was Saturday, when Dad didn't leave to teach classes but donned his carpenter overalls and worked with us. More intense yet was his annual two-week vacation from the university, taken sometime over the summer. On days that Dad was home, The List, which functioned in his absence as a sort of virtual Dad, was replaced by the real thing: there were no late starts, no lollygagging, and absolutely no inefficiency.

With an older sister in charge, you might occasionally stretch out break time, or forget a tool and have to stroll back through the neighborhood to the right garage to fetch it, or lose a half hour rummaging through one of the old houses' attics, discovering interesting junk. On days when Dad stayed and worked with us, the atmosphere at breakfast was charged with extra energy, as if the household had been plugged into higher voltage.

"OK, big day today. Cement truck is due here eight a.m., and we'll need all of us on that job!" Dad's energy and verve, always high, ratcheted up several notches as he lifted the top plate from the stack next to him, spooned one fried egg from the eleven in the skillet onto it, and handed it to Mom, who added a sausage patty from the adjoining skillet and handed the full plate around the table as Dad rapidly lifted the next plate. We'd said our before-meal prayer as usual before food was dished up, so we could eat the moment a plate of hot food landed in front of us, without waiting for the whole table to be served.

This new driveway was to be poured on the side yard between our home's driveway and our rental house next door. The addition of the new driveway would yield pavement from one house's foundation to the other. The site wasn't level and required a lot of fill before cement was poured. Previously, we'd prepared the driveway site, building forms and toting busted-up rock from our other properties to fill it in. Anyone else would have hired a professional to deliver purchased rock or sand, but Dad could find demolition concrete, field stones, and other material that wouldn't decay to use as fill under new concrete. Always, he made do with what we had, and one thing we had in abundance was labor.

That preparation done, today's agenda promised the thrilling job of pouring cement. Every Stritzel child from Maryanne to Mark would be needed to push and guide and smooth fresh concrete before it set. Pouring concrete requires exact timing. There are no do-overs. Get it wrong, and you'll look at an uneven driveway for the rest of your life. Anyone would find that annoying. Dad would find it unbearable. It couldn't happen.

"Everybody got boots?" Denise raised her voice above the cacophony of our breakfast table. "You can't wade into concrete without rubber boots!" The cacophony increased.

"I can't find mine!"

"I tried mine, but they don't fit anymore."

"I got a pair!"

We'd been organizing boots a few minutes before breakfast, diving into the floor of our little side-door coat closet, sorting through a flotsam of footwear.

"You swiped mine. Those old ones with the side buckles are mine, not yours." Clare frowned, sitting next to me at the table.

"They fit me now. You try Marla's old ones." I spread peanut butter and honey on toast.

"Not everybody will be mucking around in concrete," Maryanne reminded us.

"That's right, honeybunch." Dad gulped orange juice and looked approvingly at his eldest. "Maryanne, Denise, Marla, Greg! You four oldest will start—boots on—in the semi-fluid concrete mix that the truck will pour down the chute into the forms. I've got four shovels ready." Dad had been up and working a couple hours already. "Your job is to shovel the mass up to just above its final level. Clare-Cheryl"—he paused to mop up egg yolk with a bread crust—"you'll crouch down outside the form, one on each side of the big screed bar—that's a long two-by-six piece of lumber. Get work gloves. You'll be holding that board and pushing it back and forth over the surface of the wet concrete, to level the mass uniformly inside the forms." Dad turned from us and continued briskly. "Everybody get gloves! You three little boys get boots on and take the shorter rakes and shovels to help the older ones move the mass into place."

"What if we can't do it, even all of us together? What if it hardens too fast and we're stuck standing forever in solid concrete?" Clare's fried egg was momentarily forgotten, her fork poised midair.

"Just walk out of your boots and leave them behind." Greg scowled, wiping up the runny yolk of his egg with a corner of toast, and rolled his eyes. "For pity's sake, you'll be fine! You worry about everything."

"As the concrete sets up a bit," Dad continued, "we'll place scrap plywood on top of it. That'll give us big square pads to kneel on and wield our flat steel trowels as we finish smoothing."

A tangle of jibes filled the air. "I want to get in the concrete too! I want to do the smoothing! You can't—you'd draw in it!"

"We can change jobs as the morning goes on." Dad didn't waste time forbidding anyone from drawing in fresh concrete. He knew, as we did, that none of us would do anything so juvenile. "Don't worry, there'll be plenty of work for all. Remember . . ." He paused, and every one of us knew what the next sentence would be: "Many hands make light work!"

Dad set down his glass. "Finish your egg, Clare. You're a member of the Clean Plate Club. O Jesus, through the Immaculate Heart of Mary." And we instantly followed, eleven voices as one. Not even the imminent arrival of a cement truck took precedence over prayers. We were intoning "in union with the Holy Sacrifice of the Mass throughout the world, in reparation for our sins" when we heard the diesel thrum of a big truck rumbling down Welch Avenue. No one budged, continuing "and in particular for the intentions of the Holy Father" when we heard the rhythmic *ding! ding! ding!* of the truck maneuvering backward toward the forms of the driveway-to-be-poured. We ourselves held form through "Amen!" after which we leapt from the table, running and jabbering, pouring out our side door to pour concrete.

We divided into agreed-upon teams, snatching tools Dad had leaned against the clapboard siding of our house, and took up positions. The door of the huge truck opened wide, and a young driver, clad in heavy-duty cement-dotted workpants, swung one foot down on the running board, looked up, and paused.

He saw an army of youngsters arrayed two by two, standing amid lumber forms, dressed for battle in a faded collection of hand-me-downs, each holding a metal rake or shovel upright in a work-gloved hand like the farmer in *American Gothic*. Presiding over this crew was Dad, wearing his oldest, most-worn pair of white overalls, as befitted the task, and an odd little narrow-brimmed hat that once upon a time had been meant for picnics but had been snatched into service on his way out the door this morning to protect his bald spot from sunburn.

Dad, always weighed down by the collection of tools in his overalls, sprinted toward the driver, his hammer in the side loop slapping his leg. The overalls' weight pulled Dad's shoulders into a stoop, giving him the air of a manic gnome. "Ready to go, do you need anything before we start, you got the mix as ordered? We have hoses hooked up. All you need to do is guide the chute. That's right, swing it right into that corner. Let's start!" Dad never stopped.

The driver, no more than eighteen himself, still stood on the running board, one hand on the inside door handle, the other hooked on the cab roof, his mouth slightly open. He'd expected a jobsite staffed by regular construction guys, old or young but all adult and all male, with perhaps a cigarette hanging loosely here, a T-shirt stretched tight against beer belly there. It was a surprise to be assailed by a wound-up gnome in white overalls in charge of what looked like a summer camp for the underprivileged. The driver wasn't too surprised, though, to take a second glance at the crew and register that the three oldest members were teen girls, attractive even in ragtag work clothes.

Ever thrifty and self-reliant, Dad had arranged for just one employee to drive the truck and work the chute. He knew we could do the rest ourselves. It never occurred to him that we *couldn't* do it. Because he believed in us, we believed in us.

The young truck driver stepped off the running board and aimed the chute. The bass rumble from the mixer hit a lower note, and the first gray slurry of cement mixed with gravel and water swooshed down the chute and splashed into the form.

"Shovel, keep shoveling!" Denise cried, her boots dancing out of reach of the mass, which was spreading like cold, gray lava. "Marla, use that hoe to move it! You little boys, turn your metal rakes upside down and use the flat part, not the teeth!"

The chute swung wider, and more rivers of gray matter raced downward. Piles formed instantly. "You boys are doing great!" called Maryanne, who was not too busy shoveling to praise the Lids. Paul, Steve, and Mark were using smaller rakes, shovels, and whatever else was available to guide cement into place.

Marla stomped and twirled through wet cement, the pole of her hoe first an imaginary dance partner, then a pole vault, then a bar raised overhead. "This is fun. Watch it suck at my boots!" She planted her hoe steady and jumped.

"Stop goofing off and keep moving! This is going to set!" Clare yelled, raking fast.

"The work gets done. It always gets done!" Marla sang as she gave a twirl around her hoe as if it were a Maypole.

"Oh, calm down, you're all overexcitable," Greg grumbled, hefting shovelfuls of concrete toward the form's edges.

"And that guy is *very cute*." Marla kept her eyes on the driver and lowered her voice as she spun past Denise's ear.

"Agreed!" Denise, shoveling, spoke sotto voce and kept her head down but looked up discreetly toward the guy by the chute.

"Third that motion!" Maryanne, steadily lifting shovelfuls, tilted her head to one side and looked at him too.

"Great work, Baseball Team!" Dad was exuberant, doing the work of three of us. The job was going well. The young driver's only job was to guide the chute, but as soon as the form was full and the chute quiet, he grinned, grabbed his own shovel off the truck, and mucked in alongside, shirt off now, working in the vicinity of Maryanne, Denise, or Marla. We filled and tromped and screeded and troweled, over and over until the job was level and its surface smooth. Dad allowed Mark to press a current-year penny into one corner of the fresh concrete, to date the work. The job looked great. The job looked nearly *done*. We'd been at it nearly four hours. We were tired, but the end was in sight; all that was left was the cleanup. Maybe we'd get the rest of the day off.

"Where do you want me to dump the excess?" the driver asked Dad.

Excess? Dump? Waste? These words were like flame to the dry tinder of Dad's frugal nature.

"Nothing doing!" Dad's mind flew, imagining potential uses for the excess cement. "We can use it at one of the other houses." He raced through candidates. "The back door of 410 garage could use an entry pad! The wood back porch at 426 could use a step-down landing! We'll build forms and pour that excess in them lickety-split!" The words weren't out of his mouth before he sprinted toward the garage, which was stocked and ready with used, denailed lumber. "Come on, Baseball Team!"

We didn't think it possible that Dad had a faster speed, but that afternoon, we saw it. He was a sweaty blur, expertly building a form, shouting instructions, directing us to grab a tool or fetch a piece of lumber.

"This is a desperate situation, desperate!" He got a little wild-eyed, imagining concrete curing and hardening too soon. But it didn't. He built the forms, with us orbiting around him, and poured in every drop of excess cement. It was smooth. It was good. It was done—really done, this time.

That day, we nine regarded Dad with a kind of wonder. He was so sure and so fast, so capable, so *good* at everything. He wasn't a contractor, yet he could orchestrate the pouring of a huge drive-way—a high-stakes job with no second tries—and have it come out perfectly. Always, he knew without hesitation that we could do it: pour concrete, scrape and paint a Victorian manse, shovel heavy snowfall from a dozen properties before breakfast. Dad didn't waste a nanosecond of time or an iota of energy doubting himself or his Baseball Team. Every resource went pedal-to-the-metal toward success.

That day, we saw in Dad the power of positive thinking. Think you can? Think you can't? Either way, you're right. Dad never needed to say that. He showed us every day how to live knowing we could.

Positive thinking wasn't the only magic Dad had. Working alongside Dad could be taxing, but it was always exciting. Also—though we would never have said so—he could sometimes make work fun. The day of the pour was one of those days.

That evening around the supper table, Dad was jubilant. "That wasn't so bad, was it? That's healthy, satisfying, useful work. It's sad that so few children get the chance to gain from real-life experiences like this. You're lucky, really. You're lucky to be in a big family." And we felt it: lucky to be able to do it ourselves, and lucky to be many hands.

Decades later, Dad hired a contractor with a backhoe to break up the driveway, to make way for a new building.

"That concrete was built for the ages. It's perfect, not a crack in it," the contractor said, nodding admiringly to our brother Paul, now a middle-aged man. "I had a heck of a time! Took me hours, out there riding that backhoe, to beat that old concrete into submission! Your dad built well."

"Like the pharaohs." Paul smiled wryly. "Like the pharaohs."

1971

the waif and the amazon

Outdoors on our new, expanded concrete driveway, Dad bent over an old pockmarked door laid across two scarred sawhorses, a bright orange extension cord snaking under his feet. He guided his electric circular saw expertly into the bottom edge of the door. The soprano of the whirring steel blade whined higher as it bit into wood. Dad moved the saw forward, steadily shaving a perfect quarter inch off the base of the door, arcing up a spray of fragrant sawdust.

The saw's whine joined the cicadas' raspy song emanating from the new little trees that now lined Welch Avenue. On this warm Saturday afternoon in late August, most of us nine, like Dad, were outside working. Mom and Maryanne were inside making dinner, to be served as always at five thirty.

Paul and Steve guided noisy gas-powered lawnmowers over adjoining front yards. Denise crawled under an overgrown shrub, maneuvering a sharp pruning tool toward the base of a branch growing too close to the house. Marla was standing over Denise and leaning into the shrub to grasp the offending branch, when she saw a taxi rolling slowly down Welch Avenue, its driver reading house numbers, before coming to a stop in front of our driveway.

A *taxi*. We knew they existed, but we'd never known anyone to use one. We'd never seen one on our street. Marla let go of the branch as Denise backed out of the shrub, soil clinging to her knees. Greg and Clare stopped raking old leaves out of a flower bed. I looked up from my task of collecting yard debris. Mark stopped gathering twigs and sticks off the grass ahead of Paul and Steve, who shut off their mowers. This bright yellow taxi, with its rounded haunches and slightly curved roof, looked as though it had driven out of a television show. We couldn't imagine who would pay cab fare. Every family we knew had a car. You could ask anyone for a lift.

We stared at the cab as showers of sawdust rained down from Dad's roaring saw onto his white carpenter overalls and cracked leather work boots. *ZZZing!* The quarter-inch length cleaved away from the bottom of the old door and fell to the driveway. The saw snapped into silence, and Dad looked up.

The cabbie exited the vehicle and stepped smartly to the rear. He popped the trunk and began extricating bags and suitcases. We watched, motionless, arrayed around the front yard. The cab's back door swung open like the hatch of a spaceship, and a slim waif with dyed red-brown hair emerged onto the dappled shade of our front walk.

Our new college girl, Dawn, was seventeen, petite, slight as a willow branch, Jewish, and from Brooklyn. Her tie-dyed, ribbed, knit shirt clung tight and short, leaving six inches of bare midriff between it and her fashion-faded, hip-hugger, bell-bottom jeans. She looked stunned to find herself transported from her crowded big-city borough, dropped onto our verdant front yard, and surrounded by curious natives.

"Are you really from New York?" Mark's tone suggested she might be from the moon. "Did you take that cab all the way from the Des Moines airport? Whoa!"

"She *paid* for a cab for thirty miles?" Clare whispered into my ear, as other siblings reached to help with bags and we were jostled to the back. We could not imagine anyone wasting money on a cab at all, let alone paying for one all the way from another city.

Dad unplugged his saw and strode forward, taking charge. His carpenter overalls, weighed down with various tools in loops and pockets throughout, clanked a bit, but this affected his sure stride not at all. "I'm Joe Stritzel!" He didn't mean to boom, but he was used to addressing a large lecture hall. "Welcome to Ames!" He didn't mean to be imposing, either, but he believed in speaking up and had no truck with timidity. He extended his hand. "Welcome!"

"I'm Daaahhhrrrrrnnn," Dawn said, barely audible, shrinking back so a curtain of smooth, straight, long hair swung in front of her face.

Dad was puzzled. "Thorn?" he boomed, shaking her hand. "Your name is Thorn?"

"No, Daaahhhrrrnnnn," she replied, then louder, "DAAAH-HHRRRNNN."

"Thorn!? Thorn??" Dad, rarely confused, struggled to make out her accent.

"DAAAHHHRRRNNN!" she repeated in desperation, her Brooklynese growing thicker as she tried harder.

"Oh! Dawn!" Denise and Marla, nearer her age, suddenly got it, and jumped in as interpreters. "Hi, Dawn! Glad you're here. You have the rest of the weekend to settle in before classes start Monday. Come on in!" They reached for her suitcases and started lugging them across the grass.

Dawn looked at our house, her new home, and saw the kind of

dwelling that children draw with crayons: pitched roof, symmetrical windows flanking a front door, brick chimney. She glanced up and down the street, lined with frame houses similar to ours, as she slung one of her bags over her shoulder. "You gawt a nice place, out here in the cawntry."

"Country?" Clare was genuinely baffled. "This is Campustown."

"Whaddaya mean country?" echoed Mark. "Country is cows and alfalfa, like Uncle Thomas's dairy farm in Ohio."

"Cawntry," Dawn insisted, following us into the house. Mom left the stove and came to shake her hand, smiling. Dawn relaxed, responding to Mom's gentleness and the welcoming smell of dinner. "Cawntry," Dawn explained. "With grass and trees in frawnt."

Maryanne, Denise, and Marla led Dawn through the kitchen and up broad, carpeted stairs. "Your room is in the new addition." Maryanne huffed a bit as she dragged the biggest suitcase up the new staircase near the rear of the house. We five girls, all carrying bags, formed a constellation around Dawn as we navigated stairs into the new second-floor wing, which comprised one bathroom and five bedrooms ringing a central lounge.

Our house, when originally built in the early years of the twentieth century, offered just three bedrooms. That was fine when Mom and Dad bought it in 1954 and moved in with daughters ages three, two, and one. But ten years and six additional children later, they needed more space, and so added Mom's self-designed new kitchen, spacious laundry room, and expanded bathroom. They chose not to finish the new ceilings, leaving bright silver-wrapped insulation showing overhead among raw-yellow exposed beams, knowing more construction was inevitable. Indeed, five years later, atop that first layer of kitchen and laundry room, our parents added a second story of five bedrooms plus central lounge. We five sisters, plus an always-changing cast of college girls, poured into it, filling it immediately, leaving the three original bedrooms in the old part of the house to Mom and Dad, Greg, and the Lids. Now, in the neatest room in the new addition, with newly made bed and ironed curtains, we sisters dropped Dawn's suitcases on fresh-vacuumed carpet.

"Definitely cawntry!" Dawn looked out the window to our backyard, seeing our pair of picnic tables, the broad grassy play area ringed with half a dozen fruit trees, some studded now with reddening apples, and a fenced rear section of vegetables and berry bushes.

"Definitely town!" Marla looked out the same window to see a line of houses to the side, and the large playground and expansive brick sweep of Crawford Elementary School behind our property.

"Definitely dinnertime." And Maryanne ushered us downstairs.

Dawn settled in, quickly immersing herself in her pre–veterinary medicine program, the reason she'd chosen to move from New York City to Ames. Within days, she was laughing with us at her accent and our own, though we maintained we didn't have accents, only she did.

We served twelve to fifteen at every meal, depending on how many college girls were living with us during any given semester. Birthdays came frequently, and we celebrated each the same way, with an extra-nice dinner followed by a big homemade cake and presents afterward in the living room. On Dawn's eighteenth birthday, months later, when Mom bore a cake aflame with candles to the dinner table, Dawn burst into tears.

"Who would know my birthday, out here in the cawntry," she honked into the emergency hanky Mom handed her. "It's so nice of you!" She cried harder. The rest of us were struck dumb, having never seen anyone cry at an ordinary birthday cake. How could Dawn imagine she wouldn't have cake and presents and an enthusiastic rendition of all three verses of "Happy Birthday"? We never missed an opportunity to tack on all the verses to the old song, finishing with the refrain "God's blessings on you!"

"Of course we're going to celebrate your birthday. We do this for all of us!" Marla tucked her arm through Dawn's.

When Dawn graduated and moved out, we drove her to the airport in Des Moines, saving her cab fare. Marla cried when she left.

In stark contrast to Dawn, our next college girl, Susan, was big, brassy, blond, and from Chicago. She was older than most college students, and more worldly. At five feet eleven inches and 165 pounds, with grande-size self-confidence and a bust to match, she cut a commanding presence just entering a room. Susan had big hair, big shoulders, and a big smile. Meeting her, you just knew she was the type to keep a cool head under pressure. Coming from the big city, Susan kept current with fashion, and in the early 1970s when she came to live with us, pierced ears were in style big time.

None of us five girls or Mom had pierced ears, though Marla had undergone an attempt earlier, and I had tried wearing a kind of torturous small hoop earring that had sharp ends and was supposed to gradually pierce its way through the lobe over time. It hadn't. Mom wore clip-on earrings, which pinched painfully, for dress-up occasions.

When Susan offered to pierce all our ears at once, we signed on immediately and enthusiastically, including Mom. Mom liked to stay up-to-date, so when this convenient opportunity presented itself, she took advantage of it.

"Ear piercing is easy. I've done it dozens of times," Susan assured us. "There's nothing to it. I'll need a sewing needle, cotton balls, rubbing alcohol, a cork, a ballpoint pen, and ice cubes. Each of you needs basic gold post earrings. They must be good quality gold, no cheap metal. You'll keep them in for six weeks."

Dad might have objected to something like this, since ear piercing was not productive, efficient, or thrifty. But we could afford our own earrings, due to babysitting and such, and Mom was on board with the endeavor. Dad trusted Mom absolutely, so he only mused for a moment on the unfathomable currents of fashion.

"My mother, God rest her soul, had pierced ears as a young woman in 1915," he said, remembering our Grandma Regina. "They were in style in the twenties, then they went out of style in the forties and fifties, now they're back in."

One winter Sunday evening, we girls plus Mom gathered around our kitchen table for the mass operation. Susan gathered supplies. She surveyed Mom's collection of different-sized hand-sewing needles, stuck neatly side-by-side in a square of stiff paper, and selected one as a surgeon might select a scalpel. Dousing a cotton ball with rubbing alcohol, she swabbed the needle and advised us to rub our earlobes with rubbing alcohol, too.

"Take an ice cube from the bowl, and hold it against your earlobe," Susan instructed. "That will numb the lobe."

We tried to hold ice against our earlobes, but the slippery cubes kept squirting from our hands, skittering across the table, and sliding along the floor. With several cubes on the loose, Clare and I discovered you could play a sort of ice hockey/shuffleboard on the table. We each held a cube flat against the table, using it to knock other cubes around. Hydroplaning, the cubes ricocheted and shot off the table at speed. We laughed in delight.

"Do you want your ears pierced or not? This is serious business!" Denise held a cube against her earlobe, her voice snapping with anxiety. Melting between her fingers, the ice slipped down her sleeve. She shook it out and took another cube, gamely pressing it to her ear for a few seconds before it too squirted away down the table. After several minutes, most of our earlobes had had minimal contact with ice cubes.

"This isn't numbing anything except my fingers." Clare shook water from her hands and rubbed them together for warmth.

"OK, OK, forget the ice." Susan's hands were wet from chasing ice, too. "Pinch your earlobe, hard, between two fingernails. That'll numb it."

We corralled the ice and dumped it in the sink. Then we gathered around the table in age order, all of us dutifully pinching earlobes with sharp fingernails. It hurt. The kitchen was quiet now. No one was playing games or making jokes. Susan swabbed the needle once more with alcohol. Our recently purchased earrings lay submerged in a little bath of rubbing alcohol in the bottle cap. Susan looked up, ready to choose her first victim. Her eyes alighted on one of us, then another, like a wasp at a banquet choosing whom to sting first.

Mom glanced at the line of anxious faces. "Let me go first," she said to Maryanne. Since she was responsible for allowing us to undergo this painful procedure, she would lead the way.

"It can't hurt you, Mom!" My voice rang with nerves. "Your earlobes are too old." As a preteen, I figured that Mom, in her fifties, was so ancient she likely had no feeling left anywhere. Mom sat on the edge of her chair, leaning forward toward the table. Susan perched on a chair next to her.

"I'll be fine," Mom said, and as the needle jabbed through one of her lobes and then the other, she was. She made no sound. She barely grimaced, her eyes closing briefly, mouth pursing into a line, fists gripping the table edge. It was over within seconds. Deftly, Susan fished two gold post earrings from their alcohol bath and worked them through Mom's new piercings.

"There! Twirl them every morning and night, and during the day when you think about it, so the skin doesn't heal tight to the post." Susan was pleased the first piercing had progressed without drama. "Drip rubbing alcohol on them twice a day. In six weeks, your piercings will be healed, and you can wear any earrings you want."

Nerveless ears or not, Mom kept a good face for our sake. Not so Maryanne and Denise. Their earlobes weren't numbed, but made more sensitive by the fierce pinching.

Susan used the ballpoint pen to mark the dot where the needle should go. She held the cork behind the lobe, then with speed and authority thrust the needle through the lobe like a spear. Ear piercing is not for the timid, and Susan's modus operandi was quick and brutal. Maryanne and then Denise yelped with pain as the needle jabbed and the earrings followed. Eyes watering, they sucked in big, jagged breaths to keep their eyes from overflowing. Marla, Clare, and I, hunching forward on chairs drawn close to the table, leaning in so we could see, kept anxious eyes on our older sisters.

"Grip the hand of the sister behind you," Susan encouraged. "That'll lessen the pain of the needle." Susan's supreme confidence never wavered. Why she imagined this would affect the pain, or why we believed her when her previous advice about ice and fingernail pinching hadn't numbed anything, remains a mystery. Susan was one of those personalities who never experience a sliver of doubt, and as such could have led an army into battle. Even her barked instructions—hold ice! pinch lobes! grab a hand!—sounded military. Maryanne and Denise, somewhat recovered, swabbed their newly installed earrings with alcohol and smiled at themselves in shaky handheld mirrors.

Marla, next up, had undergone a botched piercing six months earlier, and her now half-healed lobes looked angry before Susan's needle was even close. Gritting her teeth, willing herself to be tough and fearless, Marla sat on the edge of her chair and grasped Clare's hand in a death grip as Susan quickly jabbed the needle in. But it did not go through. Scar tissue within had thrown up defensive roadblocks. Like a general encountering a bloodier battle than anticipated, Susan did not hesitate but gathered strength and pushed on. She rose slightly from her chair-edge perch, braced her knees, re-gripped her needle, and pushed hard and steady. Marla, her face crumpled, gasped and gripped Clare's hand harder. The needle finally emerged, bloody but victorious. One lobe down, one to go. Susan started on the other earlobe, steadily driving the needle, ignoring Marla's gasps. Both gold earrings, liberally swabbed with rubbing alcohol, were inserted. Marla's earlobes had survived. Not so Clare's hand.

"What is this?" Clare surveyed her red, throbbing hand. "Some sort of modern take on Civil War soldiers biting bullets during amputations?"

The pain in her hand didn't stop Clare, when she went under the needle, from using the same pain management technique on me, waiting behind her, last in line. Clare's piercings, like Mom's, Maryanne's, and Denise's, were painful but uncomplicated.

This hurts already, I thought, *and I'm still one sister away from the needle. Between my fingernail-pinched lobes and sister-crushed hand, how bad can that needle be?*

It was bad. Very bad. Since every previous patient was now bemoaning her bruised hand, but stoically not her bloody lobes, I put all my focus on holding Marla's proffered hand loosely. As the needle entered one earlobe and then the other, pain, like the closing shutter of a camera, obliterated everything but one remaining pinpoint of laser focus, that of keeping a loose grip on her hand.

"It's through!" Susan was jubilant as the needle thrust through my second earlobe into the cork.

"You didn't even tighten your grip on my hand!" Marla was surprised that my ear piercing was over.

We were done. We held up hand mirrors, still a little shakily, to admire our gold post earrings.

The next day at school, we all wore our hair tucked behind our ears. Whenever I had the chance, I ducked into the girls' bathroom at Welch Junior High to look in the mirror and admire my gleaming gold post earrings. That first day, those earrings seemed so marvelous and magnificent, so dazzling and delightful, I wondered how it was that my friends hardly noticed. I myself was entranced with my new, sophisticated look and felt I'd taken a step into the world of womanhood. We tended our lobes twice daily with alcohol. Weeks passed and our piercings healed, even Marla's.

At the end of the school year, Susan graduated from Iowa State and went on to a career as a trader at the New York Stock Exchange. Once in a while, as we twirled an especially pretty earring, we'd think of Susan. We'd imagine her there on the floor of the stock exchange, big, brassy, blond, and confident, an Amazon keeping a cool head under pressure, barking buy and sell orders in the same voice of authority she'd used during the great ear-piercing campaign at our kitchen table.

eighteen

1970

downtown, where all the
lights are bright

"When you're alone, and life is making you lonely, you can always go—Downtown!" Denise, wedged in the middle seat of our 1966 Pontiac station wagon with Marla, Greg, and Clare, started the song as we rolled past midwestern cornfields.

"When you've got worries, all the noise and the hurry, seem to help, I know," Maryanne, in the front seat between Dad and Mom, picked up the tune and supplied the next lyric to the massive hit song, composed by Tony Hatch and recorded by Petula Clark.

"Downtown!" All of us knew the next word, and from the far back seat of the station wagon, Paul, Steve, Mark, and I landed on the word with particular enthusiasm. We were thrilled, we were excited, we were On Vacation. And not just a weekend to fish at a little midwestern lake. We were going cross-country, all the way to the Atlantic Ocean. On the way, we'd stop overnight in Chicago and then spend a few days with relatives at Dad's old family farm in Ohio.

Vacation was not a concept Dad was familiar with; it sounded like some sort of modern invention that had nothing to do with him. But we knew that Mom's natal family, though hardworking, was at least familiar with the idea of a trip just for fun. We'd seen an old deckle-edged black-and-white photo of Mom as a girl, smiling and squinting into the sun, holding a hot dog on a stick over a campfire, in front of her family's Model T on a dirt road in Yellowstone National Park. Mom was the reason we owned a pop-up camper and occasionally went fishing. It was Mom who suggested, one summer in the early seventies, a two-week road trip from Ames to the East Coast.

Dad was flummoxed. What about the constant work that needed doing on the rental houses? What about all the gardens we tended? What about lost productivity? What about *cost*? But Dad liked pleasing Mom, and he wanted us to see the world, so he warmed to the idea. Neighbors could turn sprinklers on our vegetable gardens if necessary, and the houses wouldn't fall down if we suspended work for two weeks. Plus, we could stay with friends and relatives along the way, Mom pointed out. Soon Dad was in full military command mode, organizing fishing gear, hitching the camper to our station wagon, and packing tools in case of a breakdown. This was one year in which Dad's annual two-week vacation from the university would be an actual vacation rather than a pass to work even harder on our rental houses.

"So go—Downtown!" we sang. Being close-packed four to a bench seat helped our voices meld. "Things will be great when you're—Downtown!" We wiggled a bit, trying to make room where there was none. "No finer place, for sure—Downtown!" The car windows were open; the summer morning was soft and bright and full of anticipation. We passed through eastern Iowa's flat acres of soybeans and corn and tidy towns with white-painted clapboard houses set neatly side-by-side, fronted by velvet lawns and shade trees. Often our route followed interstate highway, but when it didn't, we drove down Main Streets lined with parked cars and stores offering hardware or dry goods, a grocery store, a café with a screen door. The steeple of a Lutheran church, then a Catholic one, referenced northern European immigrants.

"Don't hang around and let your problems surround you, there are movie shows—Downtown!" Denise brought harmony to our tune. We weren't surrounded by problems, just each other. Our vehicle was jam-packed, bow to stern and floorboards to dome light, with Stritzels—plus the pillows and library books most of us had brought along. At least the suitcases were in a carrier lashed atop the car. But we weren't thinking of our crammed quarters, just the next line of lyrics; our rendition wavered as we tried to remember what came next.

"Oh!" Maryanne, up in front, suddenly remembered: "Maybe you know some little places to go to, where they never close."

"Downtown!" We got it, swinging through the rest of the song, finishing with a flourish of three-part harmony.

"Sounds great!" Dad kept the accelerator steady and his eyes on the road. "Let's have another one. How about that song about the fox?"

We knew this one cold. The epic folk song "The Fox" is seven long verses, but we remembered them easily because the song tells a story about a fox that raids a henhouse. In the sixth verse, the fox returns to his wife and family with the ultimate prize, a gray goose. The lyrics include *He ran till he came to his cozy den, there were the little ones, eight, nine, ten.* We figured Dad could relate. As the fox family prepares for a magnificent supper of goose, the song continues *Daddy, Daddy, better go back again, it must be a mighty fine town-o.* We suspected he liked that line too. Of everything we sang, "The Fox" was Dad's favorite. Marla started it now, in an accommodating key, and the rest of us jumped in.

Dad, who in general thought we nine children were the bee's

knees, was particularly convinced of our vocal ability, and imagined we should sing as guest artists on *The Lawrence Welk Show*, a musical TV variety show that aired nationally from 1955 to 1971 on Saturday evenings. We enjoyed the show's ever-upbeat, fizzy, toe-tapping music, with the occasional polka thrown in for fun. The show was filmed in Los Angeles, but Welk was a North Dakotan, and his show maintained its aura of midwestern decency right through the sixties. Welk launched the Lennon Sisters, a nationally beloved and long-running quartet. Dad thought we were every bit as good as they were, if less famous. Though Dad might have been just a little biased, most of us were decent singers, and our voices blended well. In the late sixties, every teenager worth her embroidered jeans and Indian headband played guitar and sang. At the moment, Denise's guitar in its case was stowed with the suitcases in the carrier on the car's roof, so we worked our way a cappella through one tune after another.

Now, having sung our way through "The Fox" and a couple dozen more songs, we were losing our focus, and the temperature outside and inside the car was rising. "Get your *stuff* out from under my *feet!*" Greg snapped as Clare's library books slid. He shifted his position and found his bare thighs stuck to the vinyl seat. "Are you really going to read all these?" He grimaced as he shifted, pulling skin off vinyl.

"Yes," Clare said hotly. "You're the one taking up too much room!"

"It's Marla's rear end that's hogging all the room on this seat!" Denise broke up laughing, snorting through her nose and laughing like a hyena, bumping her hip into Marla's pert behind.

"You're the one with the"—Marla looked down her nose and raised her eyebrows—"*child-bearing* hips!" she hooted, flipping her own hip harder against slender Denise.

"Enough talking!" Dad drummed his fingers on the steering

wheel. "Let's hear . . . what is that one . . . ahhh . . . 'Strawberry Wine'!" Dad could never remember song titles, so his requests were a mystery. Of necessity, we'd learned to decipher. What Dad called "Strawberry Wine" was a lilting melody about living in the moment that is actually called "Today." Composed by Randy Sparks of the New Christy Minstrels, it was recorded by several artists. Its lyrics are a poignant reminder of the passage of time.

We shushed to let Denise start: "Today, while the blossoms still cling to the vine," before we joined in with, "I'll taste your strawberries, I'll drink your sweet wine." The second line, with its strawberries and wine, was apparently the only thing Dad remembered. Clare picked up her library books, and Greg shifted to make room for her. "A million tomorrows shall all pass away"—seven of us carried the melody while Denise and Marla hit a high trail of harmony— "Ere I forget, all the joy that is mine today." We ended on a soft note that faded to silence.

Mom turned around to look at us. Her gaze fell on each of us, one by one. "Now," she said simply, "is the happiest time."

When our singing voices needed a rest, Dad delivered long, oral math problems to do in our heads. He often did this in the car, where he had a captive audience. He did this at home, too, around the table after dinner, before dishes were cleared. Dad's math games were one reason friends liked to eat at our house. (Another reason was that Mom always said yes to a friend's request to stay. She figured another child to feed, when you've already got nine, is an insignificant percentage increase. Once, after Mom said yes to one of my friends, my friend phoned her own mother for permission. The other mother's voice came loudly through the phone: "No! Mrs. Stritzel has enough work to do without you!" It occurred to me then for the first time that we nine children might be considered work.) Though Dad's math problems weren't easy, the rapid pace and keen competition created excitement. Winning—shouting the answer before anyone else—was exhilarating, and our friends enjoyed the game as much as we did.

Now, from the driver's seat, in an auctioneer's rapid patter, Dad tossed the first problem back over his shoulder. "Thirty times three, minus ten, plus one, divided by nine, plus twelve," he'd fire off, building speed, "divided by seven, times three"—he was going faster now—"plus one, divided by two"—he was racing toward the finish with his trademark flourish, delivered in the jubilant tones of one who has reached the summit—"equals . . ."

"Five!" Several of us in the back seats yelled triumphantly.

"Good work!" Now Dad's eye was drawn to black-and-white cows grazing in a field, so he switched subjects, seizing the moment to teach bovine identification. "What kind of cows are they?" he tested.

"Holsteins," Maryanne answered instantly. "Too easy. Everybody knows that."

"OK." Dad drove until we passed another field filled with black cows. "How about these?"

"Black Angus." Greg, from the middle seat, spoke fastest. "Another easy one."

"Good!" Dad said, and we passed another farm or two. "What about these brown cows?"

"Jerseys." This time, Maryanne was the only one who could answer. "They're smaller than the brown-and-white Guernseys."

As our car flashed past the pastures, leaving heifers behind, Dad left them behind too, returning to arithmetic. "You older kids keep quiet on this next problem," he started. "This is for the little boys: three plus three, plus four, minus five." He spoke louder, over his shoulder, so the youngest kids in the far rear seat could hear.

❧

One reason we were happy on this trip was because we knew what was coming: root beers in frosty mugs at an A&W drive-in. Our family never ate out and never stayed in a motel. Such frivolity would have been unthinkably expensive, but even more, the whole concept was vaguely suspect and lazy. It was probably immoral. The exception was an A&W root beer, and that only on a road trip. (Earlier that day Mom, with a couple of us helping, had packed a mass lunch of bologna sandwiches, cut-up vegetables, and grapes. The drive-in was for drinks.) To turn off the baking-hot asphalt highway onto the crunching gravel lot of a brown-and-orange A&W, the station wagon listing to one side under its load as we slowly wheeled in, was to know that paradise existed on Earth and we were about to experience it.

The boxy little glass-fronted restaurant, flickering with neon, was set well back on its dusty lot, with a long strip of concrete covered by a ridged steel awning reaching toward the street. Drivers nosed up to park perpendicular to this strip, positioning their cars close to a speaker on a post. A sign read "Turn Lights On for Service!"

Dad liked efficiency almost as much as he appreciated thrift, and an A&W allowed him to demonstrate both. It wouldn't have occurred to him to ask each of us what drink we wanted to order any more than it would have occurred to any of us to ask for it. Our family often acted as one entity: individuality was needlessly time-consuming. Dad parked our rig expertly and cranked down his window.

"Eight root beers plus three baby root beers, please," he delivered into the speaker, in his in-charge professor's tone. The Lids got the baby root beers. These came free, delivered in darling miniature glass mugs. What with baby root beers' being free, plus the rest of us forever thinking of the youngest three boys as little, the Lids had baby root beers ordered for them until they were old enough to shave, at which point they finally organized and agitated for more.

Two teenage waitresses in brown-and-orange uniforms emerged from the restaurant, each bearing a tray crowded with frosty mugs. Navigating cautiously, they gently hooked the heavy trays onto our car's front partially rolled-down windows. Dad and Mom reached through their windows to access the mugs, passing them back through the car. Silence reigned for a few minutes, as we quaffed root beers and bit happily into sandwiches. But the wonder wasn't over. After our lunch and root beers, Dad ordered again into the speaker—"Eleven vanilla ice cream cones, please"—and nirvana was complete.

It never occurred to us to be annoyed at a lack of choice. We were delighted with the extra treat. Root beer *and* ice cream—such a double delight was unusual. From earliest memory, we'd known our family didn't waste money. As very small children, we'd walk right past those mechanical horses outside stores. We knew that such coin-operated attractions, like the machines that dispensed little toys in exchange for a nickel, weren't for us, and we accepted it without question. When we were older, if we went to a movie, a rarity in itself, we didn't buy popcorn. We knew the movie was enough of a treat.

Occasionally, at home after dinner, we'd share three Hershey bars for dessert. These were regular-sized Hershey bars, the whole intended for one person. But Mom would unwrap the bars, snap each into four pieces, and pass the pieces in a bowl. Each of us got one piece. We didn't know that most people ate an entire chocolate bar at one sitting.

❧

Back in our station wagon, happily fueled with vanilla soft-serve, we hit the highway again. Re-energized, Marla mentally flipped through a roster of potential songs, finally choosing her favorite, which was not a song but a spoken poem, "The Reverend Mr. Black," with only the refrains sung. Marla loved to recite from memory this epic saga about an Appalachian preacher, and during our singing sessions, she often did.

"He rode easy in the saddle, he was tall and lean," Marla began, intoning solemnly in trademark dramatic fashion that signaled to the rest of us that, like it or not, the whole poem was on its way.

"Not this again," Greg groaned.

"And at first, you'd think nothing but a streak of mean," Marla went on, paying no attention to grumbling, "could make a man so downright strong. But one look in his eyes and you knowed you was wrong." She entered the spirit of the piece, the low cadence of her voice finding the swaying rhythm of mountain dialect. We were drawn in despite ourselves, and when the time came to sing the slow, dignified refrain, we all joined in, except for Greg, who was reading one of Clare's library books.

"You gotta walk that lonesome valley," we sang, and so long hours on the road ticked by. By midafternoon, we were reprising the song "Downtown," swinging with "the lights are much brighter there," when we got lost in Chicago, and our voices deflated like a tire going flat.

"You can forget all your troubles"—Maryanne's voice, the only one left, was trailing off in trepidation—"forget all your cares, so go —Downtown . . ." Then her voice too vanished into a whisper.

The soft green landscape dotted with tidy towns had vanished. Outside the car windows were multilane highways roaring with heavy traffic, lined by warehouses and factories, and then apartment blocks, and then, as we wound deeper and deeper into the inner city, potholed streets of dilapidated frame houses and empty lots littered with blowing trash and glittering broken glass. We were looking for the home of Mom and Dad's old college friends, who were expecting us for the night, but we were nowhere near their suburban neighborhood. Instead, our station-wagon-with-camper was navigating narrow inner-city streets.

As our vehicle slowed, time seemed to slow with it. Old men rocked on sagging front porches. A woman, moving a baby from one hip to the other, shouted at children crouched over a game in the dirt. A handful of girls jumped rope on the sidewalk. Kids sat on porch railings, toes hooked behind spindles, and stopped licking popsicles to stare at us. A gaggle of teens hung around the lopped-off diagonal entrance to a little corner store, smoking, watching our packed station wagon nose uneasily down the street. Every person was black. Every person was looking. Everything was different, and we fell into silence.

My experience from growing up in Ames was that skin color made no difference, that there was no division between the races. At home in Ames, our neighborhood had one African American family. The father was a professor, the mother a homemaker, and their son my classmate. Their daughter was a couple of years younger. They were just like us, midwestern and ordinary. Our family was also acquainted with a handful of graduate students from Africa, and we knew a white anthropology professor who had spent time on that continent, married an African woman named Mary, and now lived in Ames. They went to our church. We were friends with them and enjoyed Mary's lively stories about her village, as well as her vivid native dress. We kids were baffled by the race riots we saw on the nightly news.

But this neighborhood felt different. We were the minority, and everyone was staring. In our little sphere of Campustown in Ames, race was a nonissue. Now we were out in the wider world. For the first time, for no reason I could explain, I felt a frisson of tension.

"Who would build houses so close together?" Paul, in the far back, was wide-eyed.

"You could practically reach from your upstairs bedroom window into the house next door." Mark, next to Paul, peeled one thigh off the sticky vinyl bench seat and then the other. These paint-all-gone and rotting-trim houses, set eave-by-eave close, were the same vintage as our home back in Ames, but that was the only similarity.

"No sunlight would ever make it in those side windows." I shifted uneasily between Paul and Mark, not taking my eyes off the dark aisles of bare dirt that passed for side yards between the houses. No green lawns rolled out in front from these houses, just handkerchief-size squares of hard-packed dirt with the occasional sad tuft of grass or chunk of broken concrete.

"Joe," Mom said as she lowered the map and pointed to a gas station at the corner, "time to ask for directions."

Always cognizant of prices, we gasped when we saw the sign showing gas at thirty-eight cents. At home, gas generally cost thirty-four cents a gallon, but Dad, always searching out the low price, patronized a station on the outskirts of Ames, buying it for thirty-two or lower. Just a week earlier, he'd filled up at twenty-nine cents a gallon.

Dad sucked in his breath. It was painful, but we were going to have to buy gas at Chicago prices sooner or later. Dad made a wide turn into the gas station, the undercarriage of our loaded vehicle riding low over pitted concrete stained with blotches of oil. Dad got out and entered the little service station, but before the rest of us could move, our car and camper were engulfed from behind by an approaching wave of neighborhood children. It was as if we were looking out from a submarine that had suddenly plunged into an ocean of pint-sized humanity. The laughing faces of children were everywhere; kids were pushing to get closer, looking, chattering, and pointing. It wasn't unusual for people to point and exclaim when we were all packed in the car—sometimes, on the highway, we saw people in passing cars trying to quickly count us, and we'd help out by flashing nine fingers—but this was extreme. We felt besieged.

Two girls, tight braids radiating from their heads, pushed their faces close against our car windows, jockeying to get a better look at us. Looking at the children's faces, our unease melted. We smiled back, and the exclaiming outside ratcheted up into shrieks of amazement.

"Look! Look at them!" The children were beside themselves, pointing at us wide-eyed, jostling and pushing, tossing a hand in front of a mouth to cover their astonishment. Now we couldn't help laughing too, despite our puzzlement. What about us could spark such hilarity? Our car windows were already partially open, but when we rolled them down fully, we finally understood what the children were saying.

"Look!" one girl squealed. "Look at them gold teeth!"

Our smiles had revealed silver-colored braces on our teeth. At any given time, about three of the nine of us sported orthodontia. These children had never seen braces.

With directions in hand and gas in the car, we wound our way out of the inner city and into Chicago's newly burgeoning suburbs of angular, pastel-toned houses, to the home of our parents' friends, the Connellys. Nearly twenty years had passed since our parents and the Connellys had chummed around together at Iowa State's Catholic student center. Life paths had diverged.

"Ritzy neighborhood." Maryanne raised an eyebrow as our venerable station wagon swung onto a street of new houses set on wide lawns dotted with tiny new trees and shrubs. Garages stood proud out front, front porches were nowhere to be seen, and air conditioners hummed. Sprinklers ticked lazily, tossing circular arcs of water that glittered in the low-angled sunshine. A sleek Buick Riviera adorned one driveway; a boat-sized Cadillac Fleetwood sedan rested in another. Other than the far-off figure of a boy guiding a puttering lawnmower across the green nap of a lawn farther down the street, no one was around.

"It's cocktail hour—everybody must be out back on the patios," Mom guessed, reading house numbers while Dad drove slowly along. Cocktail hour? We'd never heard Mom use that term. It sounded like something out of TV land.

"Where's my hairbrush?" Marla dug in her purse as Dad turned our rig into the correct driveway. Denise popped open a compact and smiled into its little mirror, turning her head one way, then the other. Maryanne brushed at the front of her white blouse with its neat rounded collar and smoothed her plaid shorts.

"Just get out of the car!" Greg, reaching over sisters toward the car door handle, had had enough of the vinyl seat, and we spilled out of our Pontiac.

"Hey, here you are!" Bob Connelly emerged from around the corner of the house. Like his house, he was sharp and mod and angular, his dark hair slicked back with pomade and a thin mustache crawling across his upper lip. He wore snazzy white pants, a knit striped shirt with open collar, and sandals.

"I think that's a martini," Marla breathed into Denise's ear as Bob Connelly shifted a drink floating a pimiento-stuffed olive to his left hand and reached with his right to shake Dad's hand.

"Welcome, welcome! Joe and Marcella! And all the kids." Bob

smiled big, looking as though he'd already fortified himself for the coming invasion by tossing the first martini back. "Well, it's been a while! Marilyn's out back with the canapés, and you remember our daughter Randi? Let's get those suitcases inside and get you a drink!"

Activity covered awkwardness as we opened the car-top carrier, handing down little suitcases and sleeping bags, and brought them and our pillows to the house. Of necessity, we had all packed light, and we wouldn't set up the camper for just one night's stay.

"Hello, welcome! Just leave suitcases and all those sleeping bags —goodness, there are a lot of you!—here in the living room." Marilyn, in a summer shift and white sandals, her brunette locks hairsprayed solid, came in from the back patio, setting down her drink to hug Mom, then turning to greet us. "Oh, and here's Maryanne. Remember when Randi and Maryanne were born?" Mom and Marilyn had been close when the babies were born, but the girls, seventeen now, didn't know each other.

The Connellys' living room was all sharp angles and shag rug, with a metal-legged, glass-topped coffee table supporting a just-so fan of glossy magazines. A low-slung, white couch on flaring wood legs occupied one wall. An Eames recliner, black leather on a curved wood frame, sat on its chrome base next to the sliding glass patio door. Large ceramic ashtrays with rectangular teeth to hold cigarettes adorned end tables.

"Keep moving forward," I whispered, nudging Greg and Clare. They'd stopped on the threshold in front of me because Maryanne, Denise, and Marla had stopped in the foyer ahead of them, leaving the Lids and me still outside on the front step.

"Keep going!" I hissed.

Finally we all poured in, filling the living room entirely. Once in, I saw why our three oldest sisters had hung back. Randi Connelly, long and leggy, wore a metallic micromini slung low on her hips, with a gold-buckled wide belt. Fishnet black stockings peeked out above white patent leather boots that reached her knees. A snug, gold sleeveless turtleneck, armholes cut deep, clung to her curves. Randi wore eyeliner a quarter inch thick and eye shadow of an alarming shade of blue. She shook a cigarette out of a gold metal case, lit it, and began to smoke. In the house. In front of her parents. Who did nothing, except brandish their own cigarettes in one hand, and cocktails in the other.

Our parents didn't smoke and rarely drank, save for a companionable single beer shared on a summer's evening. If any of us kids ever tried smoking, it was a fleeting experience, down in the culvert by Welch Junior High School, under the brief influence of the wrong crowd. Now, in the Connellys' stiff living room, despite our manners, our eyes involuntarily widened and mouths gaped for a moment as lazy plumes of smoke wafted upward from Randi's cigarette.

"Well . . . cocktails and canapes!" Marilyn said brightly, motioning us toward the patio door. "We have pop, and I made up some Tang." Drinks and snacks before dinner! At home, it was unthinkable to snack before dinner—you were meant to show up at the table on time, with appetite fully intact—but this was one difference we could enthusiastically endorse, and we trooped outdoors. Over food and drink, conversation picked up steam.

"We went to see that new musical *Hair* the other day." Bob Connelly drained his second martini. "It's playing in Chicago now. Great stuff, I tell ya!" He reached for a tiny pig-in-a-blanket on a frilled toothpick. "Randi saw it with friends and said we had to go." He drew the sausage off the toothpick with his front teeth. "You heard of it?"

"It was groovy." Randi popped an olive into her lipsticked mouth. "Hippies, Vietnam, and civil rights!"

"We like the songs." Denise, seeking common ground, hummed a few bars of "Let the Sunshine In."

"I haven't heard of it." Dad didn't waste time keeping up with the latest counterculture fads.

Instantly, silently, lyrics bloomed in my head. *Gimme it down to there, hair! Shoulder-length or longer, hair! Here baby, there momma, everywhere daddy daddy.* The lyrics weren't bad in and of themselves. It was their connection to free love, pot, laziness, disrespect, and general mockery that upset most of the older generation.

Burgers on the grill followed, and as the evening waned, everyone relaxed. Some of us went into the living room to shift the coffee table out of the way and roll out sleeping bags side-by-side across the shag carpet.

"Maryanne," Randi said as she approached, her freshly outlined lips pursed, one hand on hip, the other holding her after-dinner cigarette aloft, "I'm going out with friends tonight, to a sort of nightclub downtown. Mom said I should ask you to come along."

Maryanne demurred. "Oh! Thanks, but I don't have anything to wear, so I'll stay here with the group."

"You sure?" We could see Randi's look of relief even under all the eye makeup.

"Absolutely! But thanks for asking."

So it was that the Connellys' living room floor held nine full sleeping bags laid out like cords of wood in a plank road. Maryanne, lying in her bag on the carpet but still reading her library book by flashlight, felt a nudge from Denise in the bag next to her. Denise scooched her sleeping bag closer.

"You know," Denise whispered, "I can see Randi has a lot more freedom to do as she likes, but I feel sorry for her."

"I know what you mean." Maryanne lowered her book. "She makes me glad we're in our family, not hers."

"That poor girl is desperate." Marla, next to Denise, kept her voice low as she propped up on her elbow. "Desperate to be cool."

Nudging Maryanne again, Denise laughed as she lifted a few lines from "Downtown": "Just listen to the rhythm of a gentle bossa nova," she teased, singing softly, and then changed the words slightly. "You *could've* danced with *'em* too, before the night is over—Downtown, *still* waiting for you tonight—Downtown, you're gonna be all right now."

1970

on the farm

On the road the next day, we left the sins of the big city behind and headed east, our old Pontiac eating up miles on the Indiana Toll Road and Ohio Turnpike.

"Almost there, Old Betsy." Dad patted the dashboard as we turned off the interstate onto a rural road. The 1966 Pontiac station wagon had replaced our 1958 Chevy wagon a couple of years before. Dad called them both Old Betsy, the name deriving from his formative years guiding workhorses over farm fields. Proximity to the Ohio farm where he grew up, where his father and brother's family still lived, dredged up the term of endearment.

The Pontiac, trailing its pop-up camper, moseyed along between walls of green corn. June heat made wiggly waves in the air above the blacktop. Inside the car, the switch from seventy-five-miles-per-hour interstate to twenty-miles-per-hour rural road shook off our stupor brought on by the long drive. We shifted and wriggled, lifted our heads from library books, and stretched. As the miles to the farm melted away, anxiety and excitement bubbled inside us.

Dad's smile broadened, eyes crinkling with pleasure: he knew every turn, every landmark along the road in the last miles to the farm. "Seven years of waiting, but almost there!"

Dad never meant for that much time to pass between visits, but his teaching schedule, plus work on the houses, had kept us home summer after summer. We no longer knew our three cousins. Now we would spend three days with them. Would they like us? Would we fit in? Would we overwhelm them with our sheer number?

"I never know what to say to Grandpa," Clare worried, leaning forward from the middle seat toward Dad. She twirled a pigtail, the hair tight around her finger. "Grandpa doesn't talk, and when he does, he's hard to understand."

"Grandpa's kinda scary," I said, not too loud. We remembered our taciturn Grandpa Stritzel loved us, but just didn't show it. That's what Dad said, anyway. The closer I got to the farm, the more I hoped it was true. I nibbled my lower lip.

"Remember, he didn't learn English until his early twenties," Dad said. "That's when he emigrated here and met Grandma, God rest her soul, walking along the railroad tracks to church."

It was odd to think of our Grandma Regina as a young woman. We remembered her as a short, plump whirlwind of hugs, smiling and talking, nudging up wire-rim glasses on her nose before hugging us more. Being hugged by Grandma Regina was like being engulfed by a housedress, but deep down, we'd liked it.

"Hail Mary, full of grace." His hands on the wheel, Dad began a prayer for the soul of his mother. We joined in, as always, finishing in unison. Dad fell silent, nearly on autopilot on these familiar roads.

Almost there, almost there. In the hot car, restlessness and anxiety inched up. I fidgeted at my fingernails. Marla rotated her shoulders against the vinyl seat. Greg drummed his feet on Old Betsy's floorboards.

Dad saw his family's neat, white-painted farmhouse just ahead. "My folks were proud to be American," he said, "and adamant that my brother and I assimilate. We grew up speaking English."

With Dad's final turn into the driveway, Old Betsy listed sideways and swung low, as if exhausted from the two days' journey from central Iowa. Silent now inside the car, we surveyed the scene. We saw the house, a large and handsome duplex with a front porch graced by square white columns; it housed Grandpa Stritzel on one side and Uncle Thomas, Aunt Betty, and their three children on the other. Dad had told us hard work and good management over decades had grown the farm from humbler early days to its current prosperity. We knew Grandpa had built the big, beautiful house and crafted the fine detail on its columns. It rested on a gentle rise of green lawn, shaded by fruit trees and dotted with peony and iris. A tidy concrete walk led from the farmhouse side door, past a sturdy arbor swagged with Concord grapes, over a lane, and past neat vegetable and flower beds before arriving at a huge barn with an attached milking parlor. On this June afternoon in 1970, the Ohio dairy farmstead of our grandfather, aunt, uncle, and cousins was a pastoral idyll of quiet order against a backdrop of puffy clouds sailing across blue sky.

Dad braked to a gentle stop in the driveway, and Old Betsy's doors burst open. "We're here, we're here!" our chorus erupted as the vehicle began to spew children from its baking interior—but only a couple of children at first.

"Keep moving! We want out!" The Lids jostled from the far back seat, trying to climb over Denise and Marla, who had paused in their middle seat to rummage for hairbrushes to run through shoulder-length hair.

"Hold your horses! We'll all get out." Marla, one of the few of us who never needed braces, smiled into the mirror of her compact.

"Give us a minute." Denise adjusted her Indian-embroidered headband over her forehead while brushing her straight, middle-parted hair.

"It's hot! We want out now!" The Lids vaulted over the middle seat and launched themselves toward open car doors. They exploded out of the car, followed by the rest of us in a tangle of arms and legs. Spent of her load, Old Betsy seemed to exhale in relief, levitating three inches as her shocks recovered.

As we untangled ourselves on the driveway and jumped up, we looked up to see our reserved, rural relatives gathering to greet us. Denise smoothed her fringed leather vest. Marla tugged at her short-short denim cutoffs. Greg pushed his mop of hair from his eyes. I yanked up white knee socks and adjusted my seersucker halter-top, suddenly conscious that it showed a lot of bare shoulder.

Looking at our relatives was like looking back in time. The cultural storms of the sixties, roaring across the country, had skipped this pastoral pocket as completely as a stone skips water, leaving the surface unruffled.

Cousins Barbara and Susan were teens. Barbara came up the neatly edged concrete path from the kitchen garden near the side door, a trowel dangling from her gloved hand, her face wreathed in smiles. She wore a housedress à la 1955: sprigged in a tiny floral print, belted at the waist, buttoned to the neck, and dropping below the knee. An apron covered her front. Her sturdy bare calves rose from folded-down white ankle socks and tie-up, sensible shoes. Long, light brown hair was parted in the middle, gathered in an elastic at the nape of her neck, twisted up, parted again, and clamped to her head with two barrettes.

Susan was a step younger than Barbara and a step behind her on the path. Barbara had come from the kitchen garden, but Susan came from the barn. Susan wore farm dungarees and a short-sleeved, button-up work shirt; her brown hair was pulled back into an out-of-my-way ponytail. She wore little rectangular tortoiseshell glasses like Barbara. Like several of us, I realized. Myopia was one thing we had in common with our country cousins. Susan stepped off the path, scraping cow manure off her boots against the grass, a smile lighting her face.

Our youngest cousin, Thomas Owen, the same age as our Lids, came up from the barn behind Susan. Thomas Owen wore a button-down chambray work shirt, farm dungarees, and rubber boots. He sported a genuine farmer tan from working in the field. His forearms and hands were dark from the sun. His face was like an Easter egg that had been halfway dipped in dye; the lower half was deeply tanned, the upper half white, where it had been protected by his cap. His uncovered hair showed a banded circle, a permanent dent pressed in where his hat usually resided. Like his older sisters, he was beaming at us. Thomas Owen was a smaller carbon copy of his dad, our Uncle Thomas.

Uncle Thomas's receding hair was combed straight back, in a style from World War II, with an identical circular dent in it from his hatband. Like his son's, his face was two different colors, the southern hemisphere deeply tanned, the northern startlingly white. When he smiled, he was transformed with happiness, his whole face crinkling upward with joy. He hugged our dad with emotion. Uncle Thomas's speech was hard to make out—we remembered Dad's telling us Uncle Thomas had hearing loss—but after a minute or two, we caught the cadence of his speech. His joy at our arrival was so transparent and genuine that our anxiety began to ebb. Uncle Thomas wore roomy work jeans gathered in by a belt, paper bag–like, at his waist and a chambray work shirt faded from long wear.

Aunt Betty, brisk and belted in a practical housedress, sensibly shod in brogans like Barbara, did the talking. "Here you are, oh you know, I don't know!" (This pattern peppered her speech.) "Welcome to the farm! How was the trip?" The petite brown figure that was Aunt Betty bustled through a sea of children and luggage, her arms and legs protruding from the stocky middle of her housedress. Her gray hair, pulled back in a bun, framed a heart-shaped face, the creases showing joy. Aunt Betty's smiling, welcoming face was liberally sprinkled with moles, adorning nose and cheeks. With effort, none of us stared.

"Oh you know, I don't know, a busy morning making pies and now you're here," Aunt Betty said, wading in among us, her welcome percolating through her reserve. "Some of you girls can settle in with Barbara and Susan, you boys with Thomas Owen, and oh! you all have sleeping bags, that's handy, and of course all the kids can have a turn in your camper." Her chatter was like a warm river washing away the last of our awkwardness.

"Marcie, good to see you," Aunt Betty greeted Mom. We had never heard anyone call our mom any name other than Marcella. Startled, we looked at Mom. Standing on the driveway in her sleeveless piqué Jackie Kennedy A-line shift with daisy trim, Mom looked suddenly modern, stylish, and statuesque.

"You have an extra apron for me?" Mom returned Aunt Betty's hug. "I'll change into work clothes right away. It's good to be on a farm again."

"Oh you know, I don't know," continued Aunt Betty, "we can get midday dinner on now, plenty of green beans and pork chops . . ." Her words drifted over us like a welcoming blanket.

Grandpa Andrew Stritzel stood to the side, small, stooped, silent. Dad, then Mom, moved forward to hug him. To us kids, Grandpa looked as if he were from another world, and in a way he was. We could see no trace of the strong young immigrant who had worked long days building mansions in Shaker Heights. Now in old age, Grandpa was stooped to five feet four inches tall, but his news-boy cap shaded still-piercing hazel eyes. Frugal to the bone, he wore trousers that were good quality but shiny from years of wear. His ancient vest showed the fine work of some long-ago devoted seam-stress, the hand-done, bound buttonholes still sound in fabric that was just beginning to show threads. The buttons themselves, stamped of shell, were smooth from decades of use.

I tipped my head down to look up under Grandpa's cap brim at his creased face. Suddenly, I remembered our dad's only German phrase, the one that translated "Not today, but tomorrow, say all the lazy people." Looking at Grandpa, I knew where Dad got it.

Grandpa surveyed the scene. It was as if Old Betsy, tight-packed throughout the journey, had burst from pressure, unleashing a torrent of children, pillows, and stuff onto his driveway, a torrent that was about to swirl into his house, across his yard, and through his farm. Dad and Uncle Thomas lifted suitcases and sleeping bags from Old Betsy's popped-open carrier atop the car. Sharp-eyed, Grandpa counted all nine children.

"Ach, you are all here." Grandpa's voice was low and raspy. We leaned forward, trying to make out his accent.

"Yah, four boys, five girls," Grandpa said. The last word sound-ed like "gulls." His voice was gnarled, as if it emanated from the dark interior of a cobbler's shop in an Austrian village sixty years ago.

What did he think of us? We didn't know. Grandpa turned, opened the aluminum screen door on his side of the duplex, and shuffled toward his recliner.

I pulled at my halter top, trying to make it cover more skin.

❧

From afar, the hens looked placid and innocent, clucking softly and pecking at insects around their yard. Marla skipped across the chicken yard, pirouetting as she reached the henhouse, opening the door with a flourish. She and I stepped over the worn threshold of the wood frame henhouse, and the bare wood screen door banged shut behind. The change from brilliant June morning to dusky interior left us blinking. A few small windows, up high, let in shafts of sunlight, which formed themselves into sharp-edged rectangular holograms in the gloom. As our eyes adjusted, we saw along the walls long shelves, each divided into a series of open-front boxes. Each box held a nest of stiff yellow straw. Each nest held a beady-eyed hen. Each hen guarded a freshly laid egg. Those eggs were our mission. Aunt Betty had sent us to gather them, reckoning this an easy job even city kids could do.

Marla swung her empty aluminum pail. "You start with the lower line of nests. I'll take the upper," she said. We had no idea how one might extract an egg from beneath a broody hen. The one nearest me cocked its tiny head, eyeing me balefully. "OK!" Marla exhaled. "Just reach toward the hen. Come in from the side." Up close, the hens looked fiercer. Marla's tan arm slid slowly, gently, under the first hen. Her face crunched as she held her breath, her eyes closing as her fingers spread out beneath the hen. Feeling the smooth curve of an egg, she opened her eyes, and a smile bloomed across her face. "Nothing to it!" She did a little skip, placing the egg in her aluminum pail and moving to the next hen.

I approached a nest. The hen cocked her head to survey me with beady eye above sharp beak. Piercing talons on splayed feet were tucked out of sight under her fluffy body. The henhouse was silent, except for our breathing and the occasional flutter of feathers as a hen resituated herself. Dust motes swirled thick in shafts of sunlight. Ever so slowly, I reached toward the hen, closer, closer . . .

The tiny oval eye glittered evilly. The beak shot forward and pecked, hard, leaving a divot on my wrist that instantly filled with blood.

"Beast!" I dropped my bucket and rubbed my wrist.

Marla didn't have to tell me to try again. We'd been sent to gather eggs, and gather them we would. Marla, flitting from nest to nest, already had four eggs in her pail. I clenched my teeth and reached toward the hen, this time without hesitation. Get it fast; don't wait for her to peck. Under the feathers, my hand closed on a smooth egg.

"Got it!" I crowed. The warm white egg fit exactly into my cupped palm. Marveling at its warm perfection, I deposited it gently into my bucket and moved to the next nest.

Soon the bottoms of both pails were lined with two layers of eggs, and their bails hung weighty in our palms. The door banged shut as we exited the dusty henhouse, breathing deeply in the fresh air. With her free hand, Marla scooped up a bit of fresh straw that had spilled over the threshold. She tossed it skyward and spun in a circle, bucket in hand, as the shiny yellow bits, sparkling in the sun, sifted down around us. "Aunt Betty will be really happy with us!"

We left the chicken yard and crossed the lane separating outbuildings from farmhouse, nearly running now, heading up the long concrete path across green lawn. Swinging her pail, Marla skipped joyfully.

Smack! Crack! One heel connected with the bottom of her swinging pail, and neat layers of fresh eggs transformed into a mess of cracked shells and oozing yolks.

"Oh no!" Marla's exuberance evaporated, her whole being deflating. "Oh no!"

"They're not all broken." I yanked my shirttail out and wiped off some of the eggs. "Most are still whole. It's only a few."

Walking slowly now, we pulled open the aluminum side door on Aunt Betty and Uncle Thomas's side of the duplex, mounted the two stairs inside, and turned to enter the farm kitchen. A mid-century red Formica-topped table, surrounded by red-plastic-upholstered metal chairs supported by tubular rear legs like flying buttresses, held center stage on clean-scrubbed linoleum. A breeze fluttered yellow and blue curtains over screened windows. A shiny pail of drinking water from the well, ladle hung over its side, sat on the counter. We'd learned soon after arriving at the farm not to drink tap water from the faucets; it reeked of sulfur and stained sinks and tubs with dark streaks. If you wanted a drink, you dipped the ladle into this pail of sweet well water and filled a little aluminum cup. Next to the big stainless steel pail of drinking water, a radio crackled with the farm report. Aunt Betty was scrubbing potatoes at the sink, her back to us.

"Here you are with my eggs." Aunt Betty turned and saw the mess in Marla's pail. "Oh my! How did this happen? A girl your age should be more careful! Don't you know eggs can break?" she clucked in disbelief. "Little children much smaller than you can gather eggs, for goodness' sake!" Aunt Betty was genuinely distressed. "What can I do with this now?" She took the pails from us, her mind racing over how to salvage the broken eggs. We hung our heads in shame and said nothing.

In this household, it wasn't just a few broken eggs. It was waste.

twenty

1970

wait till the cows come home

"Oooohh, they're way bigger when you get up close. What if it steps on me?" Clare shrank from the broad side of a huge ruminant. She and I were helping Cousin Susan guide the gently mooing herd of forty Holsteins out of their stalls after milking the next morning. We were eager to help but were mostly in Susan's way.

"Keep your toes out from under their hooves." Susan deftly guided dozens of cows into the spacious concrete barnyard. The surface was kept scraped free of manure, and last night's rain had washed it clean. The herd massed briefly in the square yard. In a few minutes, the cows would be released to amble down a long fenced lane to a distant pasture to graze for the day. Susan patted the rough hide of one gigantic black-and-white beast. "Here, Hazel is so gentle, you can ride her! Who wants up?"

"I do!" Clare was first. Susan cupped her hands to provide a ledge, and Clare stepped nimbly in and up, swinging her leg over to land, hard, on Hazel's bony back.

"Keep free of the tail," Susan admonished as I circled Hazel's rear, viewing the cow's protruding hipbones, wondering if they could be used as handles. "Hazel doesn't mean to, but it hurts if that tail hits you when she swishes it." Susan boosted me up behind Clare.

Seeming barely burdened, the giant Holstein, swaying slightly, moved with the rest of the herd out of the barnyard down the center of the fenced grassy lane. We laughed in delight from our high, rocking perch atop Hazel as she and the herd progressed down the lane, cousin Susan growing smaller behind us.

"How do we hold on? What can we hold on to?" we yelled. "Where are the brakes?" Lacking handholds on the beast, we leaned down and clung to each other, stretched out like a human caterpillar. Atop the bony spine, we pitched and yawed in slow motion as Hazel and her many bovine sisters plodded along.

"There's nothing *to* hold on to! You'll be fine!" the tiny figure of Susan yelled after us, her voice fading.

"Whoa whoa whoa, girl!" cried Clare, up front. She had slipped down Hazel's neck as the cow stopped short and lowered her massive head to reach grass under wires and posts at the edge of the lane. I leaned forward and snatched Clare's shirt, yanking her back before she slid off the cow's head. Hazel raised her neck and slowly swung her enormous head backward toward us, long strands of grass disappearing between grinding jaws, surveying with a detached air the noisy humans arrayed along her back. Her large, brown eye blinked slowly, long fringed lashes sweeping down and up.

From our perch five feet high atop a cow, the world looked different: the sky bluer, the clouds whiter, the barn smaller. In fact, the barn, along with cousin Susan, was looking quite a bit smaller as the herd progressed down the lane. The question of how to steer a cow began to percolate through our brains. Hazel and her sisters rounded a turn in the lane and glimpsed the fresh green destination of their pasture, quickening their pace. We began to bounce and clutched wildly at the cow's neck and sides.

"Uh-oh," I said. From the rear, I was first to notice Hazel's raised tail. "Here it comes!"

Hazel stopped short. Up top, we knocked into each other like a couple of pool balls on a cowhide table. Hazel braced her legs, and let fall a series of warm plops. Steaming sections of what looked like a giant Tootsie Roll with bits of alfalfa in it extruded from her rear, dropping in slow progression.

"Oh!" Clare held her nose. "Abandon ship!"

"Get down, get down! I want off!" I yelled, as eager to dismount our ride as I had been a few minutes earlier to get on her. "Pee-yew!" Hazel had stopped next to the fence, so Clare and I used the rails to leg it down to the wet lane, formed into tufts of grass and pools of mud from the daily traffic of passing hooves. We managed to clamber down just before Hazel's tail shifted again and she loosed a high-pressure, steaming yellow stream.

"Stand back!" Clare hollered, and we leapt out of the way of the herd. We tried to land on higher tufts of grass left between deep hoofprints and cow pies, but the more pressing need was to dodge cows, who were picking up their pace, streaming around us, their eyes not on us pesky humans but on the soft green pasture ahead of them. "Get to the fence!" We jumped from tuft to tuft and then clung to fence rails as the last of the herd jostled by.

It was a long walk back to the farmhouse.

More fun was watching the cows return at the end of the day. Every day at about five in the evening, the entire herd somehow knew it was time to quit munching grass and mosey on back down the fenced lane to gather in the concrete barnyard. We kids gathered too, hanging on the fence watching cows plunge noses into three big watering troughs, or jumping down to help Uncle Thomas, Susan, and Thomas Owen.

"So this is why people say, 'Wait till the cows come home.'" Greg perched on the fence, toes hooked behind a rail. "They actually do come home."

The barn was built on a slight slope. At the rear where we stood, it was two stories, but around front the building was one story. The front of the barn featured a broad banked earth driveway that rose to meet two massive wood front doors that rolled open to the sides. Heavy wagons, stacked with neat rectangular bales of hay, could be driven in on this sturdy floor for unloading, and the bales stored there for winter feed. But here down below, at the back where the cows were kept, we—and the herd—could walk in at ground level. Dad had told us this was called a bank barn.

"Hiya, Dorothy, keep going!" Susan guided a cow to follow her sisters inside. Susan was much more at home in the barn than she was in the house.

"Come on, Rosie," young Thomas Owen cajoled another. "Rosie's a good milker like her mother, Hazel. Hazel's producing eight gallons of milk on her best days."

"Not like the old days, remember?" Uncle Thomas patted another bovine flank before turning to Dad. "With better nutrition and management, we produce much more milk now with fewer cows. Now, Nancy here, she had a bout of mastitis, but we cleared that up, and Bessie"—Uncle Thomas stroked the nose of another beast on its way inside the barn—"is a daughter of Bonnie, who was a daughter of Penny."

"Penny," reflected young Thomas Owen, "best milker we ever had for those days, sired by the bull Royal at Anderson's place down the road." The conversation swirled deeper into the foibles and habits of each bovine. Our cousins, uncle, and dad talked about lineage, milk production, and feed ratios as easily as sportswriters talk batting averages.

The rest of us stood aside. "How can they tell one from another?" Marla shook her head.

"Who knew a person could even know so much about cows?" Clare raised her eyebrows. "They know every detail about every cow. And there are forty cows!"

"You've seen one cow, you've seen 'em all," Denise murmured.

Mooing, the herd progressed into the foundation level of the barn. The floor was concrete, the walls of this first story white-painted concrete block. A heavy wood-beamed ceiling, not quite seven feet high, felt close overhead; its six-inch-thick, whitewashed planks formed the floor of the main barn above, which stored neat-stacked bales of hay. The rectangular space of the ground level was divided into three long aisles. The center aisle, six feet wide and seventy-five feet long, was lined on both sides with metal stalls, twenty on each side. The herd entered through the rear door and divided itself into two lines, each line plodding along one of two outer aisles like a bovine zipper smoothly unzipping itself. We city cousins massed in the center aisle, away from the marching cows.

"How do they know exactly where to go?" I couldn't believe the orderly parade.

"How do the cows tell?" Paul's eyes were wide.

"Don't they ever get mixed up?" Marla was amazed.

Each cow stepped smartly along on an outer aisle. Each recognized its own stall, turned a neat right angle to step in, and put its head through its open metal stanchion. Not one of the forty cows chose the wrong stall. We watched, agog at the cows' orderliness. We might not have been more surprised had one spoken. I thought of the city we'd just come from, where we'd watched masses of humans flowing in orderly progression on the sidewalks and streets and highways of Chicago at rush hour, each human heading for his front door. These cows sorting themselves out, each moving sure-footed toward its particular stanchion, weren't too different from Chicagoans streaming home after work.

Susan and young Thomas Owen worked along the center aisle, clanging shut the metal stanchions around the cows' necks in preparation for milking. The stanchions permitted movement but prevented the cow from backing out. Attached to each stanchion was a metal bowl with a grid on the bottom. When a cow pressed its nose against the grid, it triggered a flow of water into its bowl. Neat! Standing in the center aisle, Susan pitchforked alfalfa into long concrete troughs in front of each line of stanchions. Young Thomas Owen added a measured scoop of high-protein feed.

Our cousins and uncle fell to their work, the routine honed over the years. They washed each cow's udder with antiseptic solution, rinsed it, and attached an automatic milking machine. *Whoosh, whoosh, whoosh, whoosh!*—with a pneumatic hiss, Susan quickly attached four tubes of one stainless steel milking machine onto four teats of one cow, each tube fitting itself snugly around the teat. *Whoosh,* Thomas Owen fit another, Dad and Uncle Thomas fitted a third and fourth. When one cow was done milking, Dad or Uncle Thomas would carry the full, heavy milk machine, its tubes dangling down, through a door into the attached fifteen-by-fifteen-foot concrete milk parlor. This whitewashed space, separate from the barn, shone as clean as an operating theater. In the center of its spotless floor, a stainless steel milk tank glittered. Uncle Thomas opened the top hatch of the enormous tank and hefted each milking machine over it, pouring in a thick, creamy river of fresh milk.

Over the course of an hour and a half, we peeked into the milking parlor and wandered around the barn, which was humming with industry. We listened to the peaceful breathing of the great beasts, and time seemed to slow as it washed over us. The cows relaxed as they let down their milk. Chewing their feed, they grew content, and their tranquil mood spread. We helped our cousins occasionally, pushing the wheelbarrow of feed as Thomas Owen scooped, but mostly we stayed out of the way. We strolled the center aisle of the barn on the concrete path lined by bovine faces, gently rubbing bovine foreheads with our knuckles and enjoying the rhythmic chugging of the milk machines, the restful sighing of the animals, the quiet synchronicity of our relatives' movements.

The sun was slanting lower through the barn's small, four-paned windows, and the milking nearly finished, when a slim black cat twirled itself around Susan's boots, and we gathered around. "This is Edie." Susan bent to stroke the purring kitty. "She's a good mouser, so she gets to stay." The cat sat alert, head up, bright eyes locked on Susan. "Watch this," Susan said as she grasped a cow's teat and expertly aimed a thin stream of milk at the cat, which caught the milk neatly in her mouth. We laughed as Edie flicked her tongue to clean her lips.

Uncle Thomas came out of the milking parlor holding a three-legged stool and a stainless steel pail. "We saved Cora, the last cow, for you all to try milking by hand." Uncle Thomas grinned, happy to share the fun of farm life with us. His craggy face radiated warmth and joy. We no longer had any trouble understanding him.

"We get to try it?"

"Fun!"

"Is it hard?" We gathered around Cora in her stall.

I put my hand up against the animal's tough hide and felt her sturdy bones beneath. It felt like patting a rug thrown over a wood frame. But this rug was alive. Cora swung her head back, her huge liquid eyes surveying the crowd around her hindquarters, and mooed, reminding these humans to milk her *now*.

Dad situated the stool and pail. "We used to milk the whole herd by hand like this, morning and night, but we had fewer cows then." He looked up. "Cheryl, you're close by. You can go first."

I sat and hitched the stool closer, feigning confidence. Looking at the broad side of the cow was like looking up at a black-and-white movie screen. The beast was so very big. Her udder hung heavy and low, the size of a thirty-gallon plastic bag full of liquid. The pink, fleshy udder showed a tracery of thick veins bulging on its surface. Four teats, resembling four-inch-long, boiled, pale pink sausages, hung down.

"Moo—oo—oo!" Cora shifted her 1,500 pounds hoof to hoof. The movie screen swayed closer to my face. "Moo—oo—oo!" Cora was losing patience.

My slim arm reached tentatively toward the fleshy bag. My small hand grabbed a teat. I squeezed. Nothing happened.

"Do it like this." Susan leaned in, grasped a teat, and closed her fingers, not all at once, but one after the other, top to bottom, moving the milk down the teat, and a stream of milk rang against the bottom of the pail.

"Thanks! OK, got it," I said, but before I could try again, Cora swished her tail. It was just a casual flick toward a fly on her flank, but the rope of jointed bone snapped against my face like a knobby whip. "Oh!" I blinked back tears, breathing deep, steadying myself on the stool, willing myself not to cry.

"I'll hold that tail." Young Thomas Owen pinned Cora's tail against her back leg, but no one paid attention to my little injury aside from that, so I didn't either. Instead I fanned the fingers of my right hand down the teat, top to bottom and shot milk into the pail! Top to bottom, top to bottom. You couldn't just squeeze. You had to *shift* the milk down the teat. I grasped another teat with my left hand and closed my fist on one, then the other.

"Got it! This is fun!" I hit a steady rhythm, pinging the milk from each teat in turn into the pail.

We each got a chance to try, with Dad finishing to make sure Cora was fully milked, before heading up the path toward the farmhouse and supper.

Cows need milking twice daily, and they don't take any days off. The next morning, Sunday, our uncle and cousins as usual milked all forty cows before breakfast. After we'd all eaten a quick morning meal and cleaned up, we Ames Stritzels gathered in the driveway and waited for our aunt, uncle, and cousins so our two families could depart for Mass together. The aluminum screen door wheezed open, and we turned to see Uncle Thomas emerge first from the house.

We barely recognized our uncle out of his daily uniform of work jeans and chambray shirt. His generously cut beige suit, pressed and perfect, hung on his work-hardened slim frame with plenty of extra fabric in the pleated pants and big-shouldered jacket. His combed-back hair and felt fedora hat lent him the air of a dapper 1940s movie actor. Only his two-tone face and smiling eyes looked familiar. His polished shoes shone, his tie clip gleamed, and car keys rattled in his hand.

Young Thomas Owen, still a clone of his father, followed in suit and tie, also with combed-back hair. Aunt Betty, Barbara, and Susan proceeded in turn through the screen door wearing more formal versions of those 1952-style dresses, their hems dropping even lower for Sunday. Barbara, who kept the flower gardens around the house blooming, held a corsage of iris she'd snipped a few minutes earlier.

"If I have them, I wear them," she said brightly, pinning the flower to the lapel of her buttoned-up dress. The corsage was pretty; I could see Barbara knew what she was doing when it came to flowers.

I thought of news footage I'd seen a couple of months earlier.

With her handbag and headscarf, my teenage cousin reminded me of Queen Elizabeth viewing the troops. I pulled at my hem, trying to make my skirt longer. Denise glanced down at her own long-sleeved, collarless shirt with its print of peace signs and frowned. Clare skipped back into the house to get her sweater, though the morning was warm. Marla, confident as always that whatever she was wearing or doing was right, chattered with Susan.

Uncle Thomas strode toward the neat, white-painted garage and lifted the heavy one-piece wood door, illuminating a dim interior filled to the edges by the massive Mercury parked within. We hadn't thought we'd ride a tractor into town, but the powerful, luxurious sedan surprised us. He backed it, its squared-off fenders like angular metal haunches, out of the small garage onto the driveway, and we jumped out of the way.

As we distributed ourselves between the Merc and Old Betsy for the ride to church, we realized that young Thomas Owen was taking the front passenger seat of the sedan. Aunt Betty and Uncle Thomas acted as if this were normal. Wearing her 1940s hat adorned with a wisp of veil, Aunt Betty slid into the back seat with her demurely dressed daughters and the miniskirted Marla. The rest of us gaped at Thomas Owen. We'd never seen a child usurp a parent from the front seat. Perhaps it was a holdover from the chivalry of horse-and-carriage days, when women took the protected back seat, but we couldn't know that. To us, it seemed that along with 1970s fashion, women's lib had skipped this farm.

More culture shock awaited at Sunday's noon dinner. Uncle Thomas, during a slow spell the previous winter, had painted the dining room Pepto-Bismol pink. The room held a heavy, dark wood dining table, covered by a thick table protector and lace tablecloth, and straight-back dark wood chairs set on a scratchy rug, its floral pattern reminiscent of the 1930s. A dark wood china cabinet, over-full with china, occupied nearly one full wall.

We sorted ourselves out between the dining room and the kitchen, looking for places to sit. The tables in both rooms were extended with leaves.

"Oh you know, I don't know, these potatoes can go on the table. Put on bread and butter. Here are the beans." Aunt Betty bustled at the stove with Mom, both of them filling serving dishes and hand-ing them to us to put on the table. As we placed bowls and platters on the table, we looked in silent dismay at the thick, foaming full-fat milk filling every glass.

Dairy farmers to the core, our Ohio relatives served only whole milk, unpasteurized, fresh from the previous evening's milking. Of course the raw milk had been stored in the refrigerator, but any chill it had acquired there had long since dissipated, since glasses were poured fifteen minutes before dinner.

Unwilling to say anything, even sotto voce to each other, we took a collective deep breath and found our seats. We Ames Stritzels were all confirmed skim drinkers, and we drank it ice-cold. Our parents, though they'd regularly consumed whole milk growing up on farms, had switched to skim after they left home. In the 1970s, skim milk was considered less desirable, as well as cheaper than two-percent or whole milk. We had never known any other kind.

At our relatives' table now, appalled, inwardly gagging but outwardly smiling, we tried to choke down the viscous stuff as conversation swirled around us. We felt as though we were eating butter. Greg had a little pucker around his mouth. Clare looked determined as she gamely sipped. Marla followed every swallow of milk with a mouthful of white bread. Denise drank half of her glass all at once, aiming to get it over with. She looked at the glass, ruminating: for once, seeing the glass half empty was the optimistic view.

"More milk, Denise?" Cousin Barbara offered the pitcher.

"No, thank you," Denise clapped a hand over her glass and tried not to watch Uncle Thomas. His portion of milk had been heated on the stove in a saucepan and served steaming in a cup. He broke the solid skin that formed on top of the milk, moved it with knife and fork to his plate, and consumed it.

We were with family and only two states from home, but were as out of our element as if we'd landed in a far-off country where natives served fried bugs. We knew our relatives were generously sharing with us, and we knew we should be gracious and grateful. But the milk before us was so thick, so warm, so full of fat. I glanced at the Pepto-Bismol pink dining room walls, wondering if I'd need a spoonful of that later. We looked at Mom, once again wearing her Jackie Kennedy dress with daisy trim, chatting as she ate her meal and drank her milk. For a second, amid flowing conversation, we caught her eye. We saw the slightest of puckers around her mouth. But she was drinking her milk with a smile, and the knife-sharp look she shot in our direction confirmed to us that we would be well advised to do the same.

The Lids looked to us older siblings. Clare looked at me. Maryanne looked at Denise. Marla looked at Greg. An invisible ribbon of silent communication unfurled among us, spooling one to another. At home, we'd been taught to eat what was in front of us and be glad it was there. At home, we were members of the Clean Plate Club. Now we were about to become members of the Empty Glass Club. Smiling, grateful members. Even if that glass was full of raw whole milk.

❧

After three days, the visit came to an end. Once again our old Pontiac station wagon stood in the driveway with every door ajar, the luggage carrier on top open like a clamshell, our pop-up camper folded and hitched on behind. The sun shone, and a hint of breeze pushed puffs of cumulus cloud across a blue sky. Chatter swirled as we and our Ohio cousins shuttled between house and car, a human river carrying suitcases and sleeping bags.

"Let's write letters." Marla tossed her pillow into the center seat of the station wagon and turned back to Susan, who held a stack of our library books.

"I'll write news about the cows." Susan handed the books to Marla, who stowed them on the car floor where Greg's feet would rest. "Oh, and the hens!" Susan grinned as Marla knelt on the middle seat, trying to wedge the books so they wouldn't slide. "I'll definitely write you about the egg count," Susan said as she leaned into the car, "and how many get scrambled on the way from hen-house to kitchen."

We didn't notice anymore that Barbara, Susan, and Thomas Owen dressed differently than we did. When we looked at them, we no longer saw differences; we just saw our cousins, looking as sad as we were that the visit was ending. Aunt Betty came out the kitchen door, wiping her hands on her apron, her tanned face once more crinkled into smiles. Uncle Thomas, standing at the edge of the driveway, took off his cap and wiped tears from his eyes. Grandpa, shoulders bent, his vest buttoned and worn trousers neat, stood next to him. We could see in his face under the brim of his newsboy cap that Grandpa was sad to see us go.

We hugged all around, a process that took several minutes. Who knew how long it would be before we could visit again?

We piled into our places in Old Betsy and closed the car doors gently; Dad couldn't abide slamming doors or mistreatment of any sort of equipment.

"Goodbye, goodbye, goodbye!" We scrambled over each other to stick arms out the open car windows and wave. We wiggled, turning in our seats to see our Ohio relatives standing behind us, shoulder to shoulder, as Old Betsy rolled out of the driveway.

The Pontiac turned up the asphalt road and headed east, leaving the farm behind. "They're as sad as we are," Maryanne marveled as she twisted around to speak to Denise. "I thought we'd overwhelm them, but they're genuinely sorry to see us go."

"Even Grandpa." Denise tipped her head and smiled a bit. "I got to sit and talk to him. He wasn't annoyed with us, even though he seemed so at first, when we descended on him en masse. He likes us just fine. I think he's gruff because he misses Grandma."

"I know," I said from the far back. I pushed my fist into the pocket of my cutoffs and extracted a twenty-dollar bill. I spoke quietly, so Mom and Dad, chatting in the front seat, couldn't hear. "Grandpa pressed this into my hand when I said goodbye."

"Me too, me too!" Each sibling likewise extracted a folded bill from a pocket.

"I thought I should say no, but Grandpa insisted." Paul waved his twenty.

"I felt kind of bad about taking it," Greg agreed, "but he wouldn't take it back. Wow, it's a lot. It's great!"

"Work is one way to show love," Denise mused, speaking low to us siblings. "Grandpa worked hard, so his children, and now we grandchildren, would have a better life. I think those twenties represent work—and love—in portable form."

We were quiet for a moment. Maybe Grandpa was reticent because he still spoke with an accent. Maybe he understood the value of not speaking unless you could improve upon the silence. (On that score, our garrulous crew could have learned from his example.) As we rolled away from the farm that day, we began to see that love isn't always obvious, effusive, and extroverted. Sometimes, it is bent, shuffles with age, and wears a newsboy cap.

twenty-one

1970

some joker

Used to the gently undulating farmland of the Midwest, we were entranced by the sheer height of the Appalachian Mountains. From inside the Pontiac, we ogled a ramshackle cabin tucked up flat against the steep flank of a green-draped mountainside. We exclaimed with delight when we spotted a thread of smoke rising from its tipsy tin pipe of a chimney and a white-bearded man in blue denim bib overalls rocking on the front porch. To us, such hillbilly scenes looked like Saturday morning cartoons. Discovering they actually existed was a revelation.

As we drove deeper into the Appalachians, our snaky long Pontiac hugging the edge of the road, mountains soared skyward next to us. We pushed our faces against car windows, craning necks upward, gasping at the heights. As the day warmed, we rolled down windows, pulling the clean scent of towering conifers deep into our lungs. These mountains were taller, so much taller, than anything we kids had ever seen. Switchbacking through the splendid Appalachians, we stopped by a mountain stream to picnic, bursting from the car, racing to dip toes and hands in cold rushing water.

Greg, ahead of us, leapt from boulder to boulder, graceful as a gazelle, the current a thundering torrent around him. More wonders lay ahead.

Late that afternoon we pulled into Virginia Beach, on the shore of the Atlantic, the zenith of our entire two-week vacation. Dad drove slowly down the bumpy, sandy lane leading to our campground, navigating potholes carefully. Not willing to chance breaking anything on the undercarriage, he slowed further, finally moving so slowly that it seemed Old Betsy was limping toward our waiting campsite and her evening's rest. Inside the Pontiac, having glimpsed the ocean from the road earlier, we were ricocheting around like corn popping in a hot tin can.

"How is it even possible to drive this slow?" Greg, like all of us, was antsy to get out.

"You'll be fine, Greggy, we're just finding our campsite." Mom was reading numbers on posts. Each site had plenty of room for a camper and tent, a fire ring with a heavy iron grill cantilevered up one side, and a broad, heavy, wood picnic table. Late afternoon sunshine streamed through stands of scrubby pines struggling to grow in sandy soil. Though we could see other families in campers and tents and smell a cooking fire here and there, the layout and trees afforded privacy.

"That's handy. We're not far from drinking water." Mom spied the communal faucet on its square of wet concrete, dark with algae, as Dad pulled into our site, positioning Old Betsy so our camper landed exactly right on the gravel pad. Dad always parked right the first time, even in a new place. He couldn't stand the thought of wasting gas. He turned off the ignition, and Old Betsy settled with a grateful sigh.

"We make camp first!" Dad rubbed his hands together happily. He really loved having all of us together. "Many hands make—"

But we were up and out of the car, running toward the ocean. We ran through stunted pines and knobby brush, over rolling dunes, and past tufts of spiky sea grass. Spread out, sprinting in an impromptu race, laughing, out of breath and gasping, we nine topped the final rise and saw The Ocean.

Lazy, blue, rolling breakers stretched the length of the eastern horizon, curving far to the north and farther to the south. From our vantage atop the last little dune, fully half the world—no, more than half—was water. We had never seen so much water. We younger Stritzels had never laid eyes on a body of water you couldn't see across. Majestic aqua waves rolled toward us, over and over, each topped with a curling line of white foam, crashing onto white sand.

"It's a different world!" Denise breathed. And it was.

"Nothing but white sand, everywhere!" Paul hooted. "Look, they have the same red wood slatted fences we see at home for snow, but here they're for *sand*."

"Nothing but sun and sand, right up to houses on stilts!" Mark saw a line of outlandish houses up the beach. With their long stick legs exposed, they looked as if they were hiking up their skirts to go wading, and indeed might stalk off their foundations and stride into the water at any moment.

Kicking off sandals and tennies, we jumped into the foam to wade, then turned and ran up the hard, wet, packed sand, just out of reach of rushing water. Here in a strange place far from home, it was once again just us, the nine of us, the Baseball Team. The three culture shocks from the previous week—deep inner city, mod and groovy suburban Chicago, rural Ohio—fell further from our consciousness with each wave that curled toward our feet. We were us again, just us, if a bit wiser now about the world outside our own. We whooped and grabbed hands to run back as the biggest wave curled before us.

Running up the beach, a wave nipping at my heels, I saw Mom and Dad come over the crest of the last little dune. I knew Mom had cajoled Dad into coming to see the ocean before setting up camp. Mom, a dedicated worker herself, sometimes intervened to convince Dad to let up on his workload. Once, in the early years of their marriage, a circus came to Des Moines, and Mom discovered Dad had never seen one. It wasn't something his immigrant parents would have indulged in. Astonished, she joked, "You poor, deprived child!" bought tickets, and took him to the show.

Now, silhouetted against the early evening light, they swung their clasped hands and strolled the dune, watching us leap ahead of waves foaming and flooding up the beach. We jumped and ran, over and over. But it was past dinnertime, and we'd been hungry when we drove into the campground.

"If we want dinner, we'd better go set up camp." Denise jumped ahead of a wave, and she and Maryanne headed toward the campground. "Mom has chili and hot dogs in the cooler."

"Let's go build the fire." Greg ran toward dry sand, the ragged hem of his cutoff denim shorts wet. The Lids, their cutoffs wet to the waist, straggled behind.

"This wave is perfect!" Marla looked over her shoulder. "One more wade in, then I'm coming." She was the last one out of the water and over the dune.

At our campsite, the Lids and Greg pitched their green canvas pup tent. We girls first handed down suitcases and the guitar from atop the car carrier, and then popped open the camper. Two wings on either side pulled out to form two double beds; Mom and Dad took one, with Maryanne and Denise sharing the other. The little dining table inside the camper would later be lowered to form another double bed; Marla, Clare, and I would rotate between that and a sleeping bag on the tiny slot of space left on the floor. The clever design of the camper, with double beds flying out both sides, and the table lowering to perfectly join its benches, captivated us. Of course, we couldn't sit down and eat around the pygmy-sized table—we wondered if any family could—but it was fun to put it up and down. Outdoors, we unrolled the ample awning from the camper's now-raised roof and dragged the heavy picnic table under it.

"Careful with that burning marshmallow!" Clare admonished Steve as he waved a toasting stick in an attempt to put out his flaming marshmallow. Supper was over, dusk had fallen, and we were making s'mores over glowing coals. Denise tuned her guitar, testing a few chords. Clare and I dried the last of the dishes. Maryanne and Marla, inspired by the gigantic disk of a moon rising over the horizon, began singing "Moon River, wider than a mile." Steve, his marshmallow still flaming fiercely, whipped the stick, trying to quell the miniature conflagration.

"Do not do that!" Clare flung down her towel and commandeered Steve's stick, which dangled its glob of burning sugar by a goopy thread. She held it away from her bare feet, blew it out, flipped the marshmallow off away from us, and dunked the stick in a bucket of water before threading on a fresh marshmallow and handing it back to Steve.

The year before, Clare had gone on a church weekend at the YMCA camp in central Iowa. A gangly, pimply boy a year older than she—Clare called him The Idiot, suspending her usual kind nature whenever she told the story—had flung a burning marshmallow off his stick, landing it on the inside of Clare's wrist, where it met tender flesh with a lively sizzle. The incident seared a scar into her wrist and a memory into her brain; Clare became a marshmallow vigilante, a position she holds to this day.

Now, she guided Steve's hand, showing him how to caramelize the sugar in the heat, not incinerate it in the flame, before sliding it neatly onto a square of Hershey's chocolate between graham crackers.

The next morning, luxuriating in the novelty of a summer day without work, we slept late, then lingered over campfire bacon and eggs.

"Bring all the beach towels, and I want that library book," Maryanne instructed Denise and Marla, who were throwing stuff into beach bags for the two-hundred-yard walk from campsite to water's edge.

"Got baby oil for tanning?" Denise was planning to return to Ames a bronzed goddess. (Sunscreen? No one had ever heard of it. Even if we had, we would have been puzzled by the concept. The point was to get a tan. If you got a sunburn in the process, nobody was concerned.) Greg poured water on our late-breakfast campfire, whooshing up a tower of steam, as Clare and I, already in swim-suits, hurriedly wiped plates. The night before, we'd run to the camp-ground's concrete-block showers and restrooms to change clothes, but already we were learning to change in the camper. You just had to yell "Don't look!" while you did a quick change, and no one did. Living in cramped quarters necessitated politeness.

"Keep your campsite organized." Mom looked up from her knife and cutting board. She was at the picnic table, prepping veg-etables ahead of dinnertime. "You can go swimming as soon as our site's tidy."

Quickly done, we grabbed beach bags and started running across the long stretch of sand. "Oh! This sand is hot, insanely hot!" Clare squealed and hopped. We had sandals in the camper, but we hadn't worn them. Last night the sand had been cool enough; we couldn't have imagined anything as hot as the sun-baked, golden sand underfoot in the heat of day. "It's hotter and hotter!" Clare was yelping, laughing, hopping from one foot to the other.

"My feet are starting to burn!" I shrieked, laughing at the ridiculousness while cringing from the burn. By the time the heat really registered, we were halfway to the water, so going back to camp was an equally bad option.

"Ow! Ow!" Denise, Maryanne, and Greg, also barefoot, leapt skyward as they tried to run while not touching the ground. Marla, bouncing up and down, zigzagged sideways and hopped on a tiny patch of stiff grass, hoping for relief.

"It's full of stickers!" she yowled and laughed at the same time, leaping off the tuft.

"Just keep running! Ow! OW!" We hopped and shrieked our way to wet sand at the water's edge, collapsing in a heap of laughter in the cool foaming surf. After we calmed down, we inspected the soles of our feet. They looked fine.

"Still, I won't do that again. Anyone going back to camp, tell the rest of the family: Wear sandals!" Denise smoothed baby oil on her legs, to improve the sun's tanning power.

Over and over, we swam out in the water, then turned and threw ourselves into the tumbling salt surf, getting better with each attempt. If we caught the power of the wave right, we bodysurfed elegantly to a smooth shore landing. If we didn't, the wave took control, tossing us around inside it like clothes in a washing machine, before slamming us upended onto hard beach and stuffing our mouths with sand. Mom and Dad had planned to spend just one night at Virginia Beach, but we were so enthralled with the ocean, they extended our stay to three days.

We girls lived in swimsuits, and the boys in their straggly cut-offs, spending nearly all day on the beach. Our skin grew brown and dry from water and sun. Our hair was so stiff from dried salt-water that a ponytail could hold itself straight up. The world seemed nothing more than white sun, white sand, blue water, blue sky. We'd traipse back to the campsite together for a lunch of sandwiches, fruit, chips, and cookies. Even at the campground, our meals were group events, marked with a starting and ending prayer. It wouldn't have occurred to any of us to begin eating before prayers were said, or to wander back to the campsite and eat on our own.

During summer quarter, Dad wore his usual suit and tie to teach at the university. When he wasn't teaching, he was wearing long-sleeved work shirts and carpenter overalls. He seemed not to realize that such a thing as fashion existed, but if he did, he most assuredly didn't care. He owned clothes suitable for teaching, church, and carpentry work. Throw in a couple of short-sleeved shirts for picnics and such, and that was the extent of his wardrobe. He'd never learned to swim due to his Depression childhood, so he didn't own swim trunks, and he had nothing to do with such frivolous sartorial items as shorts or sandals.

And so in Virginia Beach each morning, we made sure to be at the beach ahead of Dad, to best view the spectacle of his arrival. We wanted good seats. One of us might stage-whisper to the others, "Heeere's Dad!" as Dad, oblivious, gingerly emerged from the fringe of scraggly beach shrubs onto the broad stage of sand, arrayed in the new and natty plaid swim trunks Mom had purchased specially for this trip. His torso, legs, and arms, which had rarely seen the sun, were fish-belly white. His neck and work-callused hands, in a shock of contrast, were tanned leather. His balding head was topped by a little, narrow-brimmed hat he'd acquired a decade before for church picnics. But the ultimate touch, the one most appreciated by all of us, was his feet. Mom hadn't thought of buying sandals for him. The lean-muscled, exposed white legs of Dad, who was mindful of burning sand, ended in dark ankle-high socks and the only footwear he owned aside from work boots: wingtip dress shoes.

Dad, used to constant motion at home, at first didn't know what to do on a beach. But he was a good sport, and from a beach blanket, he enjoyed watching us as we tossed ourselves, delirious with delight, into the powerful swirling surf. When the surf calmed, he even got comfortable enough to float jauntily in an inner tube himself. On our last day at the beach, Dad was bobbing gently on the tube, still-pale toes hanging in cool water, little hat perched perkily on his head.

"Hey, what's that?" Dad caught sight of something floating on the water. He looked more closely and saw it was a pair of shoes, floating side-by-side toward the far horizon, dipping up and down in synchrony like two little boats riding the ripples. "Ha, some joker left his shoes where the tide could get them!" he chuckled.

Then his face creased in consternation. "Hey! Those are *my* shoes!" The wingtips were headed out to sea. Dad leapt from the inner tube and splashed through waist-deep water to snatch up his shoes before they sailed over the edge of the known world, or at least floated into deeper water.

For decades afterward, all one of us needed to say was "Some joker left his shoes . . ." and the family would dissolve into laughter, Dad most of all.

only the brave deserve the fair

H old still, hold still!" Denise zipped the back of Maryanne's dress. "And stand up, for goodness' sake!" Denise caught the little hook in the metal eye at the top of the dress as Maryanne bent under the desk in her bedroom, scrabbling for her high heels with one hand, holding a mascara wand aloft with the other.

"Where are my heels?!" Maryanne unearthed a single, smudged white canvas Keds sneaker and backed out. "Marla!" Maryanne perched on the edge of her desk chair and leaned forward, pushing aside textbooks and sheaves of notes, pulling the little stand-up makeup mirror closer. "MARLA!" Maryanne's frustrated yell permeated the girls' second-floor wing of our house.

Maryanne opened her eyes wide, leaned into the mirror, and stroked mascara upward. "Marla—you had my black heels last!" she shouted over her shoulder toward the lounge, plunging the wand back into its tube.

"It's six twenty-five," Denise said, sliding back Maryanne's closet door and searching for the heels. "Your prom date's going to be here any minute."

In the central lounge outside Maryanne's room, Marla tucked the heavy handset of the phone snugly under her chin. "Uh-huh," she cooed into it, lifting the phone base and carrying it toward her room, retreating from the shouting. "Yeah, I could meet you at Boyd's Ice Cream in Campustown." Marla's voice held a coy note. She dragged the long cord of the phone toward her room, trying to shut the door, but the cord didn't reach, so she sat cross-legged in her bedroom doorway, leashed to the phone outlet in the lounge.

In Maryanne's room, Denise kicked off her own white sandals. "Here, you've got to wear something!" She held them out.

"I suppose everyone's staked out the living room as usual." Maryanne thrust her feet into the sandals, resigned to what awaited her in the front room below.

A long, boatlike Ford sedan made a wide turn in our driveway. In our living room, the Lids were in place.

"Here he comes!" Steve stage-whispered, heralding the arrival of the seventeen-year-old boy in his dad's car. Steve was a sentinel shrouded behind drapery, his head popping up over the parapet of the front windowsill. Greg, Clare, and I glanced up from our books; on date nights, we invariably found it necessary to do our reading in the living room.

"He's checking his teeth in the car mirror and smiling at himself!" Paul, sequestered behind another drape, lifted his head just enough to see over his windowsill. "Now he's getting out of the car and brushing at his suit. Now he's coming up the front porch."

"He's carrying a square white box!" Mark crowed, peeping out from his crouch under an end table.

DINGGG . . . DONG. Mercifully, Mom reached the front door first, turning the knob as Denise and Maryanne, finally shod, came downstairs, and Dad came in from the back door.

"Please come in," Mom said kindly.

The young man crossed the threshold and paused. He'd expected to meet his date's parents, which would be stressful enough. But as his eyes swept the room, he realized he would do this in front of a packed house. Curious-eyed siblings occupied every seat, and muffled laughter and scuffling emanated from bulging drapes. He froze. His eyes widened and he opened his mouth, but no words came out. Sweat bloomed on his forehead. Momentarily speechless, he swallowed, Adam's apple bobbing up and down, and clutched the white box.

From across the room, Dad strode forward and took charge. "Hello!" he boomed, sticking his hand forward toward the boy for a handshake. "I'm Joe Stritzel!"

Dad was never flummoxed or unsure of himself. He was, without pretense or flattery, genuinely interested in others. He never wasted a moment thinking about shyness, but if he had, he would have been baffled by it. Since it was his nature to be straightforward, he assumed everyone else was too. What was there to be scared about? He believed in a firm handshake, eye contact, and hearty greeting, whether meeting a daughter's date or a ditch digger, plumber or pope, repairman or royalty. He didn't arrange social engagements, but he was happy to go along with whatever Mom set up, and once there, he could be the life and soul of a party. He was engaging and could tell jokes with a master's sense of timing. But all this bonhomie and geniality was lost on the hapless young men who came to take us girls out on dates. Dad had such a forceful personality, they sometimes actually shook with fear in his presence.

Now, the young man in our living room quaked. "Um," he mumbled. He dropped the flower box on the end table and tugged at his tie. He pulled at his cuffs. Shifting, he rubbed the toe of one shoe on the back of the other pant leg.

Dad's proffered hand remained outstretched. Everyone paused in the now pin-drop quiet room, expectant eyes on the young man. Even the aqua-print drapes cloaking Paul and Steve hung still for a moment.

Dad began again. "I'm Joe Stritzel."

After another excruciating minute, the realization broke over the young man that he needed to grasp Dad's proffered hand and reply with his own name. Comprehension flooded his face, and he did fine shaking Dad's hand, but when he opened his mouth, out came the words, "I'm Joe Stritzel! No! Wait! I mean, I'm not Joe Stritzel, of course not." He blushed bright red, bumbling. "I'm . . . I'm . . . Pete Hochstetter!" he finally blurted, and he and Maryanne managed to get out the door.

As the Ford backed out our driveway and floated down Welch Avenue, Marla bounded into the living room, waving aloft a pair of black high-heeled pumps she'd excavated from the bottom of her closet. "Hey, didn't Maryanne want her shoes? Oh, she's gone. Guess not!" Marla headed toward the kitchen, tossing the pumps into the closet near our side door on her way to get her bike and pedal to Boyd's Ice Cream.

Late one Sunday afternoon a week or so later, the two oldest girls approached Dad as he bent over our big kitchen table, its Formica top protected by layers of newspaper, cutting a thin sheet of glass to size. A windowpane in one of the rental houses had been broken. Dad had carefully removed the broken pane and was now cutting another piece to replace it. Maryanne and Denise watched Dad position a metal straightedge on the glass, laid flat atop the newspaper. They waited, quiet, as he used a sharp glass-cutting tool to score a line, quickly, decisively, into the glass. Then he snapped the sheet of glass in two along the scored line.

"Sorry, honeybunches." Dad looked up at his two eldest. "I have to snap the glass apart while the scored line is still hot from the friction of the cutting tool." He gently laid the right-size piece of glass into the old wood sash. Without looking, Dad patted his leg, extracted a hammer from the loop on his white carpenter overalls, and gently tapped tiny metal glazier points into the wood frame to hold the new pane in place.

"Dad," Denise began, "when a date comes to pick us up, do you have to ask him all those questions about himself? Can't you just say, 'Have a nice time. Goodbye!'?"

"You don't know it, but you scare them off," Maryanne added.

Dad paused mid–hammer tap. "Scare them?" He was incredulous. "*I* scare them? Anybody scared off by me isn't worth having!" He bent again over the new pane of glass in the old sash. "Anyway, they have to get through me to get to you. This might be a way to sort them out." He looked up again at his two eldest, and paused. One of Dad's favorite sayings was on its way, and Maryanne and Denise had a feeling they knew which it was. Dad raised his hammer for emphasis, as if he were proclaiming the truth to all young men—past, present, and future—who would come courting at 412 Welch Avenue: "Remember, only the brave deserve the fair!"

Of course, Dad had once come courting himself. He came to what was then Iowa State College in 1946 on the GI Bill. Like many servicemen-turned-students, Joe Stritzel was older, twenty-four, when he started at Iowa State. A natural leader, he was active in the student club of his major, Agronomy, and in the local chapter of the Newman Center, a national association for Catholic students, at St. Thomas Aquinas Church near campus. Mom spent the World War II years working, and entered Iowa State in 1947 as an older student as well.

As first president of the just-organized Iowa State Newman Club in 1947, Joe decided to host an early autumn picnic at Brookside Park in downtown Ames, so Catholic students could get acquainted. Joe was a whirlwind of motion, organizing burgers and hot dogs, stoking fire under grills, and greeting newcomers while also acting as photographer for the event. Camera strap over his shoulder, he flipped the last burger on one huge grill, mopped his brow, stepped back from the glowing coals, looked up, and saw Marcella. Joe stopped moving, the metal spatula dangling forgotten in his hand.

A new student, Marcella was slim and statuesque in jeans and a blouse, with a stylish weathered leather jacket draped over her shoulders. She was gathering bats for a softball game, working alongside Father James Supple, a young Irish American priest newly assigned to the nascent St. Thomas Aquinas Church.

"Hey, those are done. Get those burgers off the grill!" The club vice president grabbed the spatula and nudged Joe aside.

Joe stood still, attention riveted on Marcella, who was laughing at the young priest's joke. Then Joe remembered his camera. As photographer for the event, it was most important that he take pictures of newcomers. Particularly this one. Really, it was his job to make sure new students felt welcome. Especially this one. Now that he thought of it, he absolutely must, as president, greet every new student personally. Starting with this one.

"Hi, I'm Joe Stritzel. Welcome to the Newman Club!" Joe managed, and Marcella turned, her smile illuminating the grove of fiery autumn leaves around them. "May I take your photo for our newsletter?"

"Sure." Marcella leaned against a tree.

Joe backed up to better frame the photo. He no longer heard the hum of conversation of the other students. He no longer knew they were there. The grills, the coals, the baseball bats gathered in a pile—all seemed to fade away. He looked through the camera at the young woman in the leather jacket and sharpened the focus. A breeze stirred. A handful of crimson and yellow leaves wafted down, and he released the shutter.

❧

Joe asked Marcella out at the next opportunity, to an Agronomy Club social and auction held in a gym on campus. He was enjoying chatting with his date when a fellow club member tapped his shoulder.

"Hey, Joe." The club member's face showed concern. "We need to start the auction, but the auctioneer can't make it. His car's broken down. We have more than a hundred people here, but nobody can do the auctioneering that this requires." He paused, his eyes sweeping over donated goods. "We'll have to postpone."

"Nothing doing!" Joe was appalled at the thought. "I'll do it."

Marcella raised one eyebrow—a move that her children, in decades to come, would learn meant she had her eye on you, and you'd better behave. But now, her raised eyebrow signaled consternation. "Joe," she said, tipping her head at this young man she barely knew, "do you have any idea how to auction?"

Like a lot of rural students at Iowa State in the late forties, Marcella was familiar with the rapid patter of professionals at livestock auctions. Auctioneers employed rhythmic chant—composed of numbers and "filler," or words that connect the bids while keeping buyers informed about bids and products—to keep a brisk pace, to move product, and to fan excitement in the crowd. The auctioneer's rhythm conditioned buyers into joining the call-and-response pattern while also importing a sense of urgency. Auctioneering took skill, experience, and nerve. Joe had the nerve part.

Marcella's eyebrow inched higher. "Have you ever done this before?"

"No," Joe admitted.

Marcella looked at Joe. Who was this guy who would leap into auctioneering in front of a crowd, with no experience?

"I'm leaving." Marcella was only half joking as she moved toward the coat rack.

"It's true I've never auctioneered, but I've been going to livestock auctions my whole life," Joe said quickly, following her. "My brother Thomas and I once went to an auction near Cleveland when our dad couldn't make it. I was fourteen and Thomas was twelve. Dad trusted us with the money and the decision, and we got an excellent Jersey milk cow."

"That's not auctioneering." Marcella rifled through hangers on the coat rack, searching for her leather jacket.

The club member ran toward them. "Are we postponing or going forward?" His hand clamped Joe's arm. "It's you or nobody."

Time ticked by. The murmur from the crowd grew louder. The podium on the little stage remained bare.

"It's now or never," the club member told Joe.

Joe looked at Marcella. Her hand was on that weathered leather jacket. She hadn't taken it off the hanger. He paused for a split second, then turned and sprinted up the steps to the makeshift stage. The crowd fell quiet, attention on him. Marcella dropped her hand from her jacket and watched. Joe glanced over the goods, chose an inexpensive item likely to sell quickly, and picked up the megaphone.

"Do I hear a dollar bid, a dollar bid, a dollar bid for this fine basket of garden hand tools"—and he was off and flying, years of watching and listening paying off, the rhythmic patter of his voice washing over the crowd like a wave washing up on a beach. "I see a dollar there, do I see two fifty, there's the two fifty, do I see three fifty."

Joe's can-do attitude saved the auction, and the event. Marcella was impressed, and a few weeks later, when Joe asked her to the Agronomy Club's barn dance, she said yes. The dance was at the university's agronomy research farm out in the country, quite a distance from Ames proper. Joe was used to walking wherever he needed to go or taking public transportation. But no buses went out to the country.

Joe asked a friend in his dorm, one of the few students on campus with a car, if he could rent his vehicle, a serviceable but nothing-fancy 1938 Ford sedan, for the evening. Since Joe disliked borrowing, or being beholden for a favor, his renting the vehicle was a sign of how important Marcella was becoming to him. With her on his mind, and getting caught up in negotiating a rental fee, he forgot that he did not hold a driver's license. He'd never needed one before. He was an experienced driver, having driven farm vehicles since he was twelve, and in the moment, the necessity of a license didn't occur to him.

On the evening of the dance, the Ford gleamed in the setting sun as Joe pulled up in front of Barton Hall, Marcella's dormitory. He nosed the car to the curb, keeping it just far away enough that its whitewall tires couldn't get marred. Though the event was casual, Joe had taken care with his appearance: his shirt and trousers were pressed, his shoes clean and polished. His wavy black hair, showing just a hint of early receding hairline, was combed back handsomely. He took the stone steps of the dorm two at a time, swung open the heavy oak doors, and entered the formal, spacious front lounge, joining half a dozen other young men waiting for their dates. Marcella, courteously prompt, signed out with the dorm housemother, and Joe squired her to the car.

By this time, Joe had remembered that he did not have a license, but he felt the die was cast, the event set in motion, and the date underway. He knew he was a competent driver. He decided to take the chance.

The date was a smashing success. Throughout the evening, Marcella was enchanting. Joe didn't want their date to end. He drove home slowly, mindful of his borrowed car, keeping to back country roads as long as possible, caught up in conversation with this beautiful young woman. With a rush of joy, Joe felt confident that he and Marcella might be in the early stages of going steady.

As much as he didn't want it to, the country road eventually led to Ames, and Joe turned onto South Duff Avenue, a main highway into town. He was still caught up in the glow of the evening when the sudden flash of a rotating cherry light and the wail of a police siren, right behind the Ford's curved rear fender, made him jump.

The license! As in *no* license! But he hadn't been doing anything wrong! Maybe the cop was after some other car.

"They're after some joker," Joe said, glancing in the rearview mirror and hoping very much that this was true. "But I'll pull off out of the way anyway." He did, but the patrol car pulled up behind the Ford.

The policeman would ask to see his license first thing. Perhaps, Joe thought, he could head off trouble by taking the initiative. The cop strolled up to the Ford. Joe quickly cranked down the window.

"Evening, officer," Joe began. "What did I do wrong?"

The cop put one foot on the Ford's running board, placed both hands on the car door, and leaned inside the car. His belly, round and full as a scoop of ice cream, bumped against the gray metal door. Joe winced, worried that the cop's belt buckle might scratch the car's finish. The cop sniffed, swinging his head this way and that. He wrinkled his nose and sniffed again. No smell of alcohol. He looked at Marcella, sitting demurely at the far side of the car, hands in her lap.

Indeed, these two looked like a nice young couple. And, as the young man had asked, what had they done wrong?

"All right, sonny," the policeman said to Joe, "you're driving too slow! Speed up!"

"I'm sorry, sir!" Relief flooded through Joe. "I didn't realize . . . we were talking and—"

"Think about it!" the cop snapped. "You're on a highway. Drive faster!"

The cop returned to his cruiser, having forgotten to ask to see a driver's license, and Joe was off the hook.

Marcella was way too polite to say what she was thinking, which was something like *Oh, brother!* But her assessment of Joe, stopped by a cop for driving too slow, couldn't have been too bad, because their story didn't end that night, just as it was getting started. As for what Joe was thinking, it might have been an early rendition of "Only the brave deserve the fair," because even after that embarrassing start, he was brave enough to ask her out again.

One year when our three oldest sisters were in high school, Denise was asked to prom by a young man who lived in another city. (They'd met a month before at a church retreat weekend for teens in Dubuque, two hundred miles northeast of Ames.) The boy thought he would drive to Ames on prom night, take Denise to the dance, and stay with friends in town afterward.

Denise had accepted his invitation and had come across a honey of a dress in a store window. She had saved enough from babysitting and teaching swimming lessons at Carr's Pool to buy it, so she brought it home from the store "on approval," which in those pre–credit card days meant that the merchant would take it back within three days if her mother didn't approve. In our second-floor lounge, Denise tried on the dress before all of us girls and Mom.

"Perfect!" Marla breathed as Denise twirled. The empire waist, trimmed with light-green-and-yellow braid, emphasized Denise's slim figure, and the V-necked, sleeveless style accentuated her dé-colletage. From the snug gather under her bust, a light lemon-yellow overlay of chiffon fell in a gracious drape to the floor. It was simple and gorgeous.

"Really right, really just right for you!" Maryanne enthused.

Clare and I stared. Denise, our ordinary sister, the ramrod of our work crew, looked so different from her workaday self.

"Oh, Denisey, it's beautiful! I see why you like it." Mom picked up the tag hanging from the underarm seam and pursed her lips.

Mom could look at a fashion magazine and know how to design and sew the dress shown without having to purchase the pattern. She also knew how to transform older clothes to reflect new trends. If she needed more fabric, she could delve into a supply of cast-off clothing and, with her creative eye, usually retrieve usable fabric that coordinated. Mom worked with what she had, using wit and skill rather than money to create something of beauty and function.

She taught all five of us girls how to sew, and a few years later, when junior high school sewing classes opened to boys in the mid-1970s, she helped our younger brothers Paul, Steve, and Mark learn to sew down vests, and later sleeping bags, from kits.

In our house, Mom's deluxe Singer machine had a permanent place in the first-floor laundry room. There was a second sewing station, with her previous-model Singer, for us kids upstairs in the rear wing of the house.

We used our kitchen table to lay out and cut fabric for our myriad sewing projects. It was a perfect surface for every project, and the only surface suited to the lengths needed for formal dresses, which were fairly easy to make. We sewed a lot of our regular clothing and all our party dresses. Just not on Mom's machine.

Mom's dictate that no child was ever to use her machine may have resulted from my tempestuous relationship with this craft. As a young teen in the early seventies, I sewed with a hasty and confident sense of abandon, often veering off the printed pattern instructions, zooming solo into an uncharted wilderness of chaotic creativity. I'd carry on with the surety of the naïve, sanguine that it would all work out—until right near the end, when it didn't, inevitably stalling in a tangled mess. And then I would scream.

"I can't do this. I CAN'T DO THIS!" In fury and frustration, I tore the plaid jumpsuit I was making out from the machine, a gob of snarled thread choking its inner workings. "I cannot sew! And I spent all that time cutting the fabric just right, so this blasted plaid would *match*! And now it *doesn't*!" I threw the bunched, half-sewn garment to the floor. On the printed front of the pattern envelope, the model mocked me, posturing in the oh-so-stylish zip-front jumpsuit, ready to hop into her convertible. The model's earth-toned plaids perfectly matched across seams. Fire flamed through my shoulders, which had hunched over the machine for hours. "You need to fix it!"

"Cheryl." Mom was calm. "I won't fix your mistakes. Leave it for an hour or so. Come back, use this ripper to pick out your stitching, and lay it flat. Then I'll watch and direct as you pin it."

Now, as Denise twirled before us in the lemon-yellow chiffon dress, Mom paused, choosing words carefully. "If you feel you can afford it, sometimes when you see just the right thing, you get it. Enjoy it, honey." And Denise owned the dress.

On the evening of Denise's prom, we gathered in the living room in high spirits to await her date's arrival. Paul, shoes off, jumped up on an overstuffed chair. "Let's go around the whole room without touching the floor!" Paul led Steve and Mark in an impromptu parade, hopping from upholstered chair to couch. The next armchair held Greg, deep in his library book.

"Let's pretend the carpet is water and if we touch it, we drown."

Mark passed Paul with a two-foot jump, alighting nimbly on the broad arm of Greg's chair.

"Don't land on me!" Greg looked up, eyebrows knit. Paul and Steve adroitly stepped over him.

"Get off the furniture," Clare barked as she hustled into the room, plumping the cushions behind the Lids. Mom and Dad had recently purchased the modern tall-back avocado armchair and gold couch with its stylish flat-winged arms from a fire sale, and the pieces still smelled slightly of smoke. Clare's plumping intensified the smell. "Stop making a mess! We spent all afternoon cleaning up!" She straightened magazines on the end tables, stacking copies of *Look* and *Life* neatly on top of our lone coffee-table book, *100 Great Paintings*. Mom had recently purchased this deluxe collection of art prints in the hope we would glean educational value from it. Now Clare flicked a particle of dust from its cover.

"Denise's date is due right now," I bossed the Lids. "Find something else to do." I neatened the morning newspaper, the *Des Moines Register*, and the afternoon daily *Ames Tribune* on the lower shelf of the coffee table.

The Lids sprang off the couch and started leapfrogging over each other on the carpet as Denise, stepping carefully in her long gown and high heels, descended the stairs, with Maryanne and Marla orbiting her like bridal attendants. Marla brushed a speck from Denise's shoulder. Maryanne snugged her back zipper infinitesimally up. With her hair and makeup done, Denise looked even more winsome than usual.

"That lemony chiffon really highlights the gold flecks in your green eyes." Maryanne lifted the gauzy overlay and let it drop gracefully. "It is *so* perfect."

"Let me get this smudge off your shoe." Clare dabbed her dust-cloth on Denise's patent leather toe.

"And get the smudge of lipstick off her teeth." Marla tapped her own front tooth as Clare reached her dirty dustcloth up toward the face of Denise, who feinted sideways and ducked.

Maryanne glanced at her watch. "A little late," she murmured, "but then he does have a long drive." We waited. Mom and Dad, busy as always, finished tasks elsewhere and joined us in the living room. We waited. Denise ran her tongue over her teeth, searching for the nonexistent speck of lipstick. We waited. Clare and I kept glancing out the window. The Lids ran onto the porch to look up the street. We waited. Time ticked by.

"Really getting quite late," Maryanne said quietly.

"Maybe he had car trouble." Marla cleared her throat. "It's certainly not the weather." We waited. More time ticked by.

"Maybe he has other trouble." Greg's book lay open and unread on his lap.

We waited longer, with a growing sense of unease. Dad looked stern, then angry, and Mom, increasingly distressed. In our home of constant babble and activity, where the usual atmosphere was "fifty-seven different directions," as Dad liked to say, we were all still, all quiet, all waiting.

More time ticked by.

Finally, avoiding eye contact with any of us, Denise silently went upstairs, took off her lemon-yellow dress with chiffon overlay, hung it in her closet, and closed her door. No noise was forthcoming. No sound of tears, muffled by a pillow, escaped her room. After a while, Maryanne and Marla went up, knocked on her door, and went in. At loose ends, the rest of us drifted out of the living room.

The next day, Mom hung the dress in a garment bag in the attic, where Denise wouldn't have to see it, but perhaps someday someone could wear it. Except none of us ever did. In a household where every dress was handed down, worn again and again by one sister after another, no one ever wore that yellow store-bought dress. A couple of years later, Clare and I, rummaging in the attic, came across it and took it out. The green-and-yellow floral braid snugly trimming the empire-waist bodice was unfaded, its chiffon like new, its promise still bright.

"Dad was right." Clare lifted the fabric, letting it ripple over her fingers. "Only the brave deserve the fair. That date was a chicken-heart, and he didn't deserve anyone as fabulous as our sister."

Clare, when she turned sixteen, started dating a friendly boy from a sporty, outdoorsy Ames family of four sons and one daughter. Jim's father was a respected doctor in town, his mother an active and lively hostess with expansive circles of friends. Every son played every sport and played it well; the daughter was an accomplished young equestrienne, and the family boarded her beloved horse at a farm just out of town. They lived near downtown Ames, in an attractive and gracious house facing the river and park.

"Welch Avenue?" Jim's mother looked up from her after-dinner liqueur, questioning her high school son the first time he asked to borrow the car to pick up Clare for a date. "The girl lives on Welch? Isn't that in Campustown? Does anyone except students live there?"

Jim fit into our family like a hand in a glove. On the first date, he ran the gauntlet of inquisitive siblings in our well-populated living room as easily as he ran down the basketball court before swishing a clean jump shot. Jim charmed Mom and, when he shook Dad's hand, managed to come up with his own name with no trouble.

Clare, like all of us girls, was less easygoing about the pre-date scene in our living room, particularly on one early, important date when Dad, wearing his white carpenter overalls in preparation for an evening's work on the houses, engaged Jim in conversation. Primped and prettied, Clare stood by, trying not to glance at her watch as conversation veered off on a tangent, and family life swirled around.

Dad was still talking to Jim when I loped into the living room. "Mom, Dad, I need a ride to Susan's slumber party tonight. It's out on Ross Road. Can you drive me?" I interrupted. I had left the handset of the phone lying on the kitchen desk with Susan waiting on the line. "I need to go right away."

Dad, facing a long evening's work on balky plumbing on one of the houses, had an idea. "Why don't you two take her? Aren't you going in that direction?"

"Sure," Jim said easily, as behind him Clare mouthed silently at Dad, "No! *No!*" But she knew resistance was futile: the solution hit Dad's sweet spot where saving gas and time intersected. Her younger sister, with a rolled-up sleeping bag already tucked under her arm, was as good as in the back seat of her boyfriend's car, tagging along on the first few minutes of their date. That moment highlighted not Dad's theorem exactly, but a corollary: "Only the easygoing and likable deserve the fair."

Perhaps it was just as well Jim learned from the start that dating a Stritzel girl meant engaging with the whole family. Years later, after Clare and Jim married and produced three predictably athletic and good-looking children, they'd stop to get me, my husband, and our daughters to join them on their skiing or camping trips. Just like that early date, I was still tagging along.

Back on Welch Avenue, I inevitably grew from one of the pesky younger sibs hanging around the living room on date night into a sister old enough to await her own date's arrival. Eager to avoid the whole family's involvement, I grew accomplished at greeting my date and getting us out of the house fast. "Mom-Dad-he's-here-we're-going-skating-on-the-river-be-back-before-long," I'd trill—and hustle us out the door before the *DONG* of the doorbell had faded. As my younger brothers grew up and Mom and Dad grew busier buying, selling, and working on the houses, it became easier to avoid what I saw as the date-night third degree in our front room.

During my senior year in high school, I briefly dated one of our school's football players. A gregarious guy with big popularity to go with his big hair, Damien lived in a neighborhood I'd never seen before, across the tracks and far from Campustown, in a little paint-chipped frame house on a street with no curb or sidewalk, with his dad and his dad's girlfriend, who showed up occasionally. Even though bucket seats in cars were mostly all you could find in cars now, Damien had specifically sought out a big old used car with a front bench seat, the easier to convince his girl—me, at the moment—to snuggle up next to him.

My parents, and a sister or two, knew I was dating this football player, but generally my family could no longer keep up with which sister was dating whom, and a date arriving at the front door didn't generate the level of interest it once had. Since I was a good student and happy adolescent, our ever-busier parents paid less and less attention to me, which was fine with me. Dad was now so used to boys coming to the house to take out his daughters that he no longer even made it into the living room to meet every one. Wrong-side-of-the-tracks Damien might have caused comment between Mom and Dad, but if he did, I never knew. They were primarily interested in a boy's character, and Damien was viewed no differently from any of the boys I dated. Mom and Dad treated Damien with a distracted but benign courtesy, as they did all my dates.

It also suited me that my younger brothers didn't know who, or even if, I was dating at the moment. One frosty autumn school morning, Damien drove his beater car to the Spudnut Shop near his house, got half a dozen fresh, fragrant doughnuts, then continued across town to give me a lift to school. He had football practice after school and wouldn't be able to drive me home, so I had suggested the day before that we put my ten-speed bike in his car in the morning, and I'd ride it home after school. While I was still in the house gathering my books, my brother Paul happened to glance out the front window, and saw a big man he didn't know lifting my bike into his trunk.

"Hey!" Paul shouted an alarm to rouse Mark and Steve. "Some guy's stealing Cheryl's bike!"

The three of them rushed through the front room, instantly prepared to tackle this lineman and recover the bike. But before my slight younger brothers could dash out the door, coalesce into a single form, leap off our front porch, and land on Damien like sparrows driving off a hawk, I intercepted.

"That's my boyfriend," I yelped at the Lids, "and he's giving me a ride to school!" So my flock of brothers, instead of alighting on Damien's back, landed on their feet in the driveway just as Damien closed the trunk on my bike and turned around. Everyone smiled awkwardly, I made hasty introductions, and he and I hopped in the car and flew down Welch Avenue while lifting fresh Spudnuts out of the open box on the front seat.

Only the brave deserve the fair? I was glad Damien didn't have to fight off a pack of brothers that morning, but one moonless evening a couple of weeks later, another incident brought Dad's saying to mind. Damien was backing into a parking spot, one arm around me, the other casually on the wheel, in the dark on his own streetlamp-less street. With the overconfidence typical of an adolescent, he backed up too fast while keeping up a stream of happy patter and cuddling his girl, multitasking before it was even a concept. *KEER-RUNCH!* The beater smacked into the parked car behind us. The sickening sound of metal crunching metal snapped off his line of happy talk mid-sentence. We jumped out of his battered old car, ran to the rear, crouched down on the cold, packed-dirt verge next to the crumbling concrete street, and surveyed the crumpled front fender of the car he'd just run into.

"Oh! Oh! Bummer! It looks pretty bad," I commiserated, pawing around in the depths of my purse for paper and pen. I held them out. "Here, you can leave your name and number." Damien looked at me as if I'd lost my mind.

"Name and number?" He was incredulous. "No way! That's not what we do. We cut the lights and slink out of here!" So we did.

Not exactly a case of "only the brave deserve the fair," since slinking off in the dark after smashing a fender on a parked car is hardly a display of courage. He and I had been growing apart anyway, and we didn't last much longer as a couple. Shame about the Spudnuts.

twenty-three

1972

king of the jungle

I stood riveted in the open doorway of the cheap cracker box of a house on the outskirts of Ames, where I would spend the evening babysitting. This home stood in a cluster of houses built the year before, so raw and new I could smell fresh-turned earth in the bare cornfield across the street. The house had no foyer; its flimsy front door opened directly into a beige-carpeted living room. A lumpy, overstuffed couch, single beat-up leather recliner, and TV overfilled the small space. I stared, frozen in fear, at the family pet lounging on the back of the couch. The young mother, who had picked me up at home and brought me here, didn't notice my fear.

"Baby Michael is already asleep in his room down the hall." She kicked off her tennies into a pile of detritus in a corner. I didn't move.

"Mikey will wake in a few hours," she said, stepping off carpet onto kitchen linoleum. She found her sandals under the kitchen table, thrust one on, and hopped as she pulled on the other, long hair swinging. The kitchen was little more than an alcove off the living room. "You'll hear him cry. When you do, feed him a bottle, change his diaper, and he'll go right back down." She rummaged among mail and dishes on the kitchen counter for her purse.

"Brenda, don't make us late!" her husband roared down the hall. He tornadoed into the living room. His handsome young face, framed by a short beard and blond locks that brushed his shoulders, didn't turn toward me, the thirteen-year-old babysitter in the doorway clutching a school backpack and wearing a red sweatshirt with a picture of a tiger on the front. His flared jeans swept along grubby synthetic carpet, not quite obscuring Earth shoes. He scanned the windowsill, shifted a heavy black dial phone on a spindly end table, then dug between recliner cushions. "God! Here they are!" He grabbed keys out of the cushions, shaking off crumbs. "Brenda! We'll be late to our own bar. The shift change is in fifteen minutes. We're on next, and as owners we cannot be late!"

"I'm ready, I'm ready." Brenda spoke calmly, purse hung on her shoulder, her gauzy peasant blouse showing bright embroidery at the round-scooped neck, its white fabric fluttering over jeans. She smiled at me, and I finally stepped into the house, my eyes still riveted on their pet, half snoozing atop the pilled fuzzy fabric of the couch back.

"Oh!" she glanced from me to the pet and back again. "Right! I get it." Brenda ducked into the kitchen, pushed aside dishes littered with pizza crusts, located a flyswatter under a crumpled pizza box, and stepped back into the living room. "If he nips you, tap him on the nose with this." She handed me the stick of flimsy plastic.

They swirled out the door, legged it up into their pickup, and with a squeal of tires peeled out of the driveway as the screen door on the house slammed shut behind them.

The pet was a lion. A real, uncaged, adolescent lion.

❦

In the early seventies, restrictions on exotic pets were nearly nonexistent. I'd first met this lion months earlier, when I'd gone along with my friend Polly on her babysitting job. It had been a kit then, mewing and unsteady on new legs with big clumsy paws. It had the run of the house, but mostly it dozed on the couch. When the kit wasn't sweetly snoozing, it sucked on my finger with its tiny sandpapery tongue. Polly and I were entranced. We passed the kit back and forth, cuddling it, cooing into its darling little big-eyed face while we ate popcorn and watched Mary Tyler Moore toss her beret on TV.

The job was easy; the only requirement was to occasionally check on the sleeping baby down the hall and feed him a bottle if he awoke. The parents would close their bar in downtown Ames at two o'clock in the morning, do the bookkeeping, clean the joint, return home, and finally drive their babysitter home. The going rate for a thirteen-year-old babysitter was fifty cents per hour, which over a long night like this one added up nicely.

It was one job out of dozens, and I had forgotten about the couple until they called months later. Polly was unavailable, so I was going on my own, which was the usual babysitting situation anyway. I assumed their kit had gotten too big for the house, and they'd taken it to wherever one takes overgrown lions.

They hadn't.

Now, transfixed with terror, my back plastered against the wall, I stood alone, eight feet from the king of the jungle. He reclined lazily in alpha position on the couch back. How could this animal still be here? He was the size of a Labrador. His tawny coat covered smooth muscle that rippled as he stretched and yawned, showing gleaming white incisors, unfurling a river of huge tongue.

It was seven fifty on a Saturday night. The parents wouldn't be back until four o'clock in the morning.

Fear rolled off me in waves. The lion smelled it. Idly, as if he wasn't sure why he was bothering, he lifted his head and swung it side to side, sniffing. The great heavy cranium bobbed slowly. The action made the creature look like one of those flocked animal figurines with weighted heads that people place near the rear window of their cars.

Stop! Must focus! I snapped back to reality and assessed the situation. The tiny living room felt like a boxing ring. I stood in one corner, frozen, disbelieving. In the other corner lay the feline combatant, lounging on his lofty perch, relaxed.

The lion had claws and fangs. He had sleek masses of muscle. He had on his side millennia of evolution that had honed cats into the most efficient hunters ever known.

I had a flyswatter.

His amber eyes rolled over me. His lip curled, showing those incisors again. Watching him, I noticed the phone on the leggy little end table, wedged between couch and recliner. The phone! My eyes never leaving his, I exhaled silently and inched out of my corner. The lion's head lolled to one side, but he didn't move. I took a step. He didn't move. I took another step, and another. I sidled along the wall. The lion watched, tongue hanging, panting. He didn't move.

I was nearly to the recliner. On the other side was the phone. I breathed, inched along, breathed, inched. The lion panted. A drop of saliva trembled on the end of his tongue. Slowly, I reached toward the phone. With one hand, I lifted the receiver, my eyes locked on the lion. With the other, I rotary-dialed seven digits, and at her babysitting job across town, Polly picked up on the first ring.

"You'll never believe this!" I whisper-screamed. On the lion's tongue, the quivering globule of saliva dropped. Quick as a snake, the lion coiled and sprang. I whimpered and dodged as he grabbed the phone cord in his jaw, lassoing the heavy receiver overhead before the cord slipped out of his saliva-slick jaw and the receiver flew into the wall with a solid thwack. The phone base followed, tumbling to the carpet, pulling the spindly end table over with it.

I heard the phone go dead.

The lion took one step back toward the couch, turned, and with a single graceful leap reclaimed his perch atop the back. Now cut off from the outside world, I stood rock-still in the boxing ring. Minutes ticked by. The lion lolled, head back, eyes baleful under heavy lids.

More minutes ticked by. I couldn't stand in one spot all night. My backpack full of homework was near the front door. Maybe I could get it. I saw the lion's eyelids droop. I sidled along the wall toward my backpack, trying not to breathe. The eyelids hovered at half-mast over amber eyeballs that were watching me. The lion didn't move. His lids dropped lower, lower . . . I stretched toward my backpack. The lids drifted lower yet. I hooked a finger through my backpack, lifted it, and inched back toward the cracked faux-leather recliner. As I eased into the recliner, the lion eased into sleep.

I exhaled and began doing my work on my lap as the lion dozed and a low hum of chatter emanated from the unwatched TV. I rustled no paper, made no sudden moves. I worked my way through an English assignment on literal versus figurative. Literal meant it actually happened. Figurative meant it was as if it had happened. The lion slept. I moved on to another section of English that explored irony in literature. Still the lion snoozed. I did a bit of geology homework that focused on igneous versus sedimentary rock. The lion stirred, slept again. I dug into my backpack for my math book and was deep into decimals and fractions when the baby wailed from down the hall.

Oh no. I didn't want to stir, didn't want to upset the fragile peace reigning in our little boxing ring, but I had to prepare a bottle. I eased my work off my lap. At my glacial pace, I took a full minute to move from recliner to kitchen. Keeping my head swiveled toward the lion, eyes on him, I rotated my body toward the fridge door, eased it open, and extracted a jug of milk. The lion heard the opening door's soft sigh and raised his massive head, knowing that sound meant *food*.

He sprang. This time, going for food instead of the phone, he meant business. I was facing the counter, pouring milk into the baby's plastic bottle, when the missile of the lion's body hit my back with his teeth bared. I screamed and screamed again, arching toward the counter, away from the open jaws, so that a nanosecond later, when they snapped closed, the lion bit not skin and spine but only my sweatshirt, tearing a chunk out of its red fabric.

As I arched forward, I threw the full plastic milk jug and baby bottle skyward. Both sprayed milk in wild swooping arcs before crashing to the floor. I snatched up the milk jug just before it finished glug, glug, glugging its way from full to empty all over the floor. I was breathing fast and ragged, adrenaline coursing through me, and I started to cry. I was thirteen, alone in a box of a house with a lion that had ripped into my sweatshirt with its teeth, and responsible for a baby wailing down the hall. A tear or two rolled off my cheek, plopping into the lake of milk at my feet.

Standing in that lake, I realized I was literally crying over spilled milk. Not only that, I saw irony in the fact that a lion's fangs had torn the back of my sweatshirt—a sweatshirt with a logo of a tiger on the front. I was living my English homework.

But what was this? Could the pool of milk spreading across the linoleum be a blessing? The lion spit out his mouthful of red sweatshirt. Crouching, as if by the shore of an African watering hole, he lapped at the milk. The spill was buying me time! As the lion languorously lapped, I quickly prepped the bottle, using the last of the milk in the jug, and hurried to the crying baby in his room down the hall, forgetting my own tears as I fed and cleaned little Mikey and laid him back down to sleep.

When I returned, the milk lake in the kitchen alcove had vanished. The lion lay on his perch back in the living room. He looked livelier, head raised, eyes bright, tail switching. The milk had awakened his appetite, not sated it.

It was midnight. I could not—*could not*—survive another four hours in this room with this beast. Could I somehow corral him? Off the kitchen was a flimsy hollow-core wood door, its veneer chipped at the edges. I opened it and saw a flight of wood-plank stairs down to the basement. Could I lure the lion into the stairwell and lock him in the basement?

I needed bait. I could lay a trail of bait leading from the living room couch through the kitchen and down the basement stairs. I flung open one kitchen cupboard, then the other. Where was the Wonder Bread? Every family I knew, except ours, had Wonder Bread. (Mom, deaf to our entreaties, bought whole wheat.) But oddly, these cupboards were bare. No Wonder Bread. No whole wheat bread. No box of crackers, no plastic container of homemade granola, no cornflakes, no Quaker Oats. The fridge was equally dismal: orange juice, crusty jars of condiments, a single head of browning iceberg lettuce. Did this couple survive on frozen pizza? I could start with the two pizza crusts, drying into *C*-shapes on a crumby plate. But I needed more. Opening the third and last thin, plywood cabinet, I saw a dozen Hershey bars stacked in the far corner.

It did not occur to me that lions likely didn't eat chocolate, but there was nothing else anyway. I peeled off the wrappers. The smooth chocolate showed a white bloom of age. The lion, relaxed atop the couch back, secure in his place at the top of the food chain, watched with an expression of amused indulgence. He was a predator watching his prey, knowing he could pounce and win with a single paw swipe at the last moment. Why not relax and enjoy the show first?

I laid the chocolate in a Hansel-and-Gretel trail winding from living room couch to basement stairs. The lion rolled off his perch and, with more curiosity than hunger, began to investigate.

"Here, kitty, kitty," I whispered. The lion sniffed and moved. Closer, closer. "Here cat, there's a good boy, there's a good killing machine. Come on, you like chocolate, especially old chocolate, come on . . ."

Slowly, lithely, he glided across the kitchen linoleum. He sniffed the chocolate, licked one piece, pushed it with his tongue, licked the next, moved along, sniffed the next. He wasn't eating them, but he was getting closer to the basement door. I held my breath. I allowed myself to think my plan might work. I stood rock-still, back against the kitchen counter, watching the lion's shoulders move in smooth, slow rotation under his sleek coat as he progressed along the trail. A fantasy of the lion locked in the basement blossomed in my mind. He was at the open basement door now. He placed one paw on the top step, then another. He was halfway through the door . . .

NOW! I sprang, grabbed the doorknob, and slammed the door against the lion's rump, but he was quick. Quick and quicker, from his position on the top two stairs, he turned and threw his body against the door, shoving it open as I shoved it closed. Back, forth, back, forth, I nearly had the door closed—I was desperate to hear that solid click—when the lion's heft pushed it open. I planted my sneakers against linoleum and pushed with all my might, moving the door slightly closer to closed. The lion dug his claws into the planks of the top steps and pushed back, moving the door slightly closer to open. Back, forth, back, forth, both of us panting, one of us sweating: it was a wrestling match between girl and lion with a sheet of wood between us. In a fraction of a second when the lion drew back to coil himself for another try, I saw a sliver of opportunity and flung myself against the door, but too quickly the lion sprang, all four paws off the steps for a moment, blasting the door fully ajar and knocking me to the floor.

I scrambled to my feet. The lion stalked back through the kitchen to his living room territory, eyeing me with contempt, flicking his tail as if asserting superiority over the whole human race. The lion leapt onto his couch-back perch and appeared to doze, but he was watching me. I cleaned up the chocolate, inched back into the living room, turned off the test pattern on the TV, eased into the recliner, and sat frozen. Defeat lay over me like a king-sized bedspread. Without claws, hooves, or fangs, I was useless. The lion didn't get to be king of the jungle by falling for ruses like trails of chocolate leading to basement doors.

Each of us stayed in our corners, in that boxing ring of a living room, through the rest of that long and terrible night. When the parents returned, they didn't notice my exhaustion or tear-streaked face. I forgot to mention the dead phone. It was late, and they were beat. "How was your night?" they asked perfunctorily.

It was four in the morning. I was thirteen and had been taught to be polite. "Fine," I squeaked. "Here's your flyswatter."

I did not go back to that babysitting job. Nor did my friend Polly. We never found out what became of the lion, but the episode did help my English grade.

I was sitting at our kitchen table in the evening a couple of weeks later, doing homework with a gaggle of sisters and a college girl or two. Struggling to write an epic poem for an English assignment, I'd thrown out several false starts when Denise took pity on me. She set aside her chemistry book, picked up a balled-up wad of lined writing paper, and smoothed out my latest attempt.

"Dragons?" She wrinkled her brow. "You're writing a ballad about slaying dragons?" She hitched her chair closer to mine. "You don't know anything about knights and dragons. Write about something you know."

"Write about that lion!" Marla, always up for a distraction, lifted her head from her own studies.

"Let's think of a start." Clare kept at her geometry homework, tracing neat figures with protractor and compass. "Starting is the hardest."

"How about: One night I went to babysit," Denise began.

"The family kept a lion kit," Clare continued.

Marla jumped to her feet and snagged a bag of potato chips from the cupboard. "I think there's some chive dip in the fridge." She pulled open the refrigerator door, her homework forgotten. "You'll need verses about the phone going dead, the lake of milk, and him biting into your sweatshirt. This might take a while. We'll all need sustenance."

twenty-four

1976

from pittsburgh to taiwan

Ring a ling a ling! I stood on the kitchen linoleum and wagged the heavy metal bell, its clapper reverberating up our home's back staircase. Five twenty-seven on a weeknight in autumn, early in the school year. Time to call everyone, including the four college girls living with us this year, to dinner.

"I hear it, I hear it!" snapped Charlene as she headed downstairs. A Pittsburgh native and our newest college girl, Charlene was so routinely grumpy that no one even noticed anymore. A thick tangle of black hair fell past her shoulders. The bottom edges of her flared blue jeans showed white threads where they touched the floor. Charlene, at the moment, was majoring in zoology. A conflicted soul who couldn't quite find her path, she'd changed majors twice since coming to Iowa State.

"Ah, Cheryl, thank you, I am on my way." Isabelle's soft South African accent was gracious. Isabelle was not a college student but a visiting professor renting one of the bedrooms in our house. Isabelle's short brown hair was perfectly coiffed, her eyes crinkled in a perpetual smile behind wire-rim glasses, her collared blouse pressed, her skirt and jacket neat. The delicate wire rims and impeccable manners hid a fierce intellect: Isabelle taught agricultural economics to PhD students and was in demand by universities around the globe.

My hand silencing the bell's clapper, I sprinted through the kitchen and living room toward the front staircase. This afternoon, I was on kitchen duty with Mom. I loved handling our dinner bell; we all did. Made in Switzerland of heavy gold metal carved with mountain scenes, it was designed to be worn around a cow's neck. Mom, who did not allow us to shout "Dinnertime!" in or out of the house, had us use it to summon all to evening meals.

Ring a ling ling! Holding the bell by its broad, brocade strap, I shook it up the front staircase. Five twenty-eight. The thick strap, attached in a loop to the top of the bell, showed intricate scenes of Alpine flora stitched in metallic thread and was finished on the sides with soft, red fringe.

"Smells good down here." Karen, from Australia, smiled as she came downstairs. A dairy science major, she looked like a milkmaid herself, fresh sprung from the pages of a children's book. "I had the most fascinating class today, can't wait to tell you all about it." Round and happy with short black hair and cheeks blushed pink, always cheerful as a sunny day, Karen reminded us of a bouncing ball.

"Love your mom's baked chicken!" Tiny Ellen, from Illinois, closed her eyes and drew in a deep breath as she entered the kitchen. Ellen, barely five feet tall and usually in full makeup, could pack away food like a lumberjack and not gain a pound. A physical education major, and always in motion, Ellen resembled a tiny tornado topped with a swirl of thick, jet-black hair. Her Illinois hometown was spelled Peru, but pronounced PAY-Roo, and she loved correcting us on this.

Ring a ling ling! I banged open the side door and stood out on the concrete stoop, shaking the Swiss cowbell to summon any siblings who might be outdoors. Five twenty-nine. From around the neighborhood and throughout the house, pounding feet converged on the kitchen. The Lids burst in the back door, hustling to the bathroom to wash hands. Siblings materialized from upstairs and down, indoors and out, chattering, sliding onto one long bench behind the table, jostling into chairs along its other three sides. Mom and I placed two pans loaded with crispy chicken pieces on the table next to a gigantic aluminum bowl of tossed salad and a deep pot of white rice. Talk swelled louder. I lifted the pot lid to stick in a serving spoon, and fragrant steam swirled up. Ellen from PAY-Roo, in her chair, took another deep breath, as the volume escalated.

"Keep it down to a dull roar, please." Dad, already changed out of dress shirt and tie into carpenter overalls for his evening's work on our rental houses, sat down next to Mom. Five thirty.

"Bless us, O Lord, and these Thy gifts," he began, and silence dropped like a curtain. "Which we are about to receive from Thy bounty." Heads dipped and hands folded as we all, or almost all, joined in. Charlene crossed her arms and scowled.

Mom spoke fondly of many of our college students, remembering them decades later, calling them true gems. But some who lived in our house were more challenging.

Grumpy Charlene from Pittsburgh was one. She didn't have to pray at meals with us, but did she have to scowl while we did? Mom, who figured Charlene had troubles that had nothing to do with us, never reacted to Charlene's ill temper. Instead, she responded with kindness. Charlene didn't stop snarling the whole year she lived with us. After she moved out, we forgot about her until a decade later, when Mom got a letter from her. Charlene, who apologized and thanked Mom and Dad profusely, wanted us to know she'd joined a church and now regularly said prayers herself before meals—though she did not write anything about ringing a cowbell before dinner.

Living with students from different cultures, from Brooklyn to Bombay, we routinely adjusted to different customs. In the later years, we occasionally had a Muslim college girl living with us. During Ramadan, Mom would keep her dinner hot so she could eat after sundown. No eating during daylight hours? We didn't know much about Islam, but we got that. We kids thought it sounded like something a religion would think up. It wasn't too different from Lent.

One of the college girls whom Mom remembered as a gem was Shirley Parrish, who lived with us in the early days. Shirley loved to tell about an early church-going experience. One sunny Sunday, in a somnolent little white clapboard church somewhere down a dusty road in Iowa in the 1950s, she was dozing in a rear pew, the drowsy buzzing of insects melding with the steady drone of the preacher's voice. Her head drooped to her chest as the preacher built up steam behind his message, then soft-pedaled his words, then built volume again. Her nodding head fell into sequence with the rise and fall of the pastor's rhythmic delivery. The soporific morning and the rolling cadence of his voice were lulling her over the edge into slumber when the preacher reached the fiery zenith of his message and suddenly roared, fist slamming the pulpit, "Repent! Repent! Or you will *surely perish*!" And young Shirley Parrish, in the back pew, jumped awake in shock and awe.

In contrast to Shirley, college boy John Lin was a true challenge. John came from Taiwan to live with us in the mid-seventies while he studied physics at Iowa State. By that time, our three older sisters and older brother Greg had grown up and moved out; still at home were Clare, seventeen, me, sixteen, and the Lids, in junior high. John Lin was one of several college boys who rented the basement apartment in our commodious house. Unlike the college girls who rented rooms upstairs next to our bedrooms, ate meals at our giant kitchen table with us, and shared fully in our boisterous home life, the college boys in the basement during these years used a separate entry. They walked to the university's dorm dining hall for their meals or cooked for themselves in the little kitchen in the basement apartment. We rarely saw them.

The basement apartment included a separate phone line for their exclusive use. The boys' black phone in the basement hung on a battered wood post that sported a grubby stub pencil tied on with string. Over the years, as college boys came and went, the proliferating graffiti on the bare wood post grew thicker and more incomprehensible with the scribbled numbers of pizza takeout joints, old buddies, classmates, and long-forgotten girlfriends.

But this basement phone stayed silent when John Lin's father called from Taiwan. John Lin's father only ever called our family phone on the first floor. Maybe his father didn't understand, or maybe John wanted it that way. Another concept John Lin's father never grasped was the considerable time difference between Taiwan and Ames, Iowa. Middle-of-the-night calls came in every so often, and it seemed I was always the nocturnal receptionist.

BRANG! BRANG! The phone rang, and rang, and rang. The incessant, insistent jangling went on and on, pulling me slowly but inexorably from a deep and luxurious sleep. I slept deeply, fighting against waking, clutching the pillow, willing the phone to silence.

BRANG! The caller on the other end was not giving up. The beige, heavy-plastic dial phone reverberated again and again from its place downstairs on the kitchen desk. Clare and I were in our shared bedroom upstairs in the addition, but the unholy, unending *BRANG!* was not permeating the dormant brain of my sleeping sister, and the Lids and my parents were asleep at the far end of the house.

BRANG! I didn't swear—none of us did—but if I did, now would have been the time to summon all bad words in existence and use them.

BRANG! It was beyond irritating. It was insane, infernal, infuriating. I glanced at my sleeping sister in the other twin bed. How could she sleep through this racket? I burrowed into bed, facedown, pillow gripped over my head, refusing to acknowledge wakefulness. The phone rang thirty times, seeming to wake no one but me. On the thirty-first *BRANG!* I gave up and stumbled downstairs, grabbing at the banister while clutching up my long nightgown, and fumbled for the receiver. "Hello?" I croaked.

My weak salutation was met by a torrent of Chinese, a gabbling, roaring river of idiom and vernacular flooding my ear, delivered in a furious tone at top volume from thousands of miles away: John Lin's father was calling from Taiwan.

Still fighting upward from the depths of sleep, I rasped, "John's not here." It was a university holiday, and John had gone home with a roommate. The effect was only to ratchet up the volume of John Lin's father's cascading Chinese.

I was well brought up, and yet completely ill-equipped to deal with a mad Chinese patriarch shouting across the ocean. Gamely, politely, I began to try. "Besides, it's the middle of the night here!"

My vocal entreaty against the long-distance bellowing had as much effect as a blade of grass has against a tsunami. His shouting escalated to roaring, but it made no difference to my midwestern ear. I wasn't going to understand Chinese, no matter how loudly he delivered it. The bellowing continued, my anemic responses dwindled, and eventually, after long minutes of fruitless booming, he hung up and I stumbled back upstairs.

As many times as John Lin's father called our phone, we could never find out what he wanted.

John Lin, a tall, loose-limbed, lanky lad, was a load of trouble himself, right from the moment he ambled up our front walk to sign the basement lease. With jet hair spiking in every direction, a scraggle of barely there beard, and size-ten scuffed tennies, he was one of those souls often found in academia: well-suited for the eso- teric upper reaches of quantum physics, but not up to the mundane tasks of everyday life. He seemed perennially surprised by the ne- cessity of such things as locating his classes or turning off a hot plate when done with it. He once roasted a whole chicken in our basement kitchen's oven—without a pan. He simply placed the raw chicken on the oven rack, turned the oven on, and left the chicken to cook for a couple of hours. Grease and juice splattered every- where, spewing onto the lower heating element, running down the oven walls, and pooling on the oven floor, where it burned merrily, sending plumes of black smoke curling out around the closed door. Luckily, John was still in the apartment. He gasped, threw open the door, and fanned the smoke. He owned nothing as practical as oven mitts, so he grabbed a T-shirt off the floor, wrapped his hands in it, snatched the well-roasted chicken out of the oven's maw and tossed it into the sink. Mom said it had never occurred to her that anyone would have to be told to put a chicken in a pan before putting it in the oven.

John Lin never fully grasped the concept that he would eventu- ally have to move out, and in fact even his graduation from Iowa State seemed to take him by surprise. Judging from his lack of planning, he might have been wandering across campus when he happened upon the ceremony and decided at the last minute to participate. Directly after crossing the stage and receiving his diploma, he rushed to our basement apartment and hurriedly threw a few belongings into a trunk, boxes, and bags, leaving behind a tumbled mess in the subterranean apartment. With no time or thought to ask us for a ride, he sped via taxi to the Des Moines airport, an hour's drive south, where he immediately phoned my mother. His flight was imminent, he said, but his passport was still somewhere in the chaos of our basement. Panicked, pacing, and shouting into the phone—maybe it was genetic—he beseeched Mom to bring it.

Mom and Dad did not have free time. Running a household that often numbered fifteen, operating a labor-intensive house-rental business, with Dad working full time, they were not lounging around contemplating outings to Des Moines. But John Lin's need was serious. More important, if he didn't get the passport, he would return to our house.

Mom descended into the mess in the basement to search for the passport. She could barely push open the door to his room, the floor was so covered with John's abandoned detritus.

"Oh, for crying out loud!" she muttered, wading in. Scribbled papers, torn notebooks with spiral metal spines bent askew, greasy chip bags, and opened texts, their yellow highlighted paragraphs shining in the gloom, littered the floor. No passport lay among the jumbled books.

"Glory-orski!" Mom flipped on the light, rolled her eyes, and moved her feet forward like an ice skater to get through the junk. A heap of dirty clothes, built up like a termite mound, was crowned with a single, size-ten, holey tennis shoe. The closet was empty, a few metal hangers bent far out of shape hanging from the rod, an open empty shoebox lying on its side on the floor. No passport lay among the rolls of dust.

Mom approached the desk, a broad heavy walnut affair that supported a hutch of four shelves at the back. A stack of various-sized white china plates, rimmed and crusted with ancient glop, rose teetering atop a single dorm cafeteria tray on the desk's work surface. No passport lay tucked behind the crockery.

"We're going to have to take all these back to the dorms," she groaned to herself. "How did he even smuggle those coffee cups out of the cafeteria?" Her eyes scanned the dishes, spoons, balled-up socks, and candy bar wrappers. She picked up a spoon between thumb and forefinger, held it at arm's length, and flicked a pair of gym shorts off the desktop. No passport rested beneath.

"Should I start the car?" Dad called from the top of the basement stairs.

Mom waded back and aimed her voice up the stairs. "Not yet!"

"His plane will leave soon!" Dad called down the stairwell.

"I know!" Mom turned back and faced the room, the impossible haystack of a room that, somewhere, held the needle of John's slim forest-green Taiwanese passport. This situation required help of a different sort. She stood still, closed her eyes, and called on St. Anthony, patron saint of lost items, repeating a saying we kids had learned years before in Saturday morning catechism classes.

"St. Anthony, St. Anthony, come around, something is lost and cannot be found." She wasn't praying to St. Anthony, just asking him to intercede on her behalf. When she opened her eyes, her gaze fell on a casement window high up in the concrete block wall. On its sill lay John's passport.

"Thank you," she breathed, and ran up the stairs.

Dad dashed to start the car, Mom jumped in, and they floored it down Interstate 35 to Des Moines. Pushing speed limits, they zipped up to the airport entrance, Dad throwing the car into park as Mom bounded out, running, looking for John, waving his passport in her outstretched hand. John Lin was waiting in a frenzy of tension, sprinting back and forth among airport entrances, bouncing on the balls of those size-ten feet, agitatedly running his hand over and over through madly disheveled black hair. Finally, he saw Mom. Wild-eyed and wordless, John Lin snatched his passport out of her hand and sprinted for the gate.

He made the plane, and that was best for everyone, though Mom remarked later he never did say thank you.

A few years later, a college student myself, I was with friends one evening in a bar listening to a comedian. He joked that not only do your parents not miss you, they're so glad you're gone they've probably rented out your room! Everybody laughed except me.

"My parents really did rent out my room," I said, but nobody heard me. They were too busy chuckling over parents who would view your childhood room not as a shrine but as a money-making opportunity.

"Our house was big and old," I raised my voice over the hubbub, "and closer to campus than the new dorms. The university was short on housing, so we had college students living with us during the school years, always. They walked from our house to their classes, easy."

"You had these . . . *strangers* living with you?" New friends were stunned. "In your *house?*"

"*What?* You didn't lock your doors either?" Now they really didn't believe it.

"It always felt so normal, so ordinary." I tried to convince the circle of questioning faces. "We had no theft in the entire twenty-three years college students lived in our house. Our college girls lived with us, ate with us, said prayers at meals with us. They came to feel like sisters. My parents still get letters from some of them. They were just like us."

This was how it felt, though the students who lived in our house transcended cultures across the country and around the globe. What we remember is hanging out together, when we were in junior high and high school, with our college girls in the kitchen during late study evenings. We'd make popcorn and scoop potato chips or Fritos into little tubs of sour cream from Anderson Erickson's, a regional dairy whose dip has never been equaled. We'd perch on countertops and around the table, drinking pop in the bright kitchen, our cozy camaraderie an island of light and laughter against the darkness outside.

twenty-five

1969

christmas

The Lids, Clare, and I lay in a semicircle on the carpet, chins propped on elbows, gazing up into boughs of fragrant needles. Spiraled strings of glowing, colored bulbs illuminated our faces and cast exotic light throughout our dark living room, transforming it from ordinary to magical. Snow falling this evening in early December muffled traffic outside on Welch Avenue, intensifying silence within.

"I hope we get a Hot Wheels track, the big one with loops and jumps for all our cars." Mark inhaled the pine scent.

"That would be cool," Paul agreed dreamily. "They'd go really fast on that track."

"We could set it up on top of the cabinet in the basement to make 'em go super-fast," Steve said, tilting his head and grinning, imagining a long tangle of yellow track and zooming miniature Camaros, Chargers, and Mustangs.

"It'd give you a place to keep all those cars." Clare frowned. "They're always underfoot. I'm tired of stepping on them."

"I think we might get a clock radio for our room." I closed my eyes and smiled, deeply breathing in woodsy evergreen.

"Let's have some music now." Clare jumped up and propped open the top lid of the wood cabinet that held a built-in record player. She pressed open the front door of the console and rifled through our collection of long-play vinyl albums standing on end in cardboard sleeves. Choosing one, she positioned it on the spindle and snapped the switch. Strains of Andy Williams singing "Do You Hear What I Hear?" his voice like melting honey, floated through the dark, sparkly room as Clare flopped back down next to us.

Our faces encircled the tree's fresh-cut trunk, held upright by metal pins in its red metal bowl brimming with water. I looked at the sheen of sap floating on the water's surface, then up again into the boughs. Lights glowed, tinsel glimmered, ornaments shone.

Do you hear what I hear? Andy crooned.

A lovely big orb dangled above me, its blown-glass skin so thin that light from the bulb near it shone through.

Ringing through the sky, shepherd boy, Andy caroled.

That was my favorite Christmas ornament, I decided, even better than the tiny red pipe-cleaner elf who hung on by legs twisted around a needled branch.

Do you hear what I hear? Andy sang.

A crèche scene on the glass orb was painted with brushstrokes so light, they must have been applied with a feather. I needed a closer look at that ornament.

A song, a song, high above the trees. Andy's voice was pianissimo.

I reached up, gently grasped it, and pulled. It didn't break. It didn't come off the tree, either. I pulled again. I couldn't see that the hook holding this extra-precious ornament had been twisted closed around the branch. I pulled down, harder.

With a voice as big as the sea! With a voice as big as the sea! Andy ramped up volume, and we looked up to see the tree falling toward us. In slow motion, it tipped majestically, looming forward, the tree-top angel flying down as if to get a closer look herself. We stared in horror and gasped in short breaths, no time to yell, as resinous water slopped over the rim of the tree holder, and a rush of branches and tinsel and glass ornaments and red pipe-cleaner elf zoomed toward our faces.

"Whoa! Whoa!" Maryanne materialized behind us and sprang for the tree, grasping its trunk mid-fall like a comic book hero. "How did *that* happen?" She eased it back. "Good thing I caught it before the whole thing hit the floor. Lucky we only lost two or three ornaments."

Appalled by the near disaster, I scrambled to my feet as Maryanne righted the tree. The crash would have been my fault. But Maryanne had saved me. I stepped back, trembling.

"Clare-Cheryl, get the whisk broom and sweep up those few broken pieces." Maryanne was brisk, without a thought of crime or punishment. I was off the hook, while the extra-precious ornament was still on it, still whole. I exhaled.

Maryanne shifted the tree, aiming for balance. "Paul-Steve, get towels and mop up that water. Mark, get Dad. I need him to reposition the base while I hold it."

The Child, the Child, sleeping in the night. Andy sang on about this season of mercy and forgiveness.

By Christmas Eve, with the whole house clean and bustling with happy energy, it was as if the tree had never tumbled at all.

"O Lord, stir up Thy might." Dad led all of us, seated around the kitchen table with folded hands, in the Advent prayer before supper. We always giggled when we heard this prayer; we pictured an Old Testament God stirring a big black cauldron. Denise made a mock-solemn face and rotated her clasped hands in a stirring motion. Marla widened her eyes, lowered her lashes, and made her mouth an *O* like a cherub. We ducked heads and muffled giggles into our hands.

"That by Thy protection we may be rescued from our sins," Dad carried on, paying no attention to cartoon re-enactments, "through Christ our Lord, Amen."

The normal babble of talk, the soundtrack of our house, bubbled up. The evening showed deep black outside the kitchen's picture window. Snow was forecast but hadn't yet begun.

Scotch-taped to the window was a German-made paper Advent calendar, eleven by fourteen inches, with twenty-four little paper doors set into a Bethlehem scene. Each night, one of us opened that date's paper door and explained the symbol behind it. The calendar came with a brochure that provided us with information. These paper calendars were designed to be used for one December and discarded, but we had used ours since time began. Several paper doors now clung on only by the grace of Scotch tape.

Four long, tapered candles, in traditional colors of three purple, one pink, burned bright on our little Advent wreath of plastic holly, laid flat on the table. We didn't know where the wreath had come from or when it might have been new. We assumed it had always existed, like land or ocean or air. A few of its fake berries and leaves had popped off and gone missing; hardened drops of candlewax from years past flecked the leaves that still encircled its gold-colored metal base. Tonight, as on every Christmas Eve, it rested on the table between two great steaming pots, one of oyster stew and one of shrimp soup.

Mom and Dad, working in tandem, ladled small servings of soup into bowls. Fragrant steam rose in curling tendrils. We breathed in the aroma, imagining it carried a hint of the far-off sea. We rarely had seafood that wasn't fish sticks, or tuna or salmon out of a can. Greg, in the Toast Seat, passed two baskets of savory little puffed oyster crackers. So exotic, so tasty, so fun to float the miniature crackers on the soup.

"Mmmm . . . smell that broth." Maryanne sprinkled on a few crackers and spooned up shrimp soup.

"Really a treat." Mom loved the oysters in their buttery, milky stew.

I sipped oyster broth off my spoon, leaving the weird gray blob of oyster in the bottom of my bowl for now. Not all of us were as entranced with oysters as Mom. That's why on Christmas Eve she also made shrimp soup, which everyone loved. You could try the oyster stew or not, as you wished, but if you took it, you ate it. All of it. That included the blob now lying, phlegm-like, at the bottom of my bowl. I braced myself and scooped it up, swallowing fast. Not bad.

A couple of us girls had helped Mom make the soups that afternoon, while the rest of the kids hustled to clean the house. We'd even cleared the extra-long, built-in kitchen desk, usually piled high with everyday debris, as a sign of this evening's importance. Now, sitting around the table and glancing toward the kitchen desk, we saw laid flat along its length eleven identical red flannel Christmas stockings Mom had sewed years before. On Christmas Eve, we kids gave presents to each other and to Mom and Dad, and these stockings bulged now with little wrapped gifts. Presents too big to fit piled around them. Anticipation bubbled inside me, like carbonation in a pop bottle. Would Greg like the scarf I'd sewed? Would Mom appreciate the little ceramic painted bird, stamped "Made in Japan" on the base, I'd bought at Ben Franklin's in Campustown? Would Dad enjoy the small glass jar of nuts and bolts? He always seemed pleased with this gift of hardware on Father's Day. I knew the Lids would like the Hot Wheels cars I'd gotten them.

These Christmas Eve gifts from each other were only the beginning. Long after Midnight Mass tonight, Santa would deliver the big haul that we'd open around the tree Christmas morning.

The carbonation inside me bubbled up and out. "Hurry up and finish your soup. Let's get the dishes done so we can open presents." I clattered my spoon into my empty bowl.

"Cher, I'm on dish duty with you tonight. We'll do these really fast." Clare was motivated.

"Let me out, I still have wrapping to do." Greg, pinned on the bench between sisters, jostled to get out.

"Of course you do," I said. Greg had rushed into Campustown to do his Christmas shopping that afternoon.

"Let's go, let's go!" The Lids were nearly levitating from their seats.

"Hold your horses! The presents aren't going anywhere," Dad said, and the decibel level dropped. "No need to rush. Mother, would you like another bowl of that oyster stew? I'll have more shrimp soup. Anyone else? No need to make this evening go any faster than it already is." Dad stood and picked up the ladle. Some of us passed bowls for refills. The Lids simmered down and started tossing oyster crackers in high arcs, adroitly catching them in their mouths. The soundtrack of babble swelled up again.

Dad looked around the table. We were all together. We were all home. He and Mom looked at each other. An unspoken communication, powerful as electric current, passed between them. Sitting near, I felt a jolt of emotion, as if I'd tuned in to a secret radio transmission. I looked up, startled.

"This is the last Christmas we'll all be together," Dad said quietly to Mom. The sentence was a tiny rivulet within the swirling river of chatter and noise. My siblings didn't hear him. They didn't notice, didn't pay attention.

But I heard him. "What? What do you mean?"

Dad glanced at me, saw my face etched with alarm, and said only, "Maryanne will be at college next Christmas. This is our last Christmas like this."

"Oh!" I exhaled in relief. "That's not right. Maryanne will be home from college for Christmas break next year. She'll be here, just like always."

"She'll be home for Christmas vacation, but it will never be the same," Dad said. "Our family will be different."

"No!" The intensity of my gut reaction surprised me. I pressed my palms on the Formica tabletop. "Nothing will change! We will always be together. It will always be like this." If I declared it so, maybe it would be so. I would *not* allow change. What would life be, if it weren't like this? What would each of us be, if we weren't one of nine, if we weren't our own Baseball Team? We were many hands! We made light work! With fewer hands, would we still be us?

"It will never be the same." Dad never did see value in sugar-coating the truth.

"No! Nothing will change!" But the seed of alarm in my gut thrust down a root and sent up a slim green shoot.

Still my siblings, ever boisterous, didn't hear, didn't notice, didn't pay attention.

"Cheri-lee." Mom used a term of endearment I hadn't heard since I was small. She tilted her head slightly at me and laid down her spoon. Her eyes were bright, but she didn't shed tears. "Cheri-lee. It will happen."

"No," I repeated, but the root of fear thrust deeper.

"This is the last Christmas we'll all be together like this," Dad repeated. "That is as it should be." He looked at me, but I got the feeling his words were meant for all of us. Still my siblings didn't hear, didn't notice, didn't pay attention. "Your Christmases to come will be good. Your futures will be bright. All will be well."

I breathed deep, mentally stomping the fear within, and came back to the present—and the presents.

Steve jumped and wiggled in his seat. "Time to open presents!" He could no longer sit still. "Let's see what's in the stockings!"

I fell back in with the noise and was swept along by the chatter.

"We haven't said after-meal prayers yet." Dad raised his voice to be heard. "Keep it down to a dull roar, please." Silence dropped over us. Hands clapped together.

"We give Thee thanks for all Thy benefits." Dad's voice led us all into the familiar old prayer. We'd recited it three times a day since we were old enough to speak. Tonight, it seemed to float down from heaven. The words fell on us like rain, like blessings that had been and were to come, like a benediction for the future.

"Who lives and reigns forever and ever." Reciting our prayer in unison, we were not so blessed that we didn't gain speed, as usual, as we rocketed toward the finish. Despite our warp-speed delivery, the familiar words calmed me. Forever and ever. World without end.

"Amen!" and our single voice split into the usual polyphonic commotion.

"Dishes first." Mom could always be heard even though she never raised her voice.

"Let's all pitch in tonight, even though it's not our turn. According to the schedule it's Clare and Cheryl." Maryanne got up to clear the table.

"It'll go faster if we all help." Marla jumped up to help her.

"That's right, we work together." Dad pushed back his chair.

Denise snatched up a spatula and started scraping dishes. Greg picked up empty milk glasses four at a time, their glass sides clinking, and took them to the sink before sprinting upstairs to finish wrapping. Clare gathered silverware and dropped it into the holder in our dishwasher. Paul and Steve wet sponges to wash the table, starting on opposite ends and working toward the middle. The table was so long and broad, their sponges looked like twin Zambonis polishing a hockey rink. Mark took a broom and swept crumbs along the floor and into our built-in dust drop.

Greg hustled back downstairs, arms overflowing with hastily wrapped gifts, and spilled them onto the long desk. The kitchen desk brimmed over with stockings, and each stocking brimmed over with gifts. Eleven stockings, each with its nametag, each in age order, each where it had always been.

Mom and Dad knew, as we could not, that Maryanne moving on to college was only the beginning. Careers, spouses, travel, and opportunities for all of us lay just beyond a horizon only Mom and Dad could see. The years would fly, spinning faster and faster, their centrifugal force swirling on and on into the future until we nine scattered to the four winds.

Love is the bedrock of human interaction, and that Christmas Eve, love was palpable. We heard it in the chatter, saw it in the gifts, smelled it in the fragrant broth. We felt it swirling around us like the curling tendrils of steam rising from the pots.

Mark hung the broom on its peg above the dust drop. Paul and Steve wrung out sponges and propped them to dry on the sink.

I looked at our Advent calendar on the window, its colored scene of Bethlehem village life as familiar as my siblings' faces. Behind me, noise ratcheted up as my brothers and sisters shifted all eleven red stockings, each with its nametag, each in age order, from the broad kitchen desk to the wide clean table. We didn't start opening until everyone was seated again around the table, each of us in place, each where we'd always been.

I smoothed open once more the paper doors over the Christmas Eve scene of the stable, willing the yellowed Scotch tape to hold fast. Our Advent calendar stayed up through New Year's, at least. I would make sure, this year as always, to carefully pack it away.

But there would be plenty of time for that later. I turned away from the calendar's artistic scene, the figures in its ancient story radiating eternal forgiveness, and back to the light and noise and love in the kitchen. I scrambled over a little brother or two and slid into place on the bench among my siblings, like I was sliding into home.

epilogue

I n 2012, after fifty years of work on rental houses, our family decided to tear down five of them, one of which had been our family home decades before, and build anew on the site. The century-old frame houses were increasingly difficult to keep up, and didn't offer the amenities that millennial college students sought. Yet the real estate they rested on—five lots in a row—was a prime Campustown location. And university enrollment was booming again, with the numbers of incoming freshmen setting records year after year. Once again, hordes of students wanted housing—new, luxurious housing.

Dad, ninety years old that year and sharp as ever, spearheaded the effort to take down those houses, and oversaw the design and construction of the beautiful apartment complex of twenty-seven units that arose on the site. We christened the new building The Stritz (stritzelapartments.com) and bestowed upon it the address of 412 Welch. Our new building, like the family behind it, is built for the ages.

Stritzel Family, 2014. From left: Paul, Marla, Steve, Maryanne, Mark, Dad, Cheryl, Denise, Greg, Clare.

the stritzel diaspora

After starting at Clarke College in Dubuque, Iowa, **Maryanne** eventually transferred to Iowa State, where she met a handsome college boy in one of the fraternities on Welch. They married and moved to his family's heritage farm near Collins, Iowa, where they raised corn, hogs, and six children. With her husband, Maryanne is now retired, living in town, and managing Stritzel Apartments. She amazes her grandchildren every year at the Iowa State Fair by reeling off, from memory, names of dozens of exotic hog and cattle breeds. An occasional substitute teacher, Maryanne has never filled empty class time by singing "Drunk Last Night" to her pupils.

Denise also received her undergraduate degree from Iowa State, where she met and married an engineering student. Today they live in Loveland, Colorado. Their three children include adoptees from Korea and Vietnam. Denise uses her knowledge of families and her master's degree in nursing to mentor low-income mothers of infants and toddlers. Denise, who made up her first song verses while we were working on the houses, is now known for writing epic ballads whenever one of the younger Stritzel clan gets married. She and Marla, aided and abetted by the rest of us, create a song about the bride and groom for us five aunts to perform at the wedding reception—and, may I add, we are earning a reputation.

Marla, while attending Iowa State and living in a sorority, spent one of her summers volunteering at a camp for underprivileged girls in Sechelt, British Columbia. Nearby, a young lawyer was building a cabin by hand. They met, eventually married, and went back to the land on Salt Spring Island, BC, where they built an octagonal house and raised four children as well as numerous chickens and pigs. Marla, whose sense of fun remains undiminished into her sixth decade, is revered by her five grandchildren as the best nana ever. She and her husband have lived in Vancouver and Victoria, and most recently built a home near rural Sidney, BC. They are frequent travelers, visiting Morocco one moment and India the next. Marla, an accomplished poet, occasionally attends the summer Iowa Writers' Workshop.

Greg attended Oregon State University in Corvallis before graduating from University of California, Berkeley, and working as a certified financial planner. An avid horseman, he was training horses one day when a young pregnant woman asked if he would exercise her horse while she was unable to ride. He agreed and soon learned that the young woman was recently divorced. They married and are now raising three boys in Oakland. Greg, who came to marriage and fatherhood later in life, is currently a horse trainer and riding coach.

Clare received a bachelor's degree in nursing from the University of Iowa. She married her high school sweetheart, earned a teaching certificate, and taught school while Jim attended medical school. A keen student, Clare went to law school when their elder son was in fifth grade and their twins were in first grade. After graduating with her law degree and working as a lawyer and mediator, she collaborated entrepreneurially with Marla to design and manufacture Mediator in a Box (simplehelpinabox.com), a kit that simplifies the process of mediation and helps people resolve arguments.

I, **Cheryl**, graduated from Iowa State in journalism and moved to Painesville, Ohio, to become a reporter on a daily newspaper. My college boyfriend, an engineer, moved to nearby Cleveland for his first job. For our wedding day, I chose to wear my sister Clare's wedding dress—my habit of hand-me-downs was that strong. We moved to London for his job; there I earned my MBA and two of our eventual three daughters were born. We kept moving (Cleveland, London, Cleveland, Toledo, Cleveland, Naperville in suburban Chicago, London, Naperville, and now Bellingham, Washington), and I freelanced for newspapers and magazines as we moved. With all our moves, I've gotten a lot of practice sewing window treatments, and the hard-won sewing skills from my early years have come in handy. I no longer scream in frustration when I'm sewing drapes. Not usually, anyway.

Paul, a free spirit and the only one of us still single, moved to the West Coast to work in forestry before returning to Ames to become a carpenter and buy a farm of his own just outside of town. Today he's known for fine carpentry and perfection in woodworking. An artisan, he can start with junk wood and rusty metal and create a knife of function and beauty. He taps maple trees to make syrup, bow hunts deer, and once designed and sewed a full-size, deluxe tipi. Paul, who grows corn and soybeans on his own farm, works with Dad keeping Stritzel Apartments in good repair.

Steve, who as a teen vowed he wanted a woman, a pickup, and a dog, in fact achieved all his life goals early on. He and his wife live in a country house outside Ames, where every year Steve hangs our Advent calendar, now well over half a century old. Active in the Catholic Church, Steve is a proud member of Knights of Columbus, and works in maintenance for Stritzel Apartments.

Mark graduated from Iowa State in construction engineering and owns a construction consulting business in Colorado Springs that specializes in commercial projects. He and his wife have three young-adult children and own a handful of rental houses in their neighborhood. Mark loves to hunt, fish, and organize his brothers for antelope-hunting expeditions.

Mom, after we left home, combined her knowledge of families, finance, and houses into a successful career as a realtor. In 1977, Mom and Dad bought a hundred-acre farm outside Ames; Mom designed a big new house for the property, siting it on a beautiful ridge overlooking timber and creek. They started farming corn and soybeans, planted Christmas trees on slopes not suitable for crops, and opened a cut-your-own Christmas tree farm. In 2007, just shy of her ninetieth birthday, Mom died peacefully at home, sitting on the couch one sunny afternoon. Dad and Paul were nearby. Today, whenever our family gathers, we honor her for whatever is good within us.

Dad, at ninety-seven, with twenty-five grandchildren and numerous great-grandchildren, is still going strong, working on the remaining rental houses, and farming. Every year in the weeks before Christmas, until he was ninety-three, he hitched a roomy flat trailer to his 125-horsepower 7330 John Deere tractor, hung a jaunty vintage leather strap of sleigh bells on it, and gave folks a ride over to Christmas Tree Hill on their farm. He loved welcoming people, and threw in a free lecture on agronomy as he drove them across the farm. After retiring from thirty-seven years at Iowa State, he established two Stritzel scholarships there, to be awarded in perpetuity: one for an agronomy student, the other for any agriculture student who is active at St. Thomas Aquinas Catholic Church. Dad is himself still a fixture at St. Thomas, which he's attended for seventy years. At The Stritz, Dad occasionally does maintenance, where he enjoys the problem-solving aspect of fixing this or that. It is our flagship property, and Dad's confident nod to the future.

THE END

discussion questions

Many Hands Make Light Work offers plentiful material for discussion on widely engaging social issues of cultural change while remaining a winsome memoir of a midwestern childhood.

1. For decades, the Stritzel family welcomes strangers into their home, to live, eat, and study with them. They are unknowing champions of diversity and inclusion, long before such concepts became the cultural flashpoints they are today. Growing up with this, the narrator writes that it felt ordinary and normal, though their college-student boarders transcended cultures around the globe. Why do you think this household, repeatedly absorbing people of vastly different nationalities and religions, remained harmonious?

2. What does this openness to welcoming strangers say about Mom, who conceived the idea and kept executing it successfully over the years?

3. Mom runs a household that fluctuates from eleven to sixteen people. She manages this partly by training and then organizing her children to accomplish household tasks, as age allows. Like Dad, Mom expects competence and gets it. Why do you think these children complied? Do you think it is easier to get compliance from teens if they know their contribution is essential?

4. Average family size in the United States has decreased since the mid-twentieth century. What's been lost in the shift to today's smaller families? Gained?

5. In chapter 5, "Let Them Swim," the narrator feels it's occasionally an advantage to camouflage herself among many siblings and hide from parental scrutiny. Do you feel that parental attention to children and teens has changed over the last few decades? Do you know of instances where parental attention seems excessive?

6. In *Many Hands*, the young teens ride on the open tailgate of their '58 Chevy station wagon, traveling several blocks to their summer work site. Today's focus on safety is generally positive, but can you think of instances where it goes too far?

7. Lenore Skenazy, founder of the Free Range Kids movement, captured national attention in 2008 when she let her then nine-year-old son take the New York City subway alone. Skenazy has endorsed *Many Hands*, saying: "Try not to be jealous of a childhood spent in a midwestern town that gave kids free-range, and an era that trusted all children to rise to the occasion." How do parents today balance the joys of childhood freedom with safety concerns?

8. Statistics show crime in the United States surged during the 1960s and 1970s, the decades of *Many Hands*. Today Gallup reports that despite significant declines in crime year after year, a majority of Americans believe crime is rising. What impact does perception of crime and safety have on parenting today?

9. In chapter 2, the narrator discovers that "maybe work was not the grumble-filled burden we perceived. Maybe work brought blessings of its own." Research links meaningful work with higher life satisfaction. In *Many Hands*, Dad feels it's beneficial for his offspring to work within the family business, but not outside the family where they might encounter bad influences. When is it right for children and teens to spend summers working, whether at home or in another job?

10. Do you see any parallels in modern families choosing to spend vacation time and dollars working together, such as on a dude ranch? Do you know of instances where affluent families pay to send their teens to gain experiences involving physical labor?

11. The narrator's paternal grandmother, Regina Perz, in the early 1900s quit school after eighth grade to work in a hat factory in Cleveland. She gave her paychecks to her parents to help support her eight younger siblings. How might an American fourteen-year-old today react to this expectation?

12. After the kids and Dad pour a new concrete driveway, Dad remarks it's sad so few children get the chance to benefit from real-life work experiences such as this. As a parent, would you seek this sort of experience for your children or teens?

13. Do you personally recall any youthful work experiences that were more fun than play?

14. The theme of change is especially prominent in the last chapter, when the narrator grapples with the idea that nothing lasts forever, and that everything you treasure will pass away. Three things help: Dad reassures her; she realizes for the first time that the life around her will live on in memory; and the family recites a familiar prayer, the words falling "like rain, like blessings that had been and were to come, like a benediction for the future." How do you draw solace from the past while facing an uncertain future?

15. On Christmas Eve, steam from the soup curls up and evaporates. This actual event foreshadows coming change: the only life these siblings know is about to evaporate. For you personally, what events did you only later realize marked a tectonic shift in your life?

acknowledgments

Mom liked to say, about the nine of us and the dozens of college students who lived with us over the decades, "If I had known all this was going to happen, I would have kept notes and written a book!" Thanks to Marcella Hill Stritzel for that early inspiration and so much more.

Thanks to Dad, Joseph Stritzel, for the invaluable history and memories. Likewise to my siblings, who gave generously of their time to help reconstruct the story, especially when details were disputed ("We got up at four a.m. to shovel snow." "It was five a.m." "It was four!" "Five thirty!" "Four!") To sisters Maryanne Holland, Denise Baretich, Marla Sloan, Clare Sprowell, and brothers Greg, Paul, Steve, and Mark Stritzel: I'm eternally grateful for the cosmic stroke of luck that landed us together.

I am indebted to my writing group, the Talespinners: Linda Morrow, Joe Nolting, Roy and Nancy Taylor, Victoria Doerper, Kate Miller—we've been through it, haven't we?—and our peerless teacher, Laura Kalpakian. Thanks to friend Nancy Sprowell Geise for guidance; writing buddies Lisa Dailey and Kathie Tupper; beta readers Don Logan, Gail McCarthy, Mary Youngblood, Pam Zmolek Stewart, Melissa Klein, Grace Phelan, Sandy Berner, Joyce Pedlow, Janice Riley, Kim Marcisek; editors Alma Garcia and Christina Nichols; and She Writes Press, especially Brooke Warner, Lauren Wise, and Julie Metz.

Special thanks to daughters Victoria McQuarrie, Claire Hagerup, and Regina Lionheart, for their exceedingly affordable editing assistance.

Most of all, thanks to my husband, Bob, whose belief in me never wavers.

Cheryl Stritzel McCarthy and her eight siblings grew up with a paintbrush in their hands and a song in their hearts. As soon as they were old enough to wrench a nail out of ancient lumber—so it could be used again—they were put to work renovating old houses in Ames, Iowa. Cheryl's growing-up years included babysitting for a local family that kept a lion as a pet. A real, adolescent-aged lion. Uncaged. Using a flyswatter to defend herself, she survived the lion, and today is a freelance journalist for the *Wall Street Journal* as well as the *Los*

Angeles Times and *Chicago Tribune*. The *Tribune* distributes her articles to newspapers and websites around the country, including the *Seattle Times*, *St. Louis Post-Dispatch*, *Baltimore Sun*, and *Orlando Sentinel*. She freelanced for years as a book critic for the *Plain Dealer* in Cleveland. Her previous book, *USA to UK: The Easy Way*, a lighthearted look at moving overseas, was published by British Petroleum's London headquarters for an international readership. McCarthy holds an MBA from City University in London and a bachelor's in journalism from Iowa State University. Previously at home in Shaker Heights, Ohio; Toledo, Ohio; and Naperville, Illinois, she now lives with her husband in Bellingham, Washington.

SELECTED TITLES FROM SHE WRITES PRESS

She Writes Press is an independent publishing company
founded to serve women writers everywhere.
Visit us at www.shewritespress.com.

Peanut Butter and Naan: Stories of an American Mother in The Far East by
Jennifer Magnuson. $16.95, 978-1-63152-911-5. The hilarious tale of
what happened when Jennifer Magnuson moved her family of seven from
Nashville to India in an effort to shake things up—and got more than she
bargained for.

The Outskirts of Hope: A Memoir by Jo Ivester. $16.95, 978-1-63152-964-1. A
moving, inspirational memoir about how living and working in an all-
black town during the height of the civil rights movement profoundly
affected the author's entire family—and how they in turn impacted the
community.

Not a Perfect Fit: Stories from Jane's World by Jane A. Schmidt. $16.95,
978-1631522062. Jane Schmidt documents her challenges living off grid,
moving from the city to the country, living with a variety of animals as her
only companions, dating, family trips, outdoor adventures, and midlife in
essays full of honesty and humor.

Edna's Gift: How My Broken Sister Taught Me to Be Whole by Susan Rudnick.
$16.95, 978-1-63152-515-5. When they were young, Susan and Edna,
children of Holocaust refugee parents, were inseparable. But as they grew
up and Edna's physical and mental challenges altered the ways she could
develop, a gulf formed between them. Here, Rudnick shares how her
maddening—yet endearing—sister became her greatest life teacher.

Make a Wish for Me: A Mother's Memoir by LeeAndra Chergey. $16.95,
978-1-63152-828-6. A life-changing diagnosis teaches a family that where
there is love there is hope—and that being "normal" is not nearly as
important as providing your child with a life full of joy, love, and
acceptance.

Flip-Flops After Fifty: And Other Thoughts on Aging I Remembered to Write Down
by Cindy Eastman. $16.95, 978-1-938314-68-1. A collection of frank and
funny essays about turning fifty—and all the emotional ups and downs
that come with it.